THINK BETTER AND THRIVE

MENTAL MODELS AND NOTES THAT HELP YOU MAKE THE BEST OUT OF LIFE

NAVEEN NIVERTHY

To my daughter, Aanya, who filled my life with joy.

Contents

Contents

Contents

Preface

We live in a complex world. The diversity in people, institutions, natural forces and the rise of technology has created a world that is increasingly challenging to navigate.

A mental model explains how something works in the real world. A mental model can be a concept, framework or worldview you buy into or see as working. It represents the world around us, the relationships between its various parts and a person's intuitive perception of their acts and consequences.

For example, the theory of supply and demand is used in economics Supply and demand are the driving factors that decide prices in a free market economy. The price of commodity changes depending on how much supply and demand there is for it. Another popular mental model is Abraham Maslow's hierarchy of needs. Maslow's hierarchy of needs is a model for understanding the motivations for human behaviour. It maps different motivations onto a pyramid, each level representing another human need. These include physiological needs, safety, love and belonging, esteem, and self-actualisation. Of course, a mental model is not perfect at describing the world. There are exceptions to every rule and model. But mental models give us an understanding that is much closer to reality. As historian Yuval Noah Harari puts it, "Scientists generally agree that no theory is 100 per cent correct. Thus, the real test of knowledge is not the truth, but utility." Mental models guide our perceptions and behaviours that help us navigate the world better. You use these thinking tools to understand life, make decisions, and solve problems. Learning a new mental model gives you a new way to see the world, a fresh perspective that can widen your outlook or derive new insights from known facts.

Mental models are imperfect but useful. No single mental model from humanities or sciences provides a flawless explanation of a system at work. Still, the best mental models from those disciplines have allowed us to build multi-billion-dollar corporations, global institutions, the fastest athletes, and supercomputers, taking us to the moon, mars and beyond.

The best mental models are the ideas with the most utility. They are helpful in daily life. Understanding these concepts will help you make wiser choices and take better actions. This is why developing a broad base of mental models is critical for anyone interested in reasoning and effectively.

This book is a collection of mental models that work well in tandem with each other, such that you can excel in all the five domains of life, viz. Love, Health, Work, Parenting and Spirituality.

Who is this book for?

This book is for everyone seeking happiness and striving towards it in their ways. It touches all aspects of happiness: Work, relationships, parenting, health and spirituality. This book will be helpful for those in their thirties and early forties as I have used, curated and presented in this phase of life. So, readers from this phase can connect with these ideas and relate to the examples much better. The Thirties can be challenging for most people, and it may be for good reasons that it is called the turbulent thirties. For many, the first health troubles are uncovered in their thirties. Anxiety, obesity, back pain, headaches, diabetes, hypertension, insomnia, and restlessness are only some of the health troubles that come knocking at your door. Work gets demanding, and expectations from you soar as you are not considered an amateur anymore. At the same time, you want to continue to grow in your job. You seek variety, growth, and stability. Some become overweight, and some develop anxiety. The thirties are very demanding of your energies. The thirties demand you to balance all the domains you are active in - Work, love life, health, fun, parenting, relationships, and spirituality– without letting one dominate or compromise the other. And that is why, in this book, I wish to discuss how we can turn turbulent thirties & forties into flourishing thirties and forties. If one aspect of your life is struggling while another is thriving, this book is for you.

Each of these areas is integral to leading a whole, meaningful existence. When it comes to happiness and thriving in life, we need to be a jack of all trades in a way - like the jack, you may not be the best in every suit, but we need to be better than most cards in every suit. We need to seek excellence in all five areas discussed in this book. It's important to occasionally take inventory of these areas to ensure we are not neglecting some part of our life. Picture a dashboard with these five components listed one below the other. Alongside each of these components, write down a set of scores measuring how satisfied you are in each of these facets of life on a scale of one to hundred.

Alternatively, you can ask yourself these five questions and rate yourself on a scale of 1 to 10: 1= No satisfaction, 10= High Satisfaction.

1. Work: How would you rate your engagement, enjoyment, and the meaning you derive from your work?
2. Love: Are you committing adequate time and energy to your partner, parents, siblings, friends, and other people within your social network?
3. Health: How would you rate your level of positivity and relaxation on most days?
4. Spirituality: Are you living a life of purpose and meaning?
5. Parenting: How fulfilled do you feel in your role as a parent?

This should give you an overall idea of where you stand in each of these domains with respect to happiness. This book attempts to provide you with ideas, mental models, cautionary notes and guidelines to work on yourself and improve your score in each of these areas of life. To thrive is to develop quickly and become successful. To flourish is to grow rapidly and become successful. In this book, we shall discuss how we can turn turbulent thirties into flourishing thirties.

Thriving around health and fitness means our body and mind are well integrated. Our physical and mental health makes us happier. It improves our moods, brings positivity and makes us more optimistic. But fitness is vaguely defined by most of us, and so are the ways to build the same. In the section on health, we shall discuss some effective mental models for health and fitness that can help us understand and give us ways to plan it. It is now widely accepted that the absence of psychological and physical illnesses does not imply the presence of total mental and physical health and well-being. Of course, getting some exercise and eating well is essential, but taking care of your emotional well-being is also important.

Thriving at work means constantly pushing your performance, influence and ability. When you thrive t work, you feel safe and optimistic about your future. You have a great network that nourishes you with ideas, best practices, opportunities and mentors. Thriving at work means you contribute meaningfully to your team and your employer. Succeeding at your job or career is work gives us a sense of purpose and is critical for our feeling of self-worth.

Thriving in matters of love is thriving in relationships – with your partner, family and friends. Thriving individuals can develop warm, trusting relationships with others and are willing to develop their potential to grow and expand. When you improve the strength, depth and quality of relationships, you become happier, healthier and live longer. Relationships contribute to our sense of self-worth and give us a sense of belonging. The section on love discusses some attractive mental models which can help us thrive in relationships.

Thriving as a parent means effectively applying best-practice parenting strategies and concepts from several disciplines so that you decrease power struggles, increase cooperation and collaboration in your home, and genuinely enjoy raising your children. Thriving parents have high levels of self-awareness and self-confidence to raise happy and well-behaved kids. Parenting prepares the next generation to take on the world. It is an opportunity to outlive yourself by passing on everything you value to the next generation and taking pride in watching them do better than you.

Thriving spiritually means that you have meaning and purpose in life. You act as if you make a difference, and you know you do. You feel part of something bigger than your limited self. You always see the big picture - God's perspective. You have freedom from emotional dependence and freedom from being a wanting person. You are contented, free of yearnings and ready to let go of this world and all its people and things when it's time.

Thus, the book discusses five components of thriving: health, work, love, parenting and spirituality. The book is put together such that you can read from start to finish or start with any section and read within that section. Feel free to choose a reading strategy of choice. I reiterate here that a balance of effort and success is needed in all five components for us to thrive. And this journey of thriving starts with thinking right.

Someone once said we become the books we read. I hope this book helps you think better, thrive and becomes a part of your being too!

Love,

Naveen Niverthy

ppp

Acknowledgements

I always think of myself as a curator of wisdom. In this book, I have put together best practices, strategies, mental models, tactics and notes, most of which I haven't invented. I have applied most of them in my life, and I know now that they work, but I have learnt them from others. So I am standing on the shoulder of giants and take only the credit for curating them in the form of this book. I have many people to thank here.

First and foremost, I would like to thank my daughter, who inspired me to write this book. I wish to leave this book behind as a guide for my daughter to serve her in her thirties and early forties. I would also like to thank the strengths profile assessment I took three years ago, which identified writing as an unrealized potential. The journey of this book first began in the form of a blog, which was once nothing more than my notes on parenting. Soon I started writing posts related to career, personal finance, relationship, love, marriage and spirituality. Over three years of writing the blog, I accumulated enough research and content to create this book. I would also like to thank all the readers of my blog, valueparenting.in who, time and again, appreciated the practical wisdom I shared on the blog.

I am also grateful to my Swiss employer, Oetiker group, with whom I recently completed ten years. The job has allowed me to learn and grow in a truly global culture and travel the world, soaking in values and diverse mindsets. This job also gave me a great mentor in Ashwani Keswani, a dynamic leader and a great friend who continues to motivate, support and inspire me to this date to reach ever greater heights. I am also grateful to my spiritual mentor Swamini Brahmaprajnananda for guiding me whenever I sought her counsel and to Swami Tattvavidananda, for helping me see the timeless in the traditional wisdom. I would also thank my parents, Nanda and Sarath, who, although they have no clue that I am publishing a book, have been instrumental in my growth journey, allowing me the necessary peace and space to read, study and write. I also extend my heartfelt gratitude to all my close friends Neha, Girish, Janardhan and Salil, who stood by me, kept me motivated and supported this project in their own way. I also like to thank my near and dear friends and well-wishers, who always read my blogs, appreciated and at times critiqued me but also motivated me to keep writing. I am thankful to God or Universe or good fortune, whatever you may choose to call it, that I was born and raised in a place where I had easy access to education, nutrition, security and love, which I realise is not something you can take for granted in the world we live in. Finally, I would like to thank the Notion Press team for publishing this book and making it available in physical form for distribution.

Without all these influences favouring me, my mere will to write a book would not have sufficed. I am humbled and, at the same time, grateful for the opportunity I have had to present this book to the readers in its present form.

ᗅᗅᗅ

HEALTH: Pay attention to Physical & Emotional Wellbeing

ONE

HORMONES OF HAPPINESS

If there is one aspiration that unites all humans, it is happiness. Every person - irrespective of their gender, race, religion, education, standard of living, status, or nationality – wants to be happy. And happiness is the sum of how one feels about oneself, others, and the world. Since happiness is felt, it rides on emotions – their quality and intensity. Emotions that we feel are regulated by chemicals secreted in our glands called hormones. Hormones are our body's chemical messengers. Once the glands release the hormones into the bloodstream, the hormones act on various organs and tissues to control everything from how our body functions to how we feel. And today, we know that four hormones are largely responsible for this feel-good factor in us. The four together contribute to the happy and, sometimes, euphoric feelings they produce. They also play the role of neurotransmitters i.e.they carry messages across the spaces between nerve cells. The four feel-good hormones are dopamine, serotonin, endorphins, and oxytocin. Everything we 'feel' when happy depends on whether these four hormones are secreted in balanced levels.

1. **Oxytocin:** This hormone gives us a feeling of 'falling in love with a partner and wanting to become a parent. It is induced by touch- when we're excited by our sexual partner when we cuddle with our child. It is also commonly called "love hormone" and "cuddle hormone." Its administered to expectant mothers during delivery to increase uterine contractions. After delivery, it helps move the milk and foster the parent-child bond. A promising way to boost oxytocin naturally is with exercise.

Another activity that is proven to increase oxytocin levels is music, especially when people sing in a group. This kind of music adds an element of bonding. And finally, oxytocin is also released by an act of touch. The touch could be in the form of a hug, massage, cuddling, or making love. All these acts boost oxytocin and lead to a greater sense of well-being.

2. **Dopamine** can provide an intense feeling of pleasure as part of the brain's reward system. Today we understand the relationship between dopamine and cravings. From social media to binge-watching web series, from fatty foods to sugary foods, from intoxication to caffeine, all these are dopamine-inducing behaviours. They can trigger dopamine release or a "dopamine rush," as it is also called. This feel-good neurotransmitter is also involved in reinforcing repetitive behaviour of forming habits. This is why, once we try chocolate cookies, we might come back for another one or more. Unfortunately, there is a darker side to dopamine. This comes from the intense reward people feel when they take drugs like heroin or cocaine, which can lead to addiction. Dopamine also plays a role in learning and attention, mood movement, heart rate, kidney function, blood vessel function, sleep, pain processing, and lactation.

3. **Serotonin:** Sometimes, we feel happy for no specific reason, and everything seems right with the world around us. This can largely be attributed to the release of serotonin. Besides others, the main function served by this hormone is boosting mood. Serotonin can ward off depression and provide a feeling of euphoria. Serotonin is produced by an area in the centre of the brainstem. It influences many different parts of the brain, affecting various functions and behaviours, including fear, memory, stress response, digestion, addiction, sexuality, sleep, breathing, and body temperature. The best natural way to increase serotonin is by exercising or working out. When you lift weights or pedal your bicycle, your body releases more tryptophan, an amino acid that the brain uses to make serotonin. This boost in serotonin is why many people get the euphoria known as a "runner's high," especially after an intense workout.

4. **Endorphins:** Endorphins are natural painkillers of the body. Endorphins are released in response to stress or pain in the hypothalamus and pituitary gland. This group of hormones relieves pain and creates a general feeling of well-being. Endorphins can also bust stress. We also release endorphins when we laugh, fall in love, laugh, have sex, and even enjoy delicious meals. You can increase your body's endorphin release

by engaging in activities like moderate-intensity exercise, acupuncture, breathing and focusing type of meditation, sex, playing music, singing or dancing, good belly laughter, and ultraviolet light during outdoor time. There are many ways to increase levels of endorphins naturally in your brain, including diet, exercise, and enjoying the company of the people you care about. In the quest to feel better and prevent depression, some people resort to taking endorphin supplements. Although this seems easy and tempting, for most people, supplementing these hormones is not necessary. In some cases, these supplements can cause unwanted and serious side effects.

The best way to work with hormones is moderation: avoid over-stimulating them but ensure none is under-stimulated. That is the balance that needs to be struck. When any one of them is understimulated, it could lead to a pathological condition – depression being the most common among them. So the magic words here are 'natural' and 'balanced': Engage in natural ways that boost these hormones and ensure a balanced focus on each. Better still is to find activities that help you promote all four.

All of us are pursuing happiness, which has been studied at many levels and from many vantage points. This note was meant to give us a hormone-level (body-level) understanding of happiness. The play of these hormones-their healthy release- gives us subjective feedback on the success, achievements, gifts, talents, pleasures, and love we experience. Without proper functioning, a person, even though they have all the ingredients of happiness in their life, will never be able to acknowledge it. Hence, physical health cannot be ignored, irrespective of which objects we aim to find happiness in.

Between Pleasure and Happiness, choose wisely.

The ancient wisdom of Vedanta tells us that we are frequently posed with a choice in life between Preyas and Shreyas (Sanskrit). Preyas include all desired activities by an individual at a given time. In contrast, Shreyas includes that which is desirable for all people at all times and places, namely freedom from unhappiness, the knowledge that frees one emotionally and intellectually.

For easy understanding, we can think of Preyas as 'Pleasures' while Shreyas as 'Happiness.' However, even this would need some explaining.

Why? Because many of us equate pleasure to happiness. I refer to research by Dr Robert Lustig, an American pediatric endocrinologist working with the University of California, San Francisco, who has studied how the two are very different. Here are seven ways pleasure is different from happiness:

1. *Pleasure is short-lived; happiness is long-lived*

Pleasures typically make you feel 'guilty' (maybe not for all): sugar, over-eating, binge TV, gossip, social media time, fast cars, and so on. Neither the 'feel good' from these activities nor the guilt that may come with it lasts very long. The joy that comes from holding your new-born child in your arms, walking hand in hand with your partner, a good night's sleep after a day's honest labour, the feeling of being debt-free, and living life free of guilt- all these last much longer and count as happiness.

2. *Pleasure is visceral; happiness is ethereal*

Pleasure is the stimulation of our nervous system, something we feel when our senses encounter their desired objects and cause sensations as rewards. It is gross and very much of this world. Happiness is ethereal- meaning subtle, light, something to be inferred. It does not seem to be of this world.

3. *Pleasure is taking; happiness is giving*

Invariably, we say we 'take pleasure in something- enjoy, like, adore, love, relish, delight in, savour, revel in, get a kick out of, be entertained by, be amused by. It is all about 'taking' whereas happiness is invariably given. It comes from what we give to our parents, spouse, children, work, society, nation, this world, or even to nature or this universe or our Creator. Is it any wonder that many of us find happiness in charity, acts of humanity, kindness, compassion, love, and communion?

4. *Too less or too much pleasure is unhealthy*

Pleasureis tied to the neurotransmitter dopamine. In contrast, happiness is tied to the neurotransmitter serotonin: Neurotransmitters are chemical substances made by the neuron specifically to transmit a message- these messages are precursors to how we think, feel, and ultimately act. Dopamine levels dictate our motivations and emotional arousal. The 'kick' we get out of some thoughts and activities comes from dopamine. It is released by neurons in the brain's reward centre. A certain amount is healthy, but low levels are linked to Parkinson's disease, while high levels are linked to schizophrenia.

Serotonin is a neurotransmitter produced mostly in the intestine (90%) and the rest in the nervous system. It regulates sleep, memory, learning, temperature, mood, behaviours, heart health and the function of the endocrine system, which produces hormones. One can almost instantly see the correlation between health and overall well-being. Lower levels of serotonin are linked to depression, and high levels are known to be bad too.

5. *Pleasure can be achieved with substances; happiness cannot*

The drugs most abused by humans create a neurochemical reaction that significantly increases dopamine. These include including opiates, alcohol, nicotine, amphetamines, and cocaine. On the other hand, happiness comes from a sense of balance and harmony in the mind and body. It comes through a balanced diet, exercise, optimism, hope, trust, love, and so on.

6. *Pleasure is addictive*

The extremes of pleasure lead to addiction, whether substances or behaviours. For example, dopamine is addictive and can come from your morning coffee, evening tea, post-meal dessert or cigarette, likes on social media, drugs, and anything you binge on. You do it a couple of times and crave to do it repeatedly because it is addictive. Yet there is no such thing as being addicted to too much happiness.

7. *Pleasure is experienced alone; happiness is experienced in social groups*

The guiltier the pleasure, the lonelier you are in the experience. Whereas happiness, because it is about sharing- sharing a world view, ideas, values, resources, love- is experienced in a group – as a group, as a circle of friends, as coworkers, as a community, and so on. Happiness comes from being rooted and connected to people, values, and this universe.

The path of Shreyas or happiness culminates in freedom, peace of mind, independence, fulfilment, and completeness, in other words, Moksha. The path of Preyas or pleasure culminates in loss of well-being, loneliness, arrogance, egotism, and eventually self-destruction.

I do not intend here to convey that we must actively shun pleasures. I only intend to spell out the differences between pleasure and happiness and say that we often must choose between them. Not all pleasure is bad, only that which comes at the cost of happiness. This brings us back to where we first began: to a choice, a choice that is offered to us at every step of our life-the choice between seeking pleasure or happiness. What will you choose?

ᏢᏢᏢ

TWO

EMOTIONAL INTELLIGENCE MODEL

In widespread language usage, we separate matters of the head from matters that belong to the heart. For example, logic (reason), long-term thinking, intelligence, and self-control are normally associated with the brain, whereas matters of love, emotions, and feelings are associated with the heart. This perspective is not very useful because it gives the impression that matters related to the head can be improved with skills and practice, while matters related to the heart are mainly involuntary and cannot be developed by deliberate practice. The emotional intelligence model challenges this understanding and presents matters of the heart as intelligence too. Emotional intelligence can be acquired.

Emotional intelligence (EI) is often defined as the ability to perceive, use, understand, manage, and handle emotions. Although the term first appeared in 1964, it gained popularity in the 1995 best-selling book Emotional Intelligence, written by science journalist Daniel Goleman. Goleman defined EI as the skills and characteristics driving leadership performance. People with high emotional intelligence can recognise their own emotions and those of others, use emotional information to guide thinking and behaviour, discern between different feelings and label them appropriately, and adjust emotions to adapt to environments.

Here are some tell-tale signs of people with low EI and those with high EI. For example, people with low EI often feel misunderstood, get upset easily, become emotionally overwhelmed, and have problems being assertive. In contrast, people with high EI understand the links between their emotions and their behaviour, remain calm and composed during stressful situations, can influence others toward a common goal, and handle difficult people with tact and diplomacy.

The model introduced by Daniel Goleman focuses on EI as a wide array of competencies and skills that drive leadership performance. Goleman's model outlines five primary EI constructs (for more details, see "What Makes A Leader" by Daniel Goleman, best of Harvard Business Review 1998):

1. **Self-awareness** – the ability to know one's emotions, strengths, weaknesses, drives, values, and goals and recognise their impact on others while using gut feelings to guide decisions.
2. **Self-regulation** – involves controlling or redirecting one's disruptive emotions and impulses and adapting to changing circumstances.
3. **Social skills** – managing relationships to get along with others
4. **Empathy** – considering other people's feelings, especially when making decisions
5. **Motivation** – being aware of what motivates them.

So how is Emotional Intelligence developed or acquired? Several researchers and practitioners have written a lot on this topic, and for those who wish to dive deeper into this, I recommend Daniel Goleman's books as a great place to start. But here are three key steps to follow to develop emotional intelligence:

For better Self-Awareness:

- **Recognize your emotions and name them:** What are you feeling right now? Can you name them? When in a stressful situation, what emotions typically arise? How would you like to respond in these situations? Please stop to pause and reconsider your response. Taking a moment to name your feelings and temper your reactivity is an integral step toward EI.
- **Ask for feedback:** Audit your self-perception by asking managers, colleagues, friends, or family how they would rate your emotional intelligence. For example, ask them how you respond to challenging situations, how adaptable or empathetic you are, or how well you handle conflict. It may not always be what you want to hear, but it will often be what you need to hear.

Five components of Emotional Intelligence

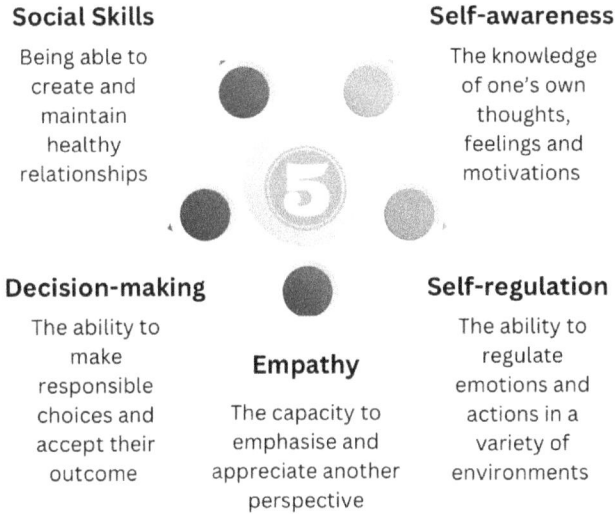

Social Skills

Being able to create and maintain healthy relationships

Self-awareness

The knowledge of one's own thoughts, feelings and motivations

Decision-making

The ability to make responsible choices and accept their outcome

Empathy

The capacity to emphasise and appreciate another perspective

Self-regulation

The ability to regulate emotions and actions in a variety of environments

Components of Emotional Intelligence

- **Read literature:** Studies show that reading literature with complex characters can improve empathy. Reading stories from other people's perspectives helps us gain insight into their thoughts, motivations, and actions and may help enhance our social awareness.

For better Self-Regulation:

- **Pausing Before Responding:** Give yourself time to stop and think before immediately replying. This could be as simple as taking a deep breath and allowing for a 20-second pause so that your feelings get out of the way of your thoughts.

- **Taking a Step Back:** Sometimes, you might need to leave the room, and that's OK. It's often better to take a walk, drink water, or call a friend than to make a snap judgment, send a scathing email, or lash out at your team.
- **Recognizing Your Emotions:** Try jotting down your feelings and what caused the distress. You'll likely start identifying patterns. If you know what triggers you the next time a similar situation occurs, you'll be better positioned to handle it in a healthy, positive way.

For improving empathy:

Practice Active listening. Active listening is preparing to listen, observing verbal and non-verbal messages being sent, and then providing appropriate feedback to show attentiveness to the message being presented. By actively listening, you can better understand people's wants and needs. This can help boost engagement, build trust, and effectively coach your team through challenges. In addition, the more your team feels appreciated, the more invested they'll be, leading to higher morale and a more robust company culture.

For better decision-making:

Be clear about what you want in life and what you don't want. Be Self-motivated. Set goals, take the initiative, rise to the challenge, and stay optimistic during turbulent times. The more positive you are, the more confident people around you will feel.

For improving Social Skills:

Take courses in Persuasion and Influencing, Communication, Conflict Management, Leadership, Change Management and Collaboration, Cooperation & Team-Working Skills. It may take time, but even little but regular effort pays incredible dividends later.

Developing emotional intelligence is a lifelong journey. The journey differs from person to person. But, according to Andrews, the above actions may lead to better self-awareness, empathy, and social skills.

ᖘᖘᖘ

THREE

LEARNING TO TAKE CHARGE OF EMOTIONS

All of us have emotions. Some of us are more sensitive than others, but we all have them. Emotions can be both positive as well as negative, and they influence how we think and act. This makes emotions a very important aspect of our personality to manage.

I had put together some affirmations to help me respond to emotions appropriately. Saying these things out to yourself can help you take charge of your emotions:

1. I am responsible for my own emotions.

I am responsible for my emotions; no other person, circumstance, or condition is responsible. All the emotions I experience are born, live, and belong in me alone.

2. I am also responsible for managing my own emotions.

How I respond to my own emotions is entirely up to me. It is up to me to formulate a mature, healthy, and effective response to my emotions instead of simply reacting. I am my emotional caretaker.

3. I am not responsible for another person's emotions or for managing their moods.

This does not stop me from being sympathetic, empathetic, and compassionate when someone I care about is hurting. I will calmly interact with distressed people, soothe their pain, and help them heal. I understand that real, lasting change only comes from the inside.

4. I will not take the bait to react when it can make things worse

I will avoid situations orchestrated to draw me in, induce a predictable reaction, start a fight, and pull me down to the other person's level.

5. I will practice consistency

Effectively managing my emotions is a skill that will take time to develop. I may sometimes fall short, fall back into old habits, get caught up or drawn into someone else's drama, and begin to feel responsible for another actor's lines. When this happens, I will remind myself that I alone am my play's author, producer, and director. I will set the stage, cast the characters, and choose the part I want. I operate the lights and curtain. And in my show, I get to take the bow.

'If' by Rudyard Kipling

The quest to thrive takes a lot of motivation and inspiration. Motivation should ideally come from inside us; it should be intrinsic, while inspiration comes from outside us. We should take learning and inspiration from all quarters of life. And poetry is no exception. I am sharing here a poem that has inspired thousands over generations. The poem is full of inspiration, motivation, and maxims for living well and is a blueprint for personal integrity, behaviour, and self-development.

> If you can keep your head when all about you
> Are losing theirs and blaming it on you,
> If you can trust yourself when all men doubt you,
> But make allowance for their doubting too;
> If you can wait and not be tired by waiting,
> Or being lied about, don't deal in lies,
> Or being hated, don't give way to hating,
> And yet don't look too good, nor talk too wise:

If you can dream—and not make dreams your master;
If you can think—and not make thoughts your aim;
If you can meet with Triumph and Disaster
And treat those two impostors just the same;
If you can bear to hear the truth you've spoken
Twisted by knaves to make a trap for fools,
Or watch the things you gave your life to, broken,
And stoop and build 'em up with worn-out tools:
If you can make one heap of all your winnings
And risk it on one turn of pitch-and-toss,
And lose, and start again at your beginnings
And never breathe a word about your loss;
If you can force your heart and nerve and sinew
To serve your turn long after they are gone,
And so hold on when there is nothing in you
Except the Will which says to them: 'Hold on!'
If you can talk with crowds and keep your virtue,
Or walk with Kings—nor lose the common touch,
If neither foes nor loving friends can hurt you,
If all men count with you, but none too much;
If you can fill the unforgiving minute
With sixty seconds' worth of distance run,
Yours is the earth and everything that's in it,
And—which is more—you'll be a Man, my son!
Source: 'Brother Square-Toes'—Rewards and Fairies by Rudyard Kipling

Here are the key lessons from this beautiful teaching poem:

To be good and succeed, we should keep calm when other people lose their cool. We should not lose our temper even if others blame us for their fault. Losing our temper does not solve our problems; rather, it intensifies them. When we keep our cool, we can think wisely and face those demanding situations, and solutions emerge.

We should have faith in ourselves, even when others doubt us. But after that, we should also give some importance to their doubt and try to find the reason for their suspicion. After all, 'To err is human...'. So, By keeping faith in ourselves, we ensure we do not demoralise ourselves or get disheartened. When we allow some consideration for others' doubts, we make room for knowing that we may be doing something wrong consciously or unconsciously.

We should work hard and be patient with the results. We should not get tired by waiting. There are several real-life examples where people missed significant opportunities only by losing their patience. Several sayings remind us, "Hurry will bury you", "Haste makes waste." and "Patience pays off."

People may lie about us to others, but we should not indulge ourselves in lies. In other words, we should always remain truthful. If we are misled or tempted to lie, people will ultimately discover the truth and won't believe us anymore. That's why it's essential to speak the truth even if that hurts us.

People may sometimes show hatred towards us, but we should not hate them. Instead, we should show our love and respect to others. No man or woman is perfect in this world. Everyone has his strengths and weaknesses. We must accept that and respect them for their excellent qualities.

If you are good at something, be proud of it but not arrogant; there is no need to show off. Do not let others feel uncomfortable in your company and avoid you. Your inflated ego may cause others to want to prove you wrong, leading to unhealthy competition.

Dream to achieve, but stay realistic. Be guided by your dreams but do not put them in the driver's seat, or else you may lose touch with reality and get lost. There is a saying, "You have to dream first before your dream can come true."

Deep thinking is essential, but they are only the means, not the end. Stay focused. Life's journey brings success and failure, joy and sorrow, and good and bad times. We should take both in our stride. People often become too happy with the success, forget the task at hand, and get too complacent or proud. This reduces their chances of reaching higher goals. Again, if we are too grieved at bad times, we may lose our faith and self-confidence. That is why both triumph and disaster are called two impostors'. So, don't be too happy or too depressed under the circumstances.

Sometimes, your words or actions may be misinterpreted or even distorted by others. Never lose your temper over it; tolerate them but ensure you have spoken the truth. We should hold our nerves even after seeing that our favourite thing we built with all our effort and time is broken. Then we must pick up the scattered parts and build them over again. Patience and resilience would help us build them again. It is said that Newton once lost papers containing his theories in a fire accident, but he was able to write them all over again. To succeed in life, one needs to push one's boundaries, get out of the comfort zone, and take calculated risks.

We should remain persistent and keep pushing forward despite illness or ageing. Never underestimate the power of one's will. If we want to achieve greatness from our hearts, the will inside us shall empower us. "When going gets tough, the tough get going."

We should mingle with people from all walks of life. We should be able to talk with ordinary people and also be able to walk with kings. The ordinary help us stay grounded while the noble empower and lift us higher.

We should build resilience; become mentally and physically tough so that no one can hurt us deeply. We must build our personality the right way so everyone supports us and can count on us in need. Practice moderation. Time is precious; if you value time, then time will value you. Time is unforgiving, as it waits for none and doesn't forgive him who wastes it. We should utilize every waking minute effectively. Life is too short.

If we can be all that is spoken of here, then we can win this earth and everything in it. And what is more, we would feel whole, contented and at peace as human beings. Kipling penned this poem for his son as he wanted to teach him how to live and lead life, pursue happiness, and inspire many generations to come. Through this book, I intend to do the same.

One area which influences many people a lot emotionally is social media. The following article will examine how social media can impact us negatively.

10 Ways Social Media Addiction Can Ruin Your Life

The world seems hooked on the five great social media platforms, viz. Facebook, Twitter, Instagram, Snapchat, and WhatsApp/WeChat. People spend billions of collective hours each day lost in their wonderland. (Tiktok may be next on the list). I am no authority on this to advise, and you need not take my advice, even if I dole out one. So rather than advising, I want to warn you of the ten ways these social media apps may ruin your life. Here they are:

1. You spend your time in a fake, made-up, and selective virtual world that gives you false hope, understanding, and experience of events, people, and their lives, making you live in an illusion.

2. You start following, feeling, and anticipating the experiences of celebrities and influencers as if they are people you know personally. Celebrities have nothing to do with you. You are as much a person as they are. You have a life of your own to live and your own experiences to have.

3. You fool yourself by rejoicing and celebrating social media likes, emojis, and commendations as real achievements and successes. And you are missing out on those successes and achievements that would have been yours in the real world if only that attention, focus, and hard work had been invested in the real world.

4. You lose the best time- hours, days, months- of your youth that could have been spent learning and shaping your career, losing many opportunities to build genuine self-esteem and self-worth.

5. You start doing things exclusively for the sake of social media. You want to have an experience only because you can photograph it, capture it in a video, add filters to it and garnish it with tags and titles so that it is impactful for your social media audience.

6. You are constantly distracted, seeking distractions to entertain yourself, and cannot focus on any task long enough to be creative, productive, and valuable.

7. You start believing that life is only meant to be enjoyed. Every day has to be seized and squeezed for the last drop of excitement. And so you lose out on taking the real journey of life. Life is about pursuing goals and working hard, even experiencing pain, to have growth, success, and happiness for yourself and your loved ones.

8. You never tend to grow out of your teenage years, always watching out for new trends, fashions, and slang. You want to look and sound smart using the latest app or filter that can enhance your social media image, the next cause to rebel against, or the next travel, restaurant, food, or celebrity to go crazy about.

9. You start manipulating or changing your real world to suit your virtual world of social reality, changing priorities and making decisions that will forever alter your life and relationships.

10. You end up in an endless cycle of regret, guilt, and escapism, not having the strength to stand up to reality and take control of your destiny in your hands.

By the time we realise this, we may have lost time, made decisions, broken relationships, and lost opportunities that we can never get back. One may regain a lost opportunity but not regain the lost time. Social media addiction deprives us of our living our limited time fully on earth. I understand social media can have some advantages but are they enough to outweigh the damage they do to us? Why walk that path at all?

Breaking the cycle of obsessive thinking

Do you often spend much time worrying about the future or thinking about the past? Are you obsessing over something that unexpectedly happened, or someone said something annoying? Brooding and ruminating over the same thoughts over hours?

I do this too, and trust me, it's very unproductive to ourselves and is often annoying to others too. It takes you away from the present moment and prevents you from giving 100% to the task.

I wanted to share how I dealt with such obsessive and nagging thoughts using lessons from my Vedanta practice. Here are the lessons one can use:

Understand that the world operates by cause and effect. Karma. Watch this play of cause and effect. Watch it work in the external world. You will see how it moves the world.

But know this, it operates in our inner world too. It moves our thoughts, feelings, and emotions.

Have you noticed why asking someone to stop crying does not work? Why can't you stop being mad when you are? Why can you not hold back those harsh remarks when they come?

Every emotion and feeling has a cause too, and it is merely the expression of that cause, like the raindrops emerging from a cloud.

Understand that that, the emotion, and that feeling you have is not you. That is not what defines you. But you are responsible for it because you engaged with its cause. So it is yours, but it is not you.

Your true nature, the real you are a witness. Witness this play like the blue sky that watches the clouds, thunderstorms, and rainbows. They come, hang on for moments, and leave like clouds.

Just accept them as they come. And accept them as they leave. Don't engage them. You are not doing it. It's happening to you. Understand this difference. So, do not identify with them or act on them.

Just let them be. Be mindful of them, just like the muddy water turns clear by staying still. You can bring back your poise, peace, and lightness.

Be responsible. Guard yourself. For thought become emotions, emotions become feelings, feelings become thought, thought becomes action, and action becomes behaviour. It is an unstoppable chain of cause and effect.

Once you become mindful of this chain and merely act as a witness to them, without engaging with them, they lose their power. When this clarity dawns upon our minds, we feel lighter, positive, and cheerful.

There are many effective ways of dealing with obsessive thinking. I chose this method because I have worked with it and found it effective. This gives you some understanding and perspective to free yourself of obsessive thinking. This freedom will help you give your undivided attention to the person or task at hand, make you more effective and bring you more success and love.

We have so far discussed emotions and emotional life. Now that we understand how closely healthy emotions are tied to physical health, we can turn our discussion toward physical health and fitness. The next chapter introduces a very comprehensive and practical model of health and fitness.

ppp

FOUR

FIVE-POINT FITNESS MODEL

———◆♡◆———

The American entrepreneur, author and motivational speaker said,

"Take care of your body. It's the only place you have to live."

Physical fitness is a state of health and well-being. More specifically, it is the ability to perform aspects of sports, occupations, and daily activities well. We can achieve physical fitness through proper nutrition, moderate-vigorous physical exercise, sufficient rest, and a formal recovery plan. However, the challenge lies in preparing a plan, choosing elements of it, and measuring progress. The five-point model for health can come in handy here.

The five-point fitness model consists of addressing five aspects of physical fitness with a single plan: Cardiovascular endurance, muscular strength, flexibility, muscular endurance, and body composition. Let us look at these components separately and see how we can combine them to build good physical health and fitness.

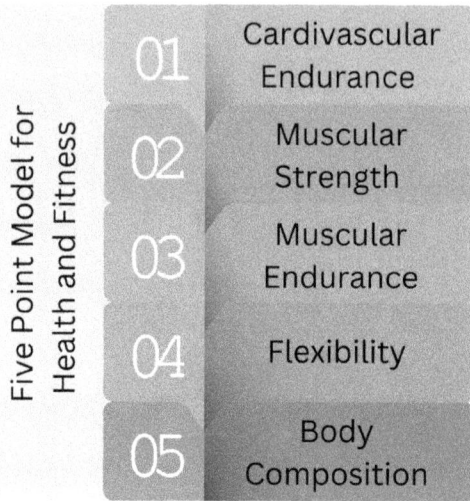

Five Elements of Fitness

1. Get Moving for Cardiovascular Endurance

According to Centres for Disease Control and Prevention (CDC), Physical activity is anything that gets your body moving. According to the current Physical Activity Guidelines for Americans, adults need 150 minutes of moderate-intensity physical activity each week and two days of muscle-strengthening activity. We know 150 minutes of physical activity each week sounds like a lot, but you can do it in stages. You can spread your activity during the week and break it into smaller chunks. For example, it could be 30 minutes a day, five days a week. Adults aged 18-64 are advised to do at least 150 minutes a week of moderate-intensity activity, such as brisk walking, and at least two days a week of activities that strengthen muscles.

Cardiovascular endurance, otherwise known as Aerobic Fitness, is the "ability to perform large muscle, dynamic, moderate to high-intensity exercise for prolonged periods" (ACSM 2000). The Heart rate is typically maintained in the range of 126-143 beats per minute throughout the aerobic exercise. A simple cardiovascular endurance test is to time yourself on a 1.5-mile (2.4-kilometre) run or jog.

Example 1	Example 2	Example 3
Moderate-intensity aerobic activity	Vigorous-intensity aerobic activity	An equivalent mix of moderate- and vigorous-intensity aerobic activity
(such as brisk walking) for 150 minutes every week (for example, 30 minutes a day, 5 days a week)	(such as jogging or running) for 75 minutes (1 hour and 15 minutes) every week	on 2 or more days a week
AND	AND	AND
Muscle-strengthening activities	Muscle-strengthening activities	Muscle-strengthening activities
on 2 or more days a week that work all major muscle groups (legs, hips, back, abdomen, chest, shoulders, and arms).	on 2 or more days a week that work all major muscle groups (legs, hips, back, abdomen, chest, shoulders, and arms).	on 2 or more days a week that work all major muscle groups (legs, hips, back, abdomen, chest, shoulders, and arms).

Physical Activity Guidelines by CDC

Regular physical activity in the form of jogging or playing a sport like a badminton is one of the most important things you can do for your health. It exercises your lung, keeps your heart healthy and boosts your mood. So, if you're ready to get the immediate benefits of better sleep, reduced anxiety, and lower blood pressure, here are ways to get started:

· Look for ways to reduce time sitting and increase time moving. For example, make it a habit to walk before or after dinner.
· Set aside specific times to make physical activity part of your daily or weekly routine.
· Start with activities, locations, and times you enjoy. For example, you might like morning walks in your neighbourhood, prefer an online class after work, or would love to play a sport.

- Try activities with others in your household for motivation and mutual encouragement.
- Start slowly and work up to more time or challenging activities.
- Use free apps and websites to find fun ways to be physically active, or join a group fitness club to add variety to your activity routine.

2. Push, pull and lift for Muscular Strength

Muscular strength is the amount of force a muscle can produce. Muscular strength is the ability of a muscle or muscle group to exert a maximal force against a resistance one time through the full range of motion. Examples would be the bench press, leg press, or bicep curl. Muscular strength is typically tested by measuring how much percentage of body weight a person can lift, pull or push. The table below tells us what qualifies a person as strong.

	Per cent of Body Weight for Men	Per cent of Body Weight for Women
Lat Pull-Down	66%	55%
Leg Extension	50%	50%
Bench Press	66%	50%
Leg Curl	33%	33%
Arm Curl	33%	25%

Adapted from Heyward, V. H. (1991). Advanced fitness assessment & exercise prescription (2nd ed.). Champaign, IL: Human Kinetics.

3. Stretch for Flexibility

Flexibility is the ability to move a joint through its complete range of motion (ACSM 2000). A typical stretching exercise lengthens or flexes a skeletal muscle to the point of tension and holds for several seconds to increase elasticity and range of motion around a joint.

Examples would be stretching individual muscles or the ability to perform specific functional movements such as the lunge. Improving flexibility can enhance the overall physical performance of other types of exercises. Some examples of stretching programs include dynamic stretches performed with activity (yoga, tai chi), static stretches without movement (holding a pose for several seconds or longer), passive stretching (using an external force like a strap or wall to hold a long pose), and active stretching (holding a pose without an external force).

The sit-and-reach test is most often used to test flexibility. Here is how it is conducted:

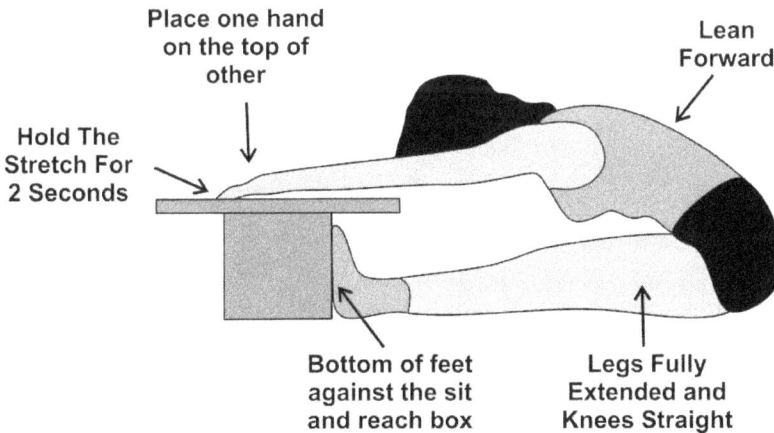

Sit and Reach Test

First, you'll need a special sit-and-reach testing box. You can also make your testing box by finding a solid box about 30cm tall. Fix a meter stick on top of the box so that 26 cm of the ruler extends over the front edge of the box toward the test subject. The 26cm mark should be at the edge of the box.

Get in position: Remove your shoes and sit on the floor with your legs stretched out in front of you with your knees straight and feet flat against the front end of the test box.

Begin the movement: In a slow, steady motion, lean forward at the hips, keep your knees straight and slide your hand up the ruler as far as you can. Stretch and repeat. Extend as far as possible, record the result in cm, rest, and repeat three times.

Calculate your results by averaging your results for your final score.

Adult Men	Adult Women	Result
34cm or above	37cm or above	Excellent
28 to 33cm	33 to 36cm	Above average
23 to 27cm	29 to 32cm	Average
16 to 22cm	23 to 28cm	Below average
Below 16cm	Below 23cm	Poor

Sit and Reach Test Scores

One of the most popular programs promoting flexibility is Yoga. In fact, it gives you much more than flexibility. All yoga forms – Hatha, Vinyasa, Ashtanga, Kundalini, Bikram, Iyengar or Yin- can provide physical and mental health benefits. The poses and postures increase flexibility, balance, and strength, all of which can help reduce the risk of injury. The focus on breathing and relaxation helps to lower anxiety and depression and to increase mental clarity and focus. Because of these effects, yoga has become increasingly popular as a therapeutic method. Yoga beautifully complements several exercise formats that help promote the other components of fitness, like muscular strength and endurance.

Push-Up Fitness Test Results

Men	Age 20-29	Age 30-39	Age 40-49	Age 50-59	Age 60+
Excellent	54 or more	44 or more	39 or more	34 or more	29 or more
Good	45-54	35-44	30-39	25-34	20-29
Average	35-44	24-34	20-29	15-24	10-19
Poor	20-34	15-24	12-19	8-14	5-9
Very poor	20 or fewer	15 or fewer	12 or fewer	8 or fewer	5 or fewer
Women	Age 20-29	Age 30-39	Age 40-49	Age 50-59	Age 60+
Excellent	48 or more	39 or more	34 or more	29 or more	19 or more
Good	34-48	25-39	20-34	15-29	5-19
Average	17-33	12-24	8-19	6-14	3-4
Poor	6-16	4-11	3-7	2-5	1-2
Very poor	6 or fewer	4 or fewer	3 or fewer	2 or fewer	1 or fewer

Push-up Test Scoring Table

4. *Muscular Endurance*

Muscular Endurance is the ability of a muscle or muscle group to exert a submaximal force repeatedly over time. The push-up test is most often used to test muscular strength and endurance.

The push-up test measures upper body strength and endurance. In this test, one pushup is performed every three seconds. The maximum number of pushups performed at this rate is recorded. Here is how it is done:

Start in the push-up position - with the hands and toes touching the floor, the body and legs are in a straight line, feet slightly apart, the arms at shoulder width apart, extended, and at a right angle to the body. Keeping the back and knees straight, lower the body until there is a 90-degree angle at the elbows, with the upper arms parallel to the floor. A partner holds their hand at the point of the 90-degree angle to the floor so that you go down only until your shoulder touches the partner's hand, then back up. The push-ups are done in time to a metronome or similar device with one complete push-up every three seconds (1.5 seconds down and 1.5 seconds up, 20 full push-ups per minute). Scoring is done by recording the number of correctly completed push-ups that you performed in time to the rhythm.

5. Eat right, fast and rest for Body Composition

Body composition measures lean body mass (all tissues other than fat, such as bone, muscle, organs, and body fluids) compared with the amount of body fat, usually expressed in per cent body fat. The most commonly used measure of body composition is BMI or Body Mass Index. BMI is calculated by taking a person's weight and dividing it by their height squared. For instance, if your height is 1.82 meters, the divisor of the calculation will be (1.82 * 1.82) = 3.3124. If your weight is 70.5 kilograms, your BMI is 21.3 (70.5 / 3.3124).

The higher the figure, the more overweight you are. Like any of these measures, it is only an indication, and other factors such as body type and shape also have a bearing. Remember, BMI is just a guide - it does not accurately apply to elderly populations, pregnant women, or very muscular athletes such as weightlifters. You can easily calculate your BMI using one of the several fitness apps that come as stock on your cell phone or an online BMI calculator. (https://www.calculator.net/bmi-calculator.html)

The best way to get back to a healthy BMI is by adopting a fasting routine like intermittent fasting. You will read about this in the following chapter. The best we can do to maintain/ improve body composition is to stay hydrated, eat right, and rest well.

An easy way to figure out how to eat right is by using the Healthy Eating Plate Model model. Nutrition experts at the Harvard T.H. Chan School of Public Health and editors at Harvard Health Publications developed it. The Healthy Eating Plate provides detailed guidance in a simple format to help people make the best eating choices. It can be applied to preparing a healthy and balanced meal plate or packing a lunch box.

That leaves us with the topic of rest –I mean quality sleep. Sleep is essential for the optimal functioning of our brain and body. Our need for sleep changes as we age. Newborns need 14-17 hours of sleep each day.

Infants need 12-16 hours each day. Toddlers require 10-14 hours each day, Pre-teens & teens about 8-12 hours each day and adults about 7-8 hours each day. Adults who sleep less than five hours a day or more than 9 hours a day can develop a risk of obesity, cardiovascular diseases and diabetes.

HEALTHY EATING PLATE

Use healthy oils (like olive and canola oil) for cooking, on salad, and at the table. Limit butter. Avoid trans fat.

The more veggies – and the greater the variety – the better. Potatoes and French fries don't count.

Eat plenty of fruits of all colors.

STAY ACTIVE!

© Harvard University

VEGETABLES

WHOLE GRAINS

HEALTHY PROTEIN

FRUITS

WATER Drink water, tea, or coffee (with little or no sugar). Limit milk/dairy (1-2 servings/day) and juice (1 small glass/day). Avoid sugary drinks.

Eat a variety of whole grains (like whole-wheat bread, whole-grain pasta, and brown rice). Limit refined grains (like white rice and white bread).

Choose fish, poultry, beans, and nuts; limit red meat and cheese; avoid bacon, cold cuts, and other processed meats.

Harvard T.H. Chan School of Public Health
The Nutrition Source
www.hsph.harvard.edu/nutritionsource

Harvard Medical School
Harvard Health Publications
www.health.harvard.edu

Copyright © 2011, Harvard University. Please see The Nutrition Source, Department of Nutrition, Harvard T.H. Chan School of Public Health, www.thenutritionsource.org, and Harvard Health Publications, www.health.harvard.edu.

Three quick tips on ensuring quality sleep

· Set a sleep schedule and stick to it. Try to go to bed at night and awaken in the morning around the same time, even on weekends. This helps to regulate the body's sleep cycles and circadian rhythms.

- Avoid screen time before bed, especially those emitting blue light, such as smartphones, tablets, and televisions.
- Create a quiet, dark, relaxing environment in your bedroom. Dim the lights and put your phone on silent mode if possible.

It would help if you also determined how well you can handle running a mile or escaping physically out of an emergency like a fire. One way to prepare a fitness program for yourself is to combine or include activities from each component into a weekly plan. You do not work on all elements on the same day but pick activities encompassing one or more of these components on different days of the week. A good balance of activity in all five components will give you the most healthy and fit version of yourself, and you will feel it. However, over-investing in only one fitness component often comes at the cost of all others. Instead, it is best to create a balanced portfolio of all the components of fitness and include them in your health and fitness plan. During the covid lockdown, I added about four kilos of additional me to myself. I sprained my back because I tried to lift my 8-year-old for a photo. My sugar cravings skyrocketed. I was not sure I could sprint for 200 meters without collapsing my lungs! The sedentary lifestyle was taking a toll on my health. So, I wanted to find a solution and return to being my fit self again. That is when I put this mental model to work and set myself a four-week target of losing the extra 'me' I was lugging around.

Here is an example of a daily five-point plan that helped me reclaim good health and fitness in ten weeks during the Pandemic

- **Cardiovascular Endurance**: I walked 10000 steps daily: Made simple lifestyle changes like taking stairs to work & to my apartment. Also, I walked while taking calls and did an hour of brisk walking in the evening to complete the remaining steps while listening to my favourite podcasts or audiobooks.
- **Flexibility:** Started the day with Sun Salutations. I did twelve Sun Salutations each morning (took 15 min)
- **Muscular Strength:** I lifted weights in my community gym twice weekly; it seemed practical and doable. I preferred doing a full body workout – exercises focusing on all the muscle groups, performing only one set of each exercise.

Height (in centimeters)	Women (in kilograms)	Men (in kilograms)	BMI 22 (in kilograms)
152	49	52	52
155	51	54	54
157	52	56	56
160	54	58	58
163	56	60	60
165	57	62	62
168	59	63	64
170	61	65	66
173	63	67	68
175	64	69	70
178	66	71	72
180	68	73	74
213	69	75	76
216	71	77	78
218	73	79	80
221	74	81	82
224	76	82	84
226	78	84	86
229	80	86	88

Metric Ideal Height Weight Chart for Adults

- **Muscular endurance:** I love cycling, so I included an hour of cycling each week in my program. Cycling brought some variety and outdoor fun, especially during pandemic days. I also did 20 pushups a day.
- **Body Composition:** No doubt that by working with the last four components, my BMI improved. But I did take additional care, like drinking eight glasses of warm water during the day and two green tea mugs in the office (replacing milk tea/coffee). I also included a portion of fruit or Salad in the meal. I avoided dessert and wheat for dinner and usually ate only until I was about 80% full. Finally, I ensured I completed 8 hours of sleep every night.

I knew it might not have been sustainable if I attempted to do anything radical, like joining a fitness club or playing a new sport during the pandemic. So, I decided to start with nothing radical and take little steps without disturbing the rest of my routines. In about ten weeks, I weighed lesser, looked better, and felt fitter. Fitness is a journey, so whatever program you choose for yourself, ensure it is sustainable in the long term. Consistency and discipline is the key. The Five points Health and Fitness model gives you a better, more comprehensive perspective of health and fitness and how to implement it in your own life. All these are measurable, so you can always measure your progress or regress. All the best with it! Next, we shall discuss an effective way to reach a healthy BMI.

ᐅᐅᐅ

FIVE

THE SUREFIRE WAY TO HEALTH AND LONGEVITY: INTERMITTENT FASTING

As Millennials, we have a lot of challenges in the sphere of spiritual, physical and mental health. Today there is a rising number of premature deaths due to high blood glucose. The single most important cause of premature deaths across the globe is high blood sugar. It causes a variety of illnesses and organ failures. Diabetes is a significant cause of blindness, kidney failure, heart attacks, stroke, and lower limb amputation. As per WHO, in 2019, an estimated 1.5 million deaths were directly caused by diabetes. Also, between 2000 and 2016, there was a 5% increase in premature mortality from diabetes, thanks to our changing eating habits. If I could give one prescription that can relieve many of our physical, mental, and spiritual ailments, it is Intermittent Fasting.

In simple words, Intermittent Fasting is the practice of alternating periods of eating and fasting. It comes in many forms, but the basic idea is to have a large time block of not eating in a day. Dr David Sinclair is a world-renowned scientist who has worked for decades studying longevity and health at Harvard Medical School. He considers ageing a medical condition, like a disease, because it causes pain, suffering, and death. He supports the practice of systematic fasting and has acknowledged several benefits of intermittent fasting, which include longevity and disease prevention.

Here is a quote from David Sinclair's book 'Lifespan':

"*After twenty-five years of researching ageing and having read thousands of scientific papers, if there is one piece of advice I can offer, one sure-fire way to stay healthy longer, one thing you can do to maximise your lifespan right now, it's this: eat less.*"

David explains how eating less food leads to slower ageing,

"*When you fast, you turn on these defences. And that's the reason I think they primarily work. It's not that blood flows better or just that insulin sensitivity changes. You really are turning on every cell's defences against DNA damage, toxins, everything that causes diseases. It seems that these defences have a way to slow down the negative effects.*"

There are many kinds of intermittent fasts, but I would like to specifically recommend one called early time-restricted feeding (eTRF), which is better supported by scientific research. Early time-restricted feeding (eTRF) is a form of intermittent fasting that involves eating dinner in the mid-afternoon and fasting for the rest of the day.

A lifestyle intervention like eTRF is the need of the hour. We all want to live longer, be healthier, and slow ageing. We want to be around to see our children grow up and become responsible adults and go on to have their own families. eTRF is the most promising, affordable, and doable prescription to help us here. It is something I have practised and seen the benefits first-hand. However, please consult your physician before taking it up yourself.

Five Key Benefits of eTRF that make an excellent case for adopting eTRF as a lifestyle choice

- Beta cells make insulin, a hormone that controls the level of glucose (a type of sugar) in the blood. eTRF increases insulin sensitivity and also improves β cell function. Insulin sensitivity refers to how sensitive the body's cells are in response to insulin. High insulin sensitivity allows the cells of the body to use blood glucose more effectively, reducing blood sugar.

Median American Eating Patterns

Early Time-Restricted Feeding

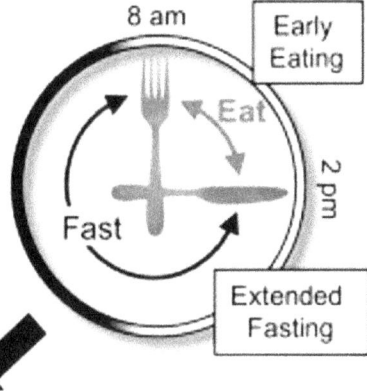

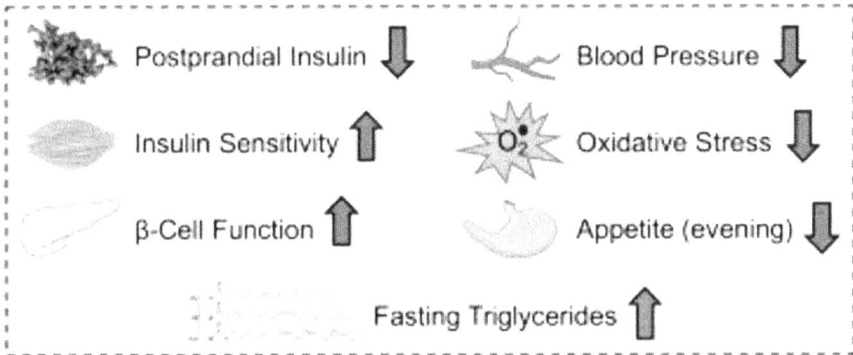

8 am

Fast   Eat

8 pm

vs.

8 am

Early Eating

Eat

Fast

2 pm

Extended Fasting

Postprandial Insulin ⬇

Insulin Sensitivity ⬆

β-Cell Function ⬆

Fasting Triglycerides ⬆

Blood Pressure ⬇

Oxidative Stress ⬇

Appetite (evening) ⬇

Early Time-Restricted Feeding Improves Insulin Sensitivity, Blood Pressure, and Oxidative Stress Even without Weight Loss in Men with Prediabetes.

- eTRF also lowers blood pressure and oxidative stress. Oxidative stress has gained attention as one of the fundamental mechanisms responsible for the development of hypertension. And hypertension is the most important risk factor in the development of cardiovascular disease.
- eTRF lowers the desire to eat in the evening, which may facilitate weight loss. This is because we are all made of food. The more we eat, the more

often we eat, the heavier we become, and the less we eat, the less often we eat, and the lighter we become.
- One of the benefits I have experienced myself with eTRF is that it soothes our minds and makes us clear & lightheaded. For a spiritual person, this is a huge benefit.
- And finally, what is remarkable about eTRF is that it can improve health even if it doesn't cause weight loss!

Research on eTRF demonstrated for the first time that the benefits of eTRF go beyond just weight loss. In a study, the participants on eTRF were fed enough to maintain their body weight. They did this to ensure that any other effects on health cannot be attributed to weight loss.
The study mentioned:

> "We conducted the first supervised controlled feeding trial to test whether IF has benefits independent of weight loss by feeding participants enough food to maintain weight. Our proof-of-concept study also constitutes the first trial of early time-restricted feeding (eTRF), a form of IF that involves eating early in the day to align with metabolism's circadian rhythms. Men with prediabetes were randomised to eTRF (6-hr feeding period, with dinner before 3 PM) or a control schedule (12-hr feeding period) for five weeks and later crossed over to the other schedule. eTRF improved insulin sensitivity, β cell responsiveness, blood pressure, oxidative stress, and appetite."

There is increasing evidence that eating for 6 hours and fasting for 18 hours can trigger a metabolic switch from glucose-based to ketone-based energy. This leads to increased stress resistance, longevity, and a decreased incidence of diseases, including cancer and obesity. You need not immediately start with the 18:6 regime but take a more gradual route to see the benefits first-hand. You can start with a 12 hour:12 system, then transition to 15:9, and later, if one feels like 18:6, could be adopted. I now use the 15: 9 discipline and am seeing progress in feeling good about myself, especially with weight loss. I also throw in moderate exercise with dumbbells on alternate days. It would be best to decide how small or big your steps are.

Here is some helpful expert advice on eTRF, which we can all use to the best of our capacity:

- ***Avoid sugars and refined grains.*** Instead, eat fruits, vegetables, beans, lentils, whole grains, lean proteins, and healthy fats (a sensible, plant-based, Mediterranean-style diet).
- ***Let your body burn fat between meals.*** Don't snack. Be active throughout your day. Build muscle tone.
- ***Consider a simple form of intermittent fasting.*** Limit the hours of the day when you eat, and for best effect, make it earlier in the day (between 7 AM to 3 PM, or even 10 AM to 6 PM, but not in the evening before bed).
- ***Avoid snacking or eating at night-time, all the time.***

As Benjamin Franklin once said, 'The best of all medicines is resting and fasting.' An intermittent fasting routine beautifully blends the two, giving our bodies enough time to rest and recover through the fasting period. The journey of Self-control begins with the simple act of fasting. Fasting helps us understand our relationship with food and our bodies. As our bodies detox, our minds are clear of chatter, and peace dawns on us. It is no wonder every religious tradition invariable includes the magic ingredient of fasting to get closer to godliness. Try it.

Even the most effective methods fail when we cannot sustain them over time. That is why it is crucial to incorporate learnings into our lives through routines. How to set up healthy routines is the topic of our next chapter.

ᐯᐯᐯ

SIX

HARNESSING THE POWER OF HEALTHY DAILY ROUTINES

———◦▷◦———

John C. Maxwell said,

> "*You'll never change your life until you change something you do daily. The secret to your success is found in your daily routine.*"

Both successful people and unsuccessful people have the same goals. Besides favours from Lady Luck and hard work, their healthy daily routines make successful people stand apart. Unfortunately, there are some negative connotations to the word 'routine' as it gives one the feeling of 'ordinary' or 'boring' or 'the regular' or 'drudgery.' Most of us believe variety is the spice of life, even though very few of us understand that it is not sustainable, healthy, or affordable to live each day very differently.

Healthy routines are great for all those who wear multiple hats and shoulder multiple responsibilities daily. Everyone wants to be successful in life. If we put some good thought behind building our routine and be open to improving it with experimentation, it can boost our productivity and efficiency and make us feel more energized, healthy, and happier.

In his NYT Bestseller Atomic Habits, James Clear said,

> "*When you fall in love with the process rather than the product, you don't have to wait to permit yourself to be happy. Instead, you can be*

satisfied anytime your system is running."

American leadership coach John C. Maxwell said,

"*If I could come to your house and spend just one day with you, I would be able to tell whether you will be successful. You could pick the day.*"

Success in any field cannot be an overnight achievement; it takes a lot of preparation, focus, and persistence. But, he continues, 'You will never change your life until you change something you do daily.' When we have goals and orient our daily lives in such a way that we always try to inch closer to our goals, even if very slowly, we can be sure of reaching success. All our goals, including fitness goals, career goals, relationship goals, or financial goals, must be part of a daily routine. Else we leave a lot to chance.

We need a daily routine to nourish all areas of life: love, parenting, work, health and spirituality. This means we include some quality time with our loved ones, some sport, or games with friends, working on priorities at the workplace, something to nourish our spiritual side, and healthy eating and physical activity. Only then is our routine sustainable, complete, and healthy. So, for example, if parenting is important to you, it should be integrated into your daily routine.

In James Clear's words,

"*You do not rise to the level of your goals. You fall to the level of your systems.*"

Goals are good only to give us direction, but our progress depends on the routines or systems we fall back on. So, whatever the goal, think of what you can do today (routine) and how you can do things every day (habit) to get there. Build a healthy daily routine and stick to it.

ᑭᑭᑭ

SEVEN

THE FOUR KINDS OF FRIENDS WE ALL NEED

———◦𝄋◦———

I came across this quote by Vladimir Lenin,

"Show me who your friends are, and I will show you what you are."

A friend is someone with whom one has a bond of mutual affection. A friendship is typically exclusive of sexual or direct family relations. Friends come in all shapes, sizes, and colours. Friends are not just people we hang out with; they become part of our sense of identity in many ways. Whether we like it or not, we invariably share traits, habits, skills, talents, values, and preferences with those we call friends.

From our cradle to our grave, we make many friends and acquaintances. But many of us believe that, like many other things, friends are like collectables. We must endlessly acquire, maintain and showcase them. As a result, our social media profiles keep brimming with friends from across the globe. Some of us have hundreds of friends on our network and still want more. This need not be so. In fact, it is stressful and takes the life out of friendships.

We should have but a handful of friends at any point in time. But before we talk about that, let us look at an interesting mental model describing the type of friends. I came across this exciting book by Geoffrey Greif called 'Buddy System: Understanding Male Friendships. In this book, he categorises friendships into four types, and it's a very helpful way to group your friends. Here they are :

Must friends

These are the ones most of us would call best friends. They are very close to you and your family, almost like family and close confidantes you can count on at any point in life. *Most friends* are with you in every significant event/celebration/setback of your life and support you unconditionally. These are the kind of friends you'd want to raise your children if you happen to die young. This could be the criteria to qualify them as one!

Trust friends

They are friends whom you can trust. You can share your fears and concerns with them, and you think can understand and guide you best in times of need. They may not be part of your inner circle, but you are comfortable sharing your challenges with them. You would like to get closer to them given a suitable opportunity or time.

Rust friends

Rust friend is someone you've known for a long time and you know very well – at least, you don't believe you can know any better even if you tried. They are typically friends you have known since your younger days, cousins. It can even be your spouse.

Just friends

Just friends keep you company on specific occasions and places, like your next cabin coworker, someone who walks the dog with you or goes to the same yoga class. This friendship is limited to the occasion or place, and you don't desire to socialise or interact with such a person outside the occasion or place. You only try to get to know the person in the context of the occasion or place.

These are the four types of friends you can have. This model can help you have a better look at your friends. You can also think of what kinds you have more or less of at present. This will tell you what kind of friends you need. A good balance of friends of each type can help one get the most happiness out of friendships. There can also be overlaps between the types in the case of some friends, and it is also possible that over time a just friend can become a trust friend , or a must friend becomes a rust friend.

Though Geoffrey Greif's book is about male friendships, it also applies to women. However, Greif points out that the big difference between male and female friendships is that women have face-to-face relationships while men have shoulder-to-shoulder relationships. As a result, women can share real intimacy, while men prefer sharing an activity- like a project, sport, or philosophy- where it is not necessary to open up about their feelings. Man or woman, boy or girl- everyone needs friends. Our friendships greatly influence the quality of our emotions and happiness.

Having said so, we must be picky about who we enlist as friends. Why? Because the personality traits, preferences, quirks, and habits of our friends rub off on us. Make friends of good character and keep away from anyone of questionable character. A Japanese Proverb goes,

"*When the man's character is not clear to you, look at his friends.*"

Friendships that do not have integrity and share similar values do not last, and they do more harm. A handful of friends of each type are enough- 4/5 of each type. We don't need more. Trim down your list, if need be, to a level you can manage. By manage, I mean you can give your friends a fair amount of your time and mind space.

It was Hubert H. Humphrey who said,

"*The greatest gift of life is friendship, and I have received it.*"

Life has given me great friends of each type, and I will be ever grateful for it. I have earned their friendships as much as they have earned mine. I encourage my daughter too to make new friends and keep good friends. With this essay and my own example, I wish this wisdom passes on to her.

What about you? How balanced is your friendship quadrant?

ᗞᗞᗞ

WORK: Career and Wealth Building

EIGHT

LIFE WITHOUT WORK IS IMPOSSIBLE

———◦♭◦———

When I had just entered secondary school, I once visited a book exhibition with my father. I remember the English books section was not the biggest as the focus was more on promoting books in the regional language. I picked the usual suspects on science, the universe and the environment, which I used to love as a school kid. My dad, however, added one book to my basket. It was called the Joy of Work by SA Sapre. I am sure he doesn't even remember it. I still have the book on the bookshelf of my parents' home. It's been over 25 years since, and it took me all these years to understand and assimilate the message in that book.

The book is based on the premise of Mahatma Gandhi's opinion that: "The source of India's troubles has been the people who are thoroughly idle'. The book expounds on the evils of idleness to begin and then stresses the importance of work for psychological, social and economic well-being. It cites interesting case studies of high achievers and greats like Swami Vivekananda, Mahatma Gandhi, Einstein, and so on to prove the point. It stresses that work is the essence of man's success in life.

The word productive is more appropriate than just work. Many people are fixated on pleasure, meaning they want to primarily spend time on pleasurable activities, which include resting, staying unemployed or engaging in passive pursuits like watching web series, or social media feeds. And among those who work, thousands dream of early retirement to escape the drudgery and commitment to work.

I believe that the least a person should do in any stage of life is be useful – perform meaningful, productive or creative tasks daily- whether it is a weekday or a weekend. Yet, unfortunately, I see several individuals of my generation who spend busy weekdays only to be suddenly hit by a couple of 'non-working' days where life loses meaning, purpose, direction and sense.

All work is valuable. Be it doing the laundry or giving a keynote speech at a conference. Work sustains order and life in the world. In the third chapter of the Gita, Krishna reiterates that life is not sustainable without work, and even peace of mind is impossible without deliberately choosing one's action (work). Because if one chooses not to take action, then the forces of nature select the action for the person. Be it a renunciant, a recluse, a pauper or a king- all must work because life is sustained by work alone. Even ants work tirelessly to find, move and store food and fight collectively against the colony's enemies. Krishna goes further to say that the higher one rises on the ladder of success, fame, power or wisdom, the more critical it is to engage in work because the world looks up to such individuals and follows their example. Therefore, work is not recommended as optional for anyone.

"*"Without work, all life goes rotten, but when work is soulless, life stifles and dies."*
Albert Camus"

No friendship, family, state, nation, community, cause, or value can survive without investing in work. The real skill is to work without getting affected by work. Draw that boundary where to stop, and develop that sensitivity to what needs to be done. Strike that delicate balance between work areas such that one doesn't compromise another too much. Pleasure in the short term and happiness in the long term should both be side effects of work rather than goals.

The great eighteenth-century American essayist and philosopher Ralph Waldo Emerson said,

"*The purpose of life is not to be happy. It is to be useful, to be honourable, to be compassionate, to have it make some difference that you have lived and lived well.*"

There are four kinds of work pursuits mentioned in India's ancient Vedic tradition:

Accumulation (*āptiḥ in Sanskrit*)

For gaining, possessing, achieving or attaining an object. E.g., build a corpus for buying a home, save for education, get that next promotion, buy that new car, travel to a new destination and so on.

Production (*utpattiḥ in Sanskrit*)

Utpattiḥ means creating, producing, manufacturing, and designing something of value, and it includes the gamut of productive tasks from counting to arranging, administration to coding, manufacturing to distribution, etc.

Transformation (*vikṛtiḥ in Sanskrit*)

It means modifying, changing, or transforming something that needs fixing or support. It includes social innovation, law-making, charitable activities, environmental conservation and social awareness that make this world a better place for generations to come.

Refinement(*saṃskṛtiḥ in Sanskrit*)

Refinement includes anything that improves on culture, including symbols, language, norms, values, and artefacts. One can also count here the various product and process innovations in the digital world because they improve lives and makes the world more efficient.

There is so much to do in this world. Please choose your area of work and jump right into it. Keep yourself engaged in one or more of these work pursuits. As Goethe rightly said,

"'A useless life is only an early death.'"

So, stay useful.

ᕱᕱᕱ

NINE

Job, Career or Calling

————•◊•————

Professor Wrzesniewski of the Yale School 1997 presented a paper arguing that people have three orientations towards their work; they see work as either a job, a career, or a calling.

This research is especially valuable for employers, managers and leaders because it tells us how people relate to their work, irrespective of their specific profession. Be it housekeeping personnel or CEOs, what matters a lot is how they perceive their work.

I used this research and turned it into a simple questionnaire to help understand whether your work orientation is of Job, Career or Calling. Try answering the following four questions by choosing from the option you agree with the most:

How much do you like your job?

A) You don't particularly like your job.

B) You like some parts of your work and don't like other aspects.

C) You love and truly value your job.

What does your job mean to you?

A) Your work is only a means to an income.

B) Your work is a means to better work/job. You look at your current job as a stepping-stone to your next one.

C) You see work as worship or what you're born to do, as a life purpose.

3. What is your primary motivation to work?

A) You work for primary Benefits: Income, Financial Stability to provide for yourself and your family's needs.

B) You do not just work for the primary benefits of Income & security but also the Secondary benefits of Status, Power, Responsibility and Growth Prospects.

C) Your work gives your life meaning. You are working to make a difference in the world, to contribute something necessary and good to the world and to improve the quality of life of people.

4. How do you look at your job after working hours?

A) You do not think of your job. You switch off from work.

B) You may continue working outside hours to go that extra mile, make that extra target, or over-deliver. You are possibly a workaholic.

C) You are always absorbed in your work, at work, off work, or on vacation. Your work is who you are, no matter where you are or what you do.

Depending on where you think you lean towards the most, your work orientation could be:

A = Job, B= Career or C= Calling

So far, so good. What next? What does all this mean? It does not mean one orientation is better than another. There are all kinds of people, and roughly 1/3rd fall into each of the three categories. But it has been observed that people with a calling orientation show higher work and life satisfaction levels. As we move from A to B to C, the productivity and creativity of people are observed to increase as well. This is what is interesting to us.

As leaders and managers, we work to constantly improve the work and life satisfaction of the people working with us (and our own). Once you know where you or your employee/s stand, you can carefully craft or re-craft a job so that people may relate to their jobs better. Job crafting means redesigning jobs by making small changes to them such that they are more meaningful to people. Jobs can be tweaked to help people exercise their strengths better and more effectively and bring out the best in them.

Without getting into too many details, here are three ways Job crafting can be done :

1. Make small changes to the number, nature or types of tasks involved in a job
2. Make changes to the number, type, intensity and nature of relationships we have at work
3. Make a change in your perspective and find meaning in your job

Here is an easy-to-use reference table for your understanding:

4 Questions	Job	Career	Calling
How much do you like your job?	You do not particularly like your job.	You like some part of their work and may not like some other aspects	You love and truly value your job
What does your job mean to you?	Your work is only a means to income	Your work is a means to better work/job. You look at your current job as a stepping-stone to your next one.	You see work as worship or what you're born to do, as life purpose
What is your main motivation to work?	You work for primary Benefits: Income, Financial Stability to provide for yourself and your family needs.	You do not just work for primary benefits of Income & security but also for the Secondary benefits of Status, Power, Responsibility and Growth Prospects.	You work gives your life meaning. You are working to make a difference to the world, to contribute something necessary and good to the world and for improving the quality of life of people.
How do you look at your job after working hours?	You do not think of your job. You switch off from work.	You may continue to work outside working hours to go that extra mile, to make that extra target, to over-deliver. You are possibly a workaholic.	You are always absorbed in your work, be it at work or off work or vacation. You work is who are, no matter where you are or what you do.

Job, Career and Calling

I would like to leave you with this thought:

You may not all have a calling yet, but it is important to start where you are and start looking at your work as more than just drudgery and a means to an end. If you have a job, start working towards a career. Being career-oriented may not make you entirely happy, but it can help you explore the world and open up to different possibilities and experiences. Then one day, you could discover your true calling and work towards making this world a better place to live.

TEN

FOUR DRIVES AND SIXTEEN DESIRES

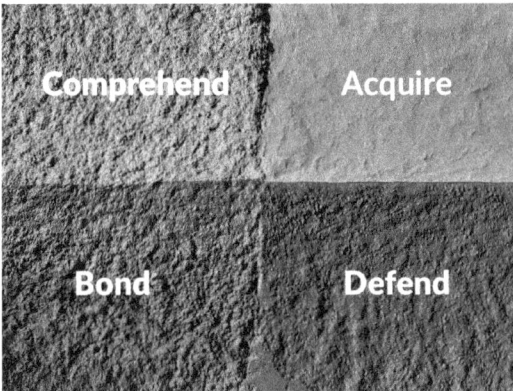

Four Human Drives

Many of us are familiar with only one model of human motivation: Abraham Maslow's Hierarchy of Needs. I have been researching some models besides this one trying to sieve new perspectives and insights. There are two more mental models, viz., the four human drives model and Steven Reiss's sixteen desires, which I plan to discuss one by one in this chapter. The two of them together can help us better understand human motivations better.

While researching this topic, I bumped into Paul R. Lawrence and Nitin Nohria's 2002 book Driven: How Human Nature Shapes Our Choices. In this book, they bring in a new (yet not so new) model of understanding human motivations. This research concluded that there are four primary human drives: the drive to acquire (obtain scarce goods, including intangibles such as social status); the drive to bond (form connections with individuals and groups); the drive to comprehend (satisfy our curiosity and master the world around us); and the drive to defend (protect against external threats and promote justice). The writers claim that these four drives underlie everything we do and are hardwired into our brains. The degree to which they are satisfied directly affects our emotions and, by extension, our behaviour. Let us take a closer look at each one of them:

The drive to acquire

We are all driven to acquire scarce goods that bolster our well-being. We experience delight when this drive is fulfilled and discontentment when it is thwarted. This phenomenon applies not only to physical goods like food, clothing, housing, and money but also to experiences like travel and entertainment—not to mention events that improve social statuses, such as being promoted and getting a corner office or a place on the corporate board. The drive to acquire tends to be relative (we always compare what we have with what others possess) and insatiable (we always want more).

The drive to bond

Many animals bond with their parents, kinship group, or tribe, but only humans extend that connection to larger collectives such as organisations, associations, and nations. The drive to bond, when met, is associated with strong positive emotions like love and caring and, when not, with negative ones like loneliness and anomie.

The drive to comprehend

We want to make sense of the world around us, to produce theories and accounts—scientific, religious, and cultural—that make events comprehensible and suggest reasonable actions and responses. We are frustrated when things seem senseless, and we are invigorated, typically, by the challenge of working out answers. The drive to comprehend makes us seek purpose and meaning in life.

The drive to defend

We all naturally defend ourselves, our property and accomplishments, our family and friends, and our ideas and beliefs against external threats. This drive is rooted in the primary fight-or-flight response common to most animals. In humans, this drive manifests as aggressive or defensive behaviour and a quest to create institutions that promote justice, that have clear goals and intentions, and which allow people to express their ideas and opinions. Fulfilling the drive to defend leads to feelings of security and confidence; not fulfilling it produces strong negative emotions like fear and resentment. The drive to defend is what makes people resistant to change. This drive makes us preserve, maintain, conserve, protect and ensure what we have gained - like profits, assets, health and wealth.

These four drives manifest in all of us – infants, children, adolescents, teens, and adults. What changes are merely the content, quality and intensity of this motivation? When taken to an extreme, each of these drives can bring misery and bind us. There is no end to what one can't aspire to acquire. There is no end to how many relationships one may bind oneself into. There is no end to how much knowledge one may obtain, and one may go to any end to defend and hold on to what one values. Where one draws that line and what quality one pursues decides one's level of well-being and fulfilment. At macroeconomic and individual levels, we are all in the race to maximise the output from these drives by constantly fueling them. But the key to happiness is to find a middle path. The key to success is to strike a balance and harmony across all four drives in a person.

Though primarily applied today at the workplace, this model can be applied in the context of all life pursuits. With this high-level understanding of human drives, we can now go one step deeper and look at desires. Motivations are expressed first as desires. So it is helpful to consider another model to help us better understand ourselves and our fellow beings.

Sixteen Desires

Plato said

> "Human behaviour flows from three main sources: desire, emotion, and knowledge."

One of the characteristic traits of humans is that they can desire. Our set of desires at any point in time also makes each of us unique. We can have tens, hundreds and even thousands of desires. But what if I told you that there are fundamentally only sixteen desires? This means every desire of every human being can be labelled with just sixteen tags. This may sound demeaning to some, as we hold our desires very close and dearly, but I see immense benefit in studying and understanding desires rather than being controlled and driven by them. It helps us stay ahead of them.

Steven Reiss, the Professor Emeritus of Psychology and Psychiatry at the Ohio State University, USA, arrived at Sixteen Basic Desires through his extensive research of over 6000 subjects. These sixteen desires encapsulate the entire spectrum of desires expressed by people. These sixteen desires can also be seen as the sixteen fundamental needs or values that drive or motivate a person.

The story goes that Steven was hospitalised during the 90s. While he was being treated, he observed the hard work and devotion that the hospital staff put in. He noticed how the nurses loved their work, which got him thinking about what is that they desired and what gave them fulfilment. What gave them happiness?

He took this topic back to his university for research and found that there is hardly any emphasis on this topic in academia, and no models were available to structure human desires. After studying over 6,000 people, Professor Reiss came up with 16 basic desires, which you can see in the table on the next page.

Professor Reiss also developed an assessment called the Reiss Profile that can be used to uncover the shape of the basic desires of an individual. This information can help identify a person's pivot of happiness. Each of us has a unique profile. The strong desires are marked in green, the weak ones in red, and those in between are marked in yellow.

For example, a person with a green value on the Reiss Profile for Power is likely to enjoy and take up leadership roles. He probably loves challenges, seeks them actively, and works hard to overcome them. On the other hand, an individual who has a weak basic desire for Power does not like to assume leadership roles and is nondirective of others and even of himself.

Acceptance	Family	Order	Social Contact
The desire to avoid failure and criticism. The need to be appreciated	The desire to raise children and spend time with siblings	The desire for structure	The desire for peer companionship
Beauty	Honour	Physical Activity	Status
The desire for aesthetically appealing experiences and for sex including courting	The desire for an upright character, to be faithful to the values of an individual's ethnic group, family or clan	The desire for muscle exercise	The desire for respect based on social standing
Curiosity	Idealism	Power	Tranquility
The desire to learn and understand	The desire to improve society and social justice	The desire for influence or leadership	The desire to be free of anxiety and pain. The need to be secure and protected
Eating	Independence	Saving	Vengeance
The desire for palatable food	The desire for Self-Reliance and the need to be distinct	The desire to collect, curate, accumulate	The desire to confront those who offend

Steven Reiss's Sixteen Desires

Irrespective of whether we employ Reiss's profile or not, it is important to understand the source of a person's motivation. The model should not be used to put people into boxes or stereotype them but rather to understand yourself and others better and more profoundly. This approach can find application in life coaching, improving sales, counselling students, sports coaching, personal training, and so on. This model can also help us find our energy sources and manage conflicts better. It also gives us a much-needed understanding of what matters most to a person. It can help us identify the factors on which a person's happiness and performance depend. And finally, it can also tell us how much energy a person should put in to make their happiness and performance sustainable.

ᑭᑭᑭ

ELEVEN

THE PARADIGM PARALYSIS OF PROFESSIONAL IDENTITY

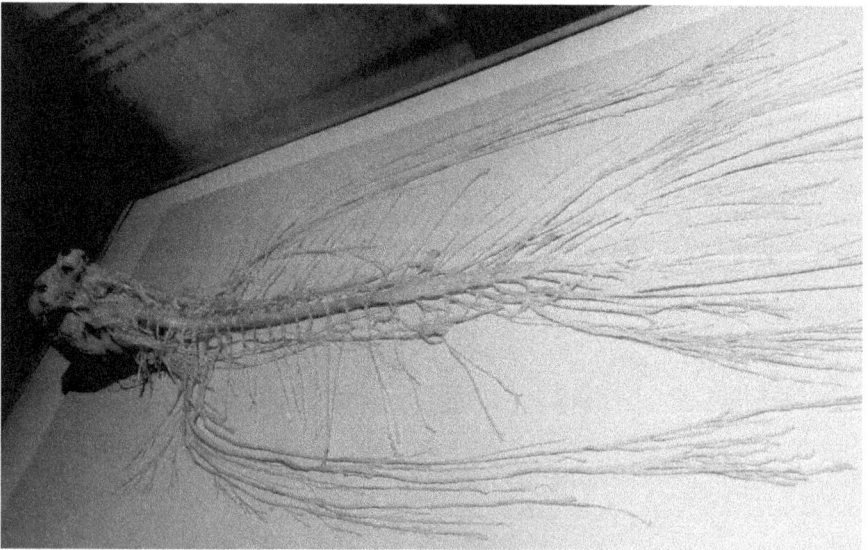

·〰·

Human Nervous System

Images can be strong, even our image of ourselves. We often get carried away by our titles, roles, industry backgrounds and designations. So much so that we need to be shaken back to our present with the help of a strong image. We need a life-transforming experience that can transport us to the present moment entirely and help us to sense the emerging future.

Here is one such image; that of our nervous system. We are so used to thinking of our insides as 'skeleton' or 'muscle' that we forget that the seat of our consciousness, our 'I-ness' and our memories reside in our nervous system. I am sure many of you may not have seen this. What you are looking at here is the seat of your mind, memory and soul! But it is surprising how less often this visual is referenced compared to other systems. It's a new paradigm.

In the same way, our professional identity paradigms are influenced largely by the industry and the functions that we have served in the past. We shape even our CVs around it. We create these silos ourselves and start believing in them, thus limiting our capabilities and future possibilities. We think because we have served in a particular industry and function for a certain number of years, we 'belong' there and may be unable to compete in other industries and functions. This is a classic example of what the futurist Joel Barker calls 'paradigm paralysis'.

Paradigms are frameworks and rules we apply to make sense of the world around us and help us solve problems. 'What may seem impossible to solve using one paradigm may be easy to solve in another', I heard Joel speak in a video I watched in one of our corporate training.

Breaking through a paradigm needs that we first become aware of it. The professional identity paradigm is just one case of paradigm paralysis that many of us live in. It can, like other paradigms, be broken too by using other paradigms. For instance, one way to break through this 'CV Identity' paradigm is to think of yourself in terms of your strengths - like character strengths (VIA character strengths) and talents (Clifton strengths). You can easily take such assessments online to uncover these. Look at yourself as these strengths and then ponder what you can do with them. Once you look at yourself using one or both of these paradigms, you will see yourself differently and uncover possibilities you may have never even considered. You may then be able to identify the skills that you may want to acquire to complement these strengths.

Many paradigms challenge us and cripple us daily- paradigms of race, gender, seniority, cognitive biases, etc. The ability to break through paradigms forms the bedrock of innovation, growth and development, and I believe every organisation and individual should strive to do this.

We are capable of so much more than we think we are. Let your past not shackle you. Think!

TWELVE

CAREER PLANNING WITH 70:20:10 MODEL

---♡---

Many of us reach a stage in our professional lives where we feel stuck. We are trying to figure out how to grow or are unsure how to take the next step towards growth. Some of us rely on our employers to show us directions. But most successful global companies are between average and poor at developing future talent. Your real developmental needs are as vague to them as to you.

The challenge is that you're competing against every individual in your industry who wants to be a high performer. If you grow more capabilities more quickly than they do, you'll perform better today, earn opportunities to perform better in the future, and a virtuous cycle will take hold. Development matters. So how can you chart the shortest, surest path to success?

Grow Yourself Faster

The research is clear about how we grow most successfully: it combines on-the-job, social, and formal learning, also known as the 70-20-10 model. This research-derived mantra says that roughly 70% of your professional growth will come from the work experiences you have, 20% will come from your interactions with others, and 10% from formal education.

Think of growth as a cycle — successfully perform, get feedback, and perform again even better. Experiences power that growth cycle, so you'll want to understand which experiences matter most and gain as many of them as quickly as possible. To begin with, you want to be very clear about

THINK BETTER AND THRIVE

your starting point and desired destination on that development journey. This is a prominent item often missing from a development plan.

Two key steps to growing faster are:

1. First, determine your starting and goal positions (From and To)
2. Get the experiences and create a personal experience map.

The challenge for many of us is that we're unsure about our origin and destination. We often think we're starting far ahead of where we objectively are and that we've arrived when we're still hundreds of miles from our goal. You can get to a more accurate assessment with a framework that Jim Shanley calls the "from/to." The from/to is two brief statements describing where you are today and your next big (not your ultimate) destination.

Examples of great from/to statements include:

· **From** being an individual contributor **to** becoming a people leader: An individual contributor brings value through technical expertise and closely following others' directions. In contrast,a people leader creates a clear strategy and delivers results through a small team.
· **From** a business strategist who can appear aloof and dismissive of those with less intellectual horsepower **to** a general manager who aligns and inspires her region through personal connections and demonstrates genuine care for people.

The directness of those statements may surprise you. However, these from/to statements are examples of successful executives who made tremendous progress once they clarified their needs. Both leaders are now CEOs — one of a $10 billion retail chain and another of a speciality eyewear company.

To get accurate from/to, you'll need to check your ego at the door and ask some trusted superiors and colleagues for their remarkably candid views of your origin and destination. Introduce the from/to concept to them. Send them the from/to examples I gave earlier, and ask them to think about your from/to. Tell them to be brutally honest because their transparency will allow you to grow faster.

Use their input to create your final from/to. Which of their statements seem most direct and make you most uncomfortable? Is the "to" far enough away so that it will be a meaningful challenge to achieve? Whose opinion do you trust the most? With a clear from/to, you can now focus on accelerating your growth.

Create Your Experience Map

The 70-20-10 ratio says that experiences best accelerate your development. This means you'll want to understand which experiences will build your career and, more importantly, the few, most powerful experiences that can close your 'from/to' gap. A regularly updated personal experience map will help you chart your path.

A personal experience map shows which experience you want to acquire in the next two to five years to grow your career. It's a practical planning document that describes how you will produce the highest-performing you.

Two types of experiences will accelerate your development — functional experiences and management experiences. Functional experiences help make you great at something, i.e. marketing, supply chain, R&D. They allow you to prove that you're highly competent at what you do. Management experiences will help you prove that you can perform or manage various challenging situations. For example, you've been a great marketer in one region and proven that you can lead marketing when you have a new team, in a turnaround situation or in a different geography. When you successfully achieve these challenging experiences, you prove to your company that you're a versatile leader who deserves a chance for larger, more important roles.

You can create your experience map after you:

Interview experts in your field

The best and brightest in your field can help you understand which experiences will get you into the top 10% and become an expert. Interview those leaders to learn which experiences will build your functional excellence. The interviews will provide the raw material to create your experience map.

- **Identify experts inside and outside your company.** Interview the best in your field, not just the best in your company. For example, if you want to be a chief financial officer (CFO), identify five CFOs you admire or are well-regarded in your industry. If your goal is to be great at early-stage pharma R&D, it's the same process. Find the leaders on the industry "best" lists (best chief marketing officer, chief information officer, etc.), from their articles in trade magazines, on lists of speakers at relevant conferences, or from referrals of leaders in your company.

- **Request an interview.** Email each leader, asking for an informal conversation in which they can help develop someone in their field.
- **Ask for insights.** During your call, ask them, "What are the key functional experiences [not necessarily jobs] that you believe will produce the highest-quality [general manager, IT architect, finance director]? Or, "Describe what you would see on the résumé of someone outstanding at _____." If you're having trouble getting quality information, ask them about the most valuable experiences they've had in their careers.

Build your map

Review your interview notes and list the experiences that your interviewees described. Only some things you hear will be helpful; some information will overlap or contradict what another interviewee said. Your goal is to sort through this information to find the few experiences that will most accelerate your career.

An experience should describe a meaningful business outcome — open a new production facility, lead a large team through a business turnaround, or close books for a business unit. It should be a significant building block of your functional or leadership capability; your accomplishment should mean something to others in your field.

The functional experiences you need to be a high performer will be unique to your profession. In contrast, management experiences will be very similar across professions because management experiences grow generic capabilities valuable to all managers, no matter their function. For simplicity, you can use these experiences when you create your map:

- **Life-cycle experiences**: Lead in different parts of your company or product evolution: a turnaround situation, a startup, a steady-state environment, a developing market or a fully mature one.
- **Managing experiences**: Upgrade a poor-quality team, lead a large team, manage a team where you have influence but not authority, lead in a

matrixed environment, lead in a highly political environment.

- **Geographic experiences:** Have experiences outside your home geography where the local language is not your native language.

Select four to seven functional experiences and three to four management experiences you believe will benefit you most and list them on your experience map. The map should be focused and realistic — a reference sheet that you'll regularly use to plan your growth and assess your progress.

The personal experience map is now your guide to continue growing your high-performing self. Creating it will be one of your best investments of time. Please review the content of your map any time you switch jobs or companies and at least every six months to ensure that it remains a current, helpful guide.

Growing yourself faster is challenging, but it's made far simpler when you're clear about your origin, destination, and the fastest, experience-driven route between the two.

ᐁᐁᐁ

THIRTEEN
HOW RELATIONSHIPS RISE AND FALL

———•ᚦ•———

Mark .l Knapp (born on July 12th, 1938) is a renowned professor at the University of Texas and is especially known for his works in nonverbal communication research and evolving interactions. He developed a model for relational enhancement, which routes the interpersonal development between two people. Knapp's relationship model explains how relationships grow and last and how they end. This model is categorised into ten different stages, which come under two interrelating stages: Knapp's relationship escalation model and Knapp's relationship termination model. This model helps us to understand how a relationship grows and fall apart. The speed and time between each step may be different in each case, and sometimes, you may even skip a stage.

Coming together: Knapp's Escalation Model

1. Initiation

This very short stage is about making an impression. Judging a person at this stage would not be accurate. People at this stage will be concerned with making favourable impressions. Physical appearance plays a significant role in impression-making, such as the dress they wear, the perfume they use and their overall appearance.

Example 1 – If a boy finds a girl attractive and wants to converse with her, he will introduce himself with a formal greeting – how are you? What is your name?

Example 2 – In business relationships, overall amiability is essential. They ask about demographics, profession and other shared aims. Therefore, it is crucial in business to create a good impression at the initial stage itself.

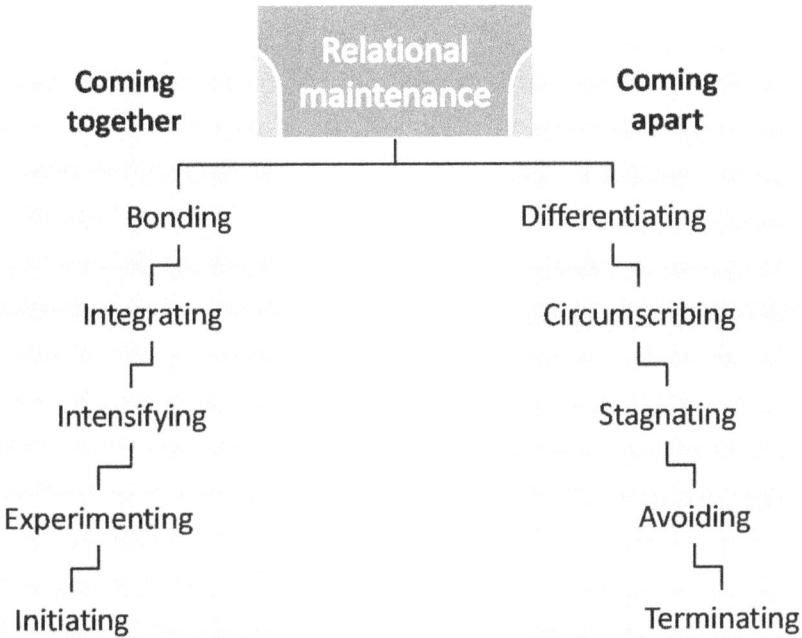

```
                    Relational
Coming              maintenance          Coming
together                                 apart

      Bonding                      Differentiating

      Integrating                  Circumscribing

      Intensifying                 Stagnating

   Experimenting                   Avoiding

   Initiating                      Terminating
```

Knapp's Relationship Escalation Model

2. Experimentation

This stage is about exploring to know each other well. Experimentation is also called the probing stage because each person will analyse the other for information or a common interest to decide whether to maintain a relationship among them. Most of the relationships wind up here due to the different interest levels.

Example 1 – When the boy sees the girl, the next time, they will discuss to find out about their common interests and ask questions like- which is your favourite food? Or which is your favourite car?

Example 2 – Exploring how a partner will benefit another person's business in business relationships.

3. Intensifying

In this stage, the relationship intensifies and becomes less formal. People will start revealing their personal information and analysing the other person's impression. They find various ways to nurture a relationship and strengthen it, such as giving gifts, spending more time together, asking for dates, expecting a relationship commitment etc.

Example 1 – The boy asks the girl on a date. During their date, they talk about their lives and how the boy got the job and his personal experience, and the girl also reveals about her parents, her previous experiences, etc.

Example 2 – In this stage in business, negotiation and commitment activity may be involved, which leads to an increase in the amount of information and trade.

4. Integration

At this stage, people will start to make their relationship closer than before. In their personal life, people may fall in love or find a close friend. The level of intimacy can progress to a further relationship.

Example 1 – After several months, they labelled their relationship as boyfriend and girlfriend.

Example 2 – In this stage of the business relationship, they will start profiting from their agreement, resulting in financial benefit.

5. Bonding

In this stage, a person will tell the world about their relationship. They make their relationship recognised and will honour their commitment legally. The relationship is indefinite and only to be broken through a formal notice, agreements or death etc.

Example 1 – The boy proposes, and the girl agrees to marry him.

Example 2 – The bonding stage of business relationships comprises partnerships and long-lasting relationships, which can lower business expenses and result in more profit.

Coming apart: Knapp's Relationship Termination Model

When a relationship progresses, there will be misunderstandings and conflicts, and the so-called 'indefinite relationship' might fail to persist. Like coming together, there are five stages in coming apart.

6. Differentiating

While progressing in a relationship, sometimes, due to other external pressures, people will start thinking individually rather than with a partner. For example, they may start developing different hobbies or other endeavours. As a result, the relationship will begin to fade, breaking the everlasting bond. The partners often express a feeling of dislike for each other.

Example 1 – The boy comes up with the idea of leaving his current job and doing something else that he has always wished to do. The girl rejects the idea with some reasoning. So, pressure is created inside the relationship.

Example 2 – In business, meetings are crucial to know the partners' stands and other opinions. Due to work pressure, meetings are less frequent. They start to think more as individuals than as partners.

7. Circumscribing

After differentiating, partners will limit their conversations and set boundaries in their communication. Often people will never communicate the topic, fearing an argument. Instead, they will have their own space and activities.

Example 1 – The girl started talking more about general topics like food, climate etc. and started avoiding the conversation about quitting the job. The boy does the same.

Example 2 – In business, issues regarding quality might arise due to the communication gap, and conflicts can lead to alternative contract units.

8. Stagnation

The relationship will decline even more if it reaches the stagnation stage. Communication will be more limited. The only reason the partners don't separate is due to children or other unavoidable causes. The relationships in this stage will not continue or improve.

Example 1 – The girl finds that there is not much to talk about in general and will remain silent even though they live in the same house. So there is a serious communication gap between the girl and the boy.

Example 2 – In business relationships, there will be a communication gap when one party or both partners feel neglected or insignificant.

9. Avoidance

At this stage, the partners intentionally avoid any contact and will be physically detached. They restrict themselves from any forms of communication to avoid a conversation or an argument.

Example 1 – One day, the boy packs his bags and walks out of the house. All this time, the girl would have avoided the boy and would not attempt to stop him.

Example 2 – The stagnation stage will result in both partners avoiding each other as it affects their fundamental functioning.

10. Terminating

This is the final stage of coming apart. The relationship ultimately terminates. The partners will take different paths and will go on with their lives.

Example 1 – The boy approaches an advocate for a divorce.

Example 2 – In the termination stage, the partnership is broken, and the two parties move on with their ventures.

Knapp's Relationship development model can be applied effectively to many types of relationships: romantic couples, friends, business partners, roommates, and colleagues. We can use the model in each of these cases to understand and explain how relationships develop, maintain, and deteriorate. Pick three relationships from your life as examples; a successful one, one which you think has failed and one which you are working to improve. Then, apply Knapp's model, draw insights from past successes and failures, and apply them to these relationships you are working to improve.

ppp

FOURTEEN

WORKING WITH OTHERS

---◆♭◆---

Being effective in any kind of collaboration, be it with children, students, friends, associates, co-workers or even loved ones is a skill. The few people who can do this well can lead themselves and others well. Developing this essential leadership skill requires a deliberate focus on the dynamics at play in any social setting. Here, I find the SCARF model very useful. Built by Dr David Rock in 2008, the SCARF model describes how we can work effectively with people by understanding their social styles. These social styles, in turn, influence how we respond to others.

The model is based on three central observations:

1. We treat social threats and rewards with the same intensity as physical threats and rewards
2. The capacity to make decisions, solve problems and collaborate with others is generally reduced by a threat response and increased under a reward response
3. The threat response is more intense and more common. It often needs to be carefully minimised in social interactions.

SCARF stands for Status, Certainty, Autonomy, Relatedness and Fairness. Research suggests that these five domains activate the same reward circuitry that physical rewards (money etc.) or physical threats (pain, etc.) activate. For example, a perceived threat to one's status activates similar brain networks to a threat to one's life. In the same way, a perceived increase in fairness activates the same reward circuitry as receiving a monetary reward.

Here is a table providing a brief explanation of the model. It also tells us how reward response and threat response are activated in the case of each of the domains.

Domain	How *Reward Response* is activated	How *Threat Response* is activated
Status is a sense of our personal worth; where we are in relation to other people.	On providing positive feedback, public acknowledgement of contributions	On criticism, providing unsolicited advise
Certainty is the sense of what the future holds for us.	Setting clear boundaries, expectations and goals, having realistic timelines.	Lack of transparency, dishonesty and unpredictability.
Autonomy is the sense of control over our lives.	Providing choices, delegating, empowering.	Micromanaging, being authoritative
Relatedness is the sense of safety that we feel with others.	Sharing friendly gestures, socializing, and having mentoring programs.	Fueling internal competition within groups or teams, working in functional/business/ relational silos
Fairness is the sense of what is impartial and just.	Transparent decision making, open communication, candidness and following clear rules/policies.	Unequal treatment/rules/ policies/guidelines; lack of communication

The SCARF Model by Dr David Rock

The model enables people to more easily remember, recognise, and potentially modify the core social needs that drive human behaviour.

My experience with this model has been great, and I especially see it as effective when we employ all the domains together and not in isolation. However, you will also learn by experience that each person has a different level of each of these five needs, and if you are sensitive, you can notice them in your transactions. You can employ this model at your workplace with your team, at workshops and leadership events, and it works. Once you get the hang of it, it comes naturally to you and becomes part of your skill set. Like all good things, it comes by practice, and you can employ it in several domains of life - relationships, parents, friends work and parenting. The application of this model in parenting will be discussed in the parenting section.

FIFTEEN

YOUR SOCIAL ROLES

Social roles are the part we play as members of a social group. Based on my observations, I have put this life roles hierarchy into five layers of a pyramid - the 5 Cs. The pyramid means that most of us operate at the bottom while very few operate at the top. We need all five roles to have a progressive and thriving society. These layers represent a hierarchy of intellectual progression.

Consumer

We are all consumers. We spend our days reading, listening, eating, and buying. We don't just buy things we need but also things we do not need to make us happy. Progress and prosperity mean the constant consumption of newer and better things. We work to afford the newest clothes, the nice car, and the expensive dinner out. Consumption is thus the most common social behaviour we see around us.

But none of this will add lasting happiness to our lives. True happiness comes from helping others — from carving out our own contribution path rather than our consumption path. It comes from the confidence that you can succeed in your dream. As long as you remain only a consumer, you will not have the fulfilment you desire. A consumer can never get enough. They can never be truly happy. They will always look at the world, thinking about what they can get from it instead of what they can give to it.

Contributor

A contributor is connected to the economy and society. A contributor strives to make something valuable to others. They receive their payment monetarily. The contributor mindset allows you to view the world through the opposite lens of the consumer. This lens will keep you striving to find new ways to provide value and allows you to see how others are doing the same. An individual contributor may be a small cog in the machine of commerce and economy and hence appear insignificant. But when each cog is doing its job in the right place and the right time, it keeps the world going. The contributors put food on the table at the end of the day. They keep the machinery of the production, logistics, trade, supply chain, distribution and retail running. The contributors make up the majority of our taxpayers. They are the backbone of any economy. Starting in the job market on a career path means beginning your journey as a contributor.

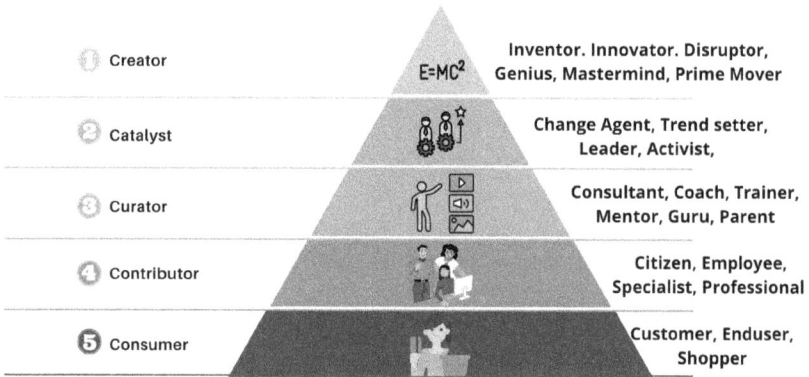

Social Roles Hierarchy

Curator

What makes a museum great? It's the things you don't see, the stuff that's not on the walls or in the showcases. It's the art of saying no and making the most of the best. That's the job of a curator. It is essentially an editing process. The curator also brings together the artefacts and stitches them into a narrative. He juxtaposes seemingly different artefacts and puts them into a story. The mission of a curator is to educate or teach children and adults about anything that is of real value, like art, culture, thinking, ideas, best practices and so on. Curators will make learning fun and enjoyable if they are passionate about their work. A curator can come in many forms: a teacher, a mentor, a coach, a guru, an author or a trainer.

Catalyst

A catalyst is an agent that provokes or speeds significant change or action: a catalyst champions and rallies people around a cause. The cause necessarily involves a change- in attitude, mindset, thinking or behaviour, or worldview. Take the catalyst out, and you will not have any change or transformation. Instead, a catalyst can enthuse a group of people, orient them toward a common goal and motivate them to accomplish them.

Creator

A creator is an innovator, an inventor. Innovation can certainly be an adventure. It requires the courage to face uncertainty and a willingness to take risks. The outcome is never entirely clear. Yet creators must be proactive in the pursuit of it. The path is unknown, so they must be imaginative in seeking it out. They cannot be sure what will be required to succeed, so they must be resourceful and strategic. And because failure is always one possible outcome, they must have faith in themselves, their capabilities, and their ideas' potential. They need to be willing to explore and experiment. They need to be adventurous.

From my experience, everyone from a clerk to a business owner or inventor or a CEO is fulfilling one of these roles. So I created this model for my use: first, to understand what kind of a role I am currently playing in my life and, secondly, to decide in which direction I should try to move. You can try the same exercise.

ϷϷϷ

SIXTEEN

TRADE-OFFS IN LIFE: WE CANNOT HAVE IT ALL

Many of us wish to have it all in life. Most of us have ever updated, and growing list of needs, wants and desires. And we want to make no compromises and have no regrets. We learn pretty late that there is a trade-off for everything in life, and most of us understand the concept of trade-off the hard way- through experience. The definition of trade-off is an exchange where you give up one thing to get something else that you also desire.

Here are five key trade-offs we all must make in our lives:

Money vs Time

90% of all jobs and promotions are a trade-off between money earned and the time required. At junior levels, you clock in mandated hours of attendance for your fixed salary. As you grow in responsibility and compensation, the demands on your time eat into your daily hours, weekends, and holidays. To solve this trade-off, you need to change or expand your skillset. For example, compare a super-specialist doctor to a general practitioner at a hospital. The specialist earns more for less of his time. With more valuable skills, you can choose between more money or more free time, depending on what is critical in your current stage of life.

Generalist Vs Specialist

In the real world, most professionals are either Generalists or Specialists. Generalists know a lot of subjects, which is why they tend to have loosely defined roles with flexible KPIs within organisations. A general medicine practitioner, for instance, might attend to patients of varying age groups presenting with a broad range of symptoms. In contrast to this is a specialist's role. It takes more time to be a specialist in any discipline, which is why specialists often earn more, even at entry-level jobs. They have tightly defined job roles, and organisations often employ fewer specialists than generalists, meaning that the dependence on specialists is high, making them more valuable and difficult to replace. However, there is a flip side to being a specialist for several reasons, such as career inflexibility, limited opportunities pool, and the fear of being replaced by automation or emerging technologies.

Safety vs Economy

I don't know how many of us have noticed this trade-off between economy and safety. This trade-off is quite evident in cars: large cars can carry many people (five or more), and since they have larger crumple zones, they may be safer in an accident. However, they also tend to be heavy (and often not very aerodynamic) and hence have a relatively poor fuel economy. On the other hand, small cars like the Smart Car can only carry two people, and their lightweight means they are very fuel-efficient. At the same time, the smaller size and weight of small cars mean that they have smaller crumple zones, which means occupants are less protected in case of an accident. In addition, if a small car has an accident with a larger, heavier car, the occupants of the smaller car will fare more poorly. Thus, car size (large versus small) involves multiple trade-offs regarding passenger capacity, accident safety, and fuel economy.

Speed Vs Accuracy

The complex relationship between an individual's willingness to respond slowly and make fewer errors compared to their willingness to respond quickly and make relatively more errors is described as the speed-accuracy trade-off. Either you can accomplish a lot in a specific time with many errors or accomplish little within the same time with near perfection.

Career Success Vs Family Success

Many of us face this trade-off, while only a few have made peace with it. A career gives you financial stability, whereas a family gives you social stability. These are two sides of the same coin. If you have a career, you will miss your family, and if you have your loved ones, you may regret not having a great career. Yet, both are important in one's life. So, a practical solution would be to raise fewer children while also focusing on your career. It is still hard but manageable.

These are only some examples of trade-offs. A trade-off involves a sacrifice to obtain a desired product or experience. Understanding the trade-off for every decision you make helps ensure you use your resources, whether it is time, money, pleasure or energy, efficiently. Every minute of every day, you and the people around you are making trade-offs. Whether it is picking your next investment, next job or deciding whether to have your next child or partner, there will be trade-offs.

What do you do when you cannot do everything you want? Understanding your value structure is the best way to decide what you need to trade against. It is wise to give up a lower value for a higher one or, put another way, maximise a higher value at the cost of a lower value.

One of the secrets to living a fulfilling life is to understand the trade-offs in life. Acknowledging that gaining something desirable also leads to losing something desirable makes us truly grounded and contented.

ÞÞÞ

SEVENTEEN

FIVE COMPONENTS OF PERSONAL FINANCE

———◦♡◦———

Most of us adults believe that money is a harsh reality of life. But the fact is that reality is neither harsh nor benign. It simply is a fact of life. It is our lack of objectivity that makes it look harsh or otherwise. The sooner we have this objectivity, the better our prospects of living a financially healthy life. To make the most of your income and savings, it's essential to become financially savvy—it will help you distinguish between good and bad advice and make intelligent financial decisions. Alongside this page, you can see a simple mental model that can help us understand personal finance better. The personal finance model has five components: Income, Spending, Saving, Investing and Protecting.

I have curated and shared the most important lessons on managing personal finance here:

Protection

Buy sufficient insurance to cover you and your dependents for health, life, accidents, and other risks. The most popular thumb rule says one should have a sum of 8-10 times his yearly income as term cover or life insurance. This rule is far from perfect, but it still can be used as starting point. A modified version of this rule says that if you are in your early 30s, insurance coverage should be 12-15 times your annual income & if you are in your 50s, take 6-8 times. This is a more practical method of estimating term cover value.

The Five Components of Personal Finance

Source: Investopedia

Saving

Savings is the income left over after spending. Everyone should aim to have savings to cover large expenses or emergencies. This means not using all your income, which can be difficult.

Income

It is the starting point of personal finance. It is the entire amount of cash inflow that you receive and can allocate to expenses, savings, investments, and protection.

Investing

Involves purchasing assets, usually stocks, bonds or mutual funds to earn a return on the money invested. The aim is to increase personal wealth beyond the amount invested.

Spending

The outflow of cash and typically where the bulk of income goes - towards rent, mortgage, groceries, hobbies, eating out, home furnishings, home repairs, travel, and entertainment.

Protection

Methods to protect people from unexpected events, such as illnesses or accidents, and as a means to preserve wealth. Protection includes life and health insurance and estate and retirement planning.

Components of Personal Finance

Income

Money is always the by-product of our hard work, growth and success. Money follows success, not otherwise. Money can be a symptom of success but not the cause of success. Never make it into an aim of life. Aim for love, happiness, fulfilment, well-being and peace of mind, not money.

Live a lifestyle that you can afford with your limited income. Lifestyle upgrades should follow income growth instead of the other way around.

Spending

Money can buy freedom, pleasures, insurance, and comforts essential to happiness and well-being. So, it deserves a place of importance and respect in our lives.

Rent a home until you are not sure where you want to live and retire in the long term. Your next big opportunity may be in another town or city, and you need to be able to make that change quickly.

Do not use credit to buy comforts. Comforts are best funded by hard-earned money. Reward yourself for your successes with something more comfortable or luxurious. Also, do not spend to de-stress. It is a vicious circle and hard to come out of. De-stressing should be as simple as a good night's sleep, yoga, meditation, a good workout or a cup of hot green tea.

Use the money to free up your time if needed but not the other way around. Automate all fixed expenses like rent, utilities and EMIs.

You would also like to own a car someday because it represents mobility, freedom and safety. However, in financial terms, a car is a depreciating asset – today morning, you purchase a vehicle for INR 1 Million & by the evening, it will be worth INR 0.8-0.9 million. And, after five years, it will not be worth even half the value. Nevertheless, some of us need cars. Then the question arises, what car should you buy?

As a general rule, the value of a car should be at most 50% of the owner's annual income. Whenever you purchase a used car or buy a new one, plan to use it for ten years. While buying a car with a loan, stick to the 20/4/10 rule – Minimum 20% down payment, loan tenure not more than four years & EMI should not be higher than 10% of your income.

Someday, you would also like to buy a house. A house's value should equal 2-3 times your family's annual income. So if you & your spouse are earning a total of INR 2 million – you should buy a house in a range of INR 4-6 million rupees.

Most middle-class families go for a mortgage when buying a house. Then the question arises, how much should the monthly payouts be (equated monthly instalments EMIs in India)? Experts agree that your EMIs should be at most 36% of your Gross Monthly Income at any point in time. It should be even lesser, almost 28% of your gross income, when you are close to your retirement.

Saving

Start small. You may start by saving 10% of your income. If you are planning early retirement, start by saving 20% of your monthly income. Another thumb rule says if you are in your early 30s, Save 10% for maintenance, 15%

for adding comforts later on, and 20% to escape your daily work life and enjoy. If you are late by a decade, add 5% more in each category.

Save for the rainy day. Bad times do not come invited, but occasionally they do come. Therefore, it is best to reserve some cash to cover tough times. This is also popularly called an emergency fund. Emergency Fund helps people in case of a sudden loss of income, medical emergencies, etc. The most commonly recommended thumb rule for building an emergency fund says one should save equal to three to six months of monthly expenses. If the government employs you, you can keep it for three months. If the private sector employs you, the higher the savings, the better. Try your best not to use this amount for day-to-day needs/wants. If you are retired, you should have equal to one year of expenses in the emergency fund.

Aim to become financially independent as an individual, at least by retirement. A financially independent person has enough income to pay one's living expenses for the rest of one's life without having to be employed or dependent on others.

You should have 20 times your income saved for retirement and plan to replace 80 per cent of pre-retirement income. Here we assume that the retirement age is 60 and the average life expectancy is 80 years.

And finally, be grateful for whatever wealth or goodwill you may get as an inheritance, and at least try to conserve it if you cannot grow it further.

Investing

First and foremost, invest in your education. Education is the most reliable investment and yields the best return on investment. If you need more education to get an edge, it's the first place to invest.

Money is earned, and wealth is accumulated. Wealth is built over several years of disciplined saving and investing. Save before you spend. Start saving, start small but make it into a habit. Leverage the power of compounding. Once you start investing money, automate the investing. Do not waste your time micro-managing money. Instead, delegate tasks to portfolio or wealth managers to free your time.

Equity and Index Mutual Funds are among the most recommended and popular instruments. They spread the risk across companies in their portfolio and can have stable returns in the long term.

Allocate your money properly between debt instruments and equity. You can use the following thumb rule for the same. The percentage of equity in your portfolio should be around 100, subtracted by your age. In other words, debt should be equal to your age. E.g., if you are 30, you should have 30% of your investments in debt & 70% (100 – your age) in equity. However, please note that this rule needs to be tailored to your risk appetite, risk tolerance, or how far out your goals are.

Then you may ask how much rate of return we can expect from different investments. Use the rule of 10/5/3. As per this thumb rule, you can expect a 10% return from equity, a 5% return from bonds or fixed deposits & 3% from liquid funds. Try combining the rule of 72 with this rule – you will get some fantastic numbers.

Sometimes Rules of thumb will give you a false sense of security or wrong guidance – so take them with a pinch of salt. But at any given point, it is better to at least have financial planning based on a thumb rule than to have no financial planning. Also, you may not be able to implement them strictly, but you can try to be close to them or gradually aim to get close to them over months or years.

An interesting thumb rule to calculate when your investment will double in value is the rule of 72: It's a straightforward & most common rule – if you divide 72 by the rate of return, you will get the number of years in which your money will double. For Eg. If you expect a return of 12%, your money will double in 6 years (72/12=6) & what if the rate of return is 8%? Then 72/8=9 years. You can also use this in reverse order. At what rate will your money double in 5 years? The answer is 72/5=14.4%

Times today are more challenging and competitive for all of us. The fear of missing out can put our real priorities and growth at risk. But, on the other hand, the quicker we learn from our mistakes and those of our earlier generations, the better our prospects of financial success.

ᕈᕈᕈ

EIGHTEEN

ECONOMICS IN TEN PRINCIPLES

———— ·ɒ· ————

There is a reason why children, when asked 'what do you want to grow up to be?', never answer 'Economist'. The reason is that children have not been told or made to think about the economy or economics. Children think that all good things in this world are in limitless supply, even though they may not have everything. Economics is the science of managing scarcity, balancing supply and demand and enabling society, company, country or individual to thrive by making the right choices. Suppose we are willing to explore economics. Then the question arises: where do we start? How much of economics should we know? Quite a daunting task, isn't it?

To answer this question, we turn to the work of Harvard economics professor N. Gregory Mankiw. His book 'Principles of Economics is an introductory economics textbook for college students. In this text, he describes in detail the ten principles of Economics that we should all know about to get a sense of how the economy works. I have summarised them here in simple words so that you can get a quick overview of them.

1. People Face Trade-offs

A trade-off in a situation in which the achieving of something you want involves the loss of something else which is also desirable. To get one thing, we usually have to give up something else. An example of this is choosing between leisure time and work; when you choose leisure time, you cannot really be working, and while you are working, you are not really enjoying leisure time.

2. The Cost of Something is What You Give Up Getting It

Technically this is also called Opportunity cost. It is the value of the action that you do not choose when choosing between two possible options. If we take up any project, investment, purchase or decision, we must consider the opportunity costs involved. For instance, the opportunity cost of studying at university for three years is the three years of pay you do not earn during that time. In other words, it is the second-best alternative foregone.

3. Rational People Think at the Margin

Marginal changes are small, incremental changes to an existing plan of action. Marginal benefit (for the consumer) and marginal cost (from the producer) are two measures of how the cost or value of a product changes. A marginal benefit is the maximum amount of money a consumer is willing to pay for an additional good or service. The consumer's satisfaction tends to decrease as consumption increases. Let us say you wish to eat a dessert after a meal, and so you order a cup of strawberry ice cream for 3$. For the ice cream maker, the marginal cost of ice cream, i.e., the cost of producing an additional cup of ice cream, let's say, does not change. But as a consumer, you already have had a cup of ice cream, so your willingness to pay for an additional cup is lower than 3$. You may be willing to pay only 2$ for an additional scoop. That is why two scoops of ice cream typically cost less than double that of a single scoop.

4. People Respond to Incentives

An incentive is something that causes a person to act. Because people use cost and benefit analysis, they also respond to incentives. When the government wants you to invest money into the economy by buying houses, it gives you tax-saving benefits as an incentive. It also works the opposite way. If you want to stop people from doing something undesirable, make it expensive. If the government wants to discourage people from smoking, it levies higher taxes on cigarettes, which increases cigarette prices and dissuades people from smoking to save money.

5. Trade Can Make Everyone Better Off

Only some countries, states, districts, companies or even people are equally good at everything it does or produces. Trading allows the exchange of goods/services that each entity can best produce. , E.g. Trade allows countries to focus on producing what they are good at and trade that against something they aren't so good at. India imports oil from the Gulf countries and exports food, grains and other commodities in trade.

6. Markets Are Usually a Good Way to Organize Economic Activity

A market is where people buy or sell products, commodities or services. Markets are where the demand is met with supply as if an 'invisible hand' decides pricing and consumption. For example, Amazon is a great marketplace to buy or sell products because it presents a huge variety and choices to the consumer and is a very convenient platform to sell for traders. It is a win-win for both, hence an efficient way to encourage economic activity.

7. Governments Can Sometimes Improve Economic Outcomes

Governments can create the "rules of the game" for citizens, businesses, civil society and even the government to protect the markets, protect the rights and safety of citizens and ensure the delivery of public goods and services. These actions are called market regulation and are intended to help the economy grow. Common examples of regulation include limits on environmental pollution, laws against child labour or other employment regulations, minimum wage laws, regulations requiring truthful labelling of the ingredients in food and drugs, and establishing minimum testing standards for safety.

8. The Standard of Living Depends on a Country's Production

A country that produces a lot or produces more valuable goods and services will be able to pay higher wages. That means its residents can afford to buy more of its plentiful production. Its residents will be able to afford more comfort and security. The more goods and services produced in a country, the higher the standard of living.

9. Prices Rise When the Government Prints Too Much Money

If you print more money, the amount of goods stays the same. With more money printed, households will have more cash and money to spend on goods. If more money is chasing the same amount of goods, companies will increase prices, causing inflation.

10. Society Faces a Short-Run Trade-off Between Inflation and Unemployment

Unemployment generally refers to individuals who are employable and actively seeking a job but cannot find a job. There can be many causes for unemployment, like increasing technology or automation requiring fewer people to do the same or even more work. In the short run, suppliers will want to increase their production of goods and services when prices increase. They need to hire more workers to produce those goods and services to achieve this. More hiring means lower unemployment while there is still inflation. So, for governments, it is a tight walk to decide exactly how much money to print so that inflation doesn't hurt and unemployment doesn't rise too much.

Gregory suggests these ten principles of economics "supposedly represent the heart of economic wisdom". The book was first published in 1997 and had nine editions as of 2020, standing the test of modern times. Even though I do not recommend reading the entire book, I recommend getting an overview, as it makes great learning for children and adults alike.

ᐁᐁᐁ

NINETEEN
FOUR TYPES OF LUCK

1 Blind Luck

2 Luck by Persistence

3 Luck by Hunting

4 Luck by Invitation

Four Types of Luck

There are three critical ingredients to success: Hard work, Timing and Luck. Here I would like to flesh out the topic of luck. It is a commonly held belief that luck is outside our sphere of influence; hence, we cannot control it. However, this belief is only partially true. I want to discuss what I learnt about luck and its different types. Here are the four types of luck that I learnt about:

1. *Blind Luck*

The first type of luck is blind luck. In blind luck, one gets lucky because something totally out of their control happened. You may then call it a stroke of fortune or fate. When blind luck favours you, you are born with a silver spoon in your mouth or fortune lands on your lap without you even wanting it or trying to have it. Being born to wealthy parents or inheriting a large fortune are examples of blind luck.

2. *Luck by Persistence*

The second type is luck which comes through hard work, persistence, hustle, and motion. In this kind of luck, you are running around creating opportunities. You are generating enough force, hustle, and energy for luck to find you. You walk, fall, stand up, and try to walk again until you reach a point when good things start happening to you, like getting into shape to win that next assignment, building critical skills through hard work, or working for that next promotion. It is all about sheer persistence by which you eliminate competition.

3. *Luck by Hunting*

The third way is to become good at spotting luck. Creating luck by hunting requires very keen observation, patience, and focus. If you are skilled in a field, you will notice when a lucky break happens in your field, and other people who are not attuned to it won't notice. So, you become sensitive to spotting luck, and once you spot it, you immediately grab it and use the opportunity to grow. So, if you are a salesperson and you know some big opportunity is coming up, you would diligently shortlist the most desirable prospects, study them, understand them and woo them. You put yourself where you may get lucky.

4. *Luck by Invitation*

The final kind of luck is the rarest, hardest kind, where you build a unique character, brand, and mindset, which causes luck to find you. For example, suppose you are the best deep-sea diver in the world. You are known for taking on deep-sea diving attempts that others won't even dare to attempt. This news reaches the ears of a treasure-hunting company, and they invite you to help them find that sunken treasure ship that nobody could get to in the past. So now, their luck rubs on to you. Their luck just became your luck. They will come to you to get the treasure, and you will get paid for it. Luck by invitation means creating a unique position and name for yourself in your team, company, or business community. When opportunities arise, people will find you as they know you are the right person for the job.

While it is easy to talk about the four kinds of luck, it is not easy to move from relying on blind luck to luck by persistence. But by being aware of the four kinds of luck, there is hope that you can slowly hunt for luck or let luck find you.

ᗁᗁᗁ

TWENTY

USE THE MONEY TO FIND FREEDOM, NOT BONDAGE

If I were to pass on a piece of financial advice to my daughter, it would be to never get into debt for luxuries or experiences. Do not borrow money to buy a better car, a bigger house, a vacation, or a retreat. In borrowing for the present pleasure, we rob ourselves of future peace and happiness. With the growth of banking and financial institutions, living with debt has become the norm today. As a result, paying EMIs has become an integral part of middle-class life in India and a culturally accepted, expected and sometimes respected norm.

Benjamin Franklin said

"Rather go to bed supperless, than rise in debt."

Any pleasure which is addictive can become bondage. And the addiction that is paid by debt is a double-edged sword. I understand that it is not easy to live debt free- the impatience to yield to the temptation to own the next gadget/phone/car is tremendous. But it is not impossible. We can resist every kind of temptation with the sword of wisdom. The best policy is to adjust your lifestyle to your earnings, even if they are humble or meagre. Pretending to be rich makes you poor faster. Using credit to make lifestyle changes starts a hard-to-end vicious circle.

There is immense peace in living within one's means. Living a simple life and keeping good mental and physical health is far more valuable than buying lifestyle diseases with borrowed money. Adam Smith said,

"*What can be added to the happiness of a man who is in health, out of debt, and has a clear conscience?*"

This kind of living does not rule out or demean the importance of seeking security. When buying a house, taking a loan may still make sense. For most other things, it is best to buy when we can afford them. A decent place to live, a personal conveyance, holidays with family and so on are all worthy expectations, but it is better to earn them patiently. Someday, you can make a big purchase out of your savings or investments. Thomas Jefferson said,

"*Never spend your money before you have it.*"

One of the lessons I learnt from my spiritual mentor is to use the money to buy freedom rather than bondage. Buying freedom means using our earning capacity to help us prioritise and focus on our most valuable pursuits. Making simple changes like paying for external help for household chores, car washing, laundry etc., can leave one with much-wanted leisure time, which we can use for hobbies, reading, fitness, family, and many other productive pursuits. Spending on automation and systems can also help boost productivity at work and home.

However, the most important motivation to live debt-free is the values it inspires in us – patience, hard work, goal orientation, confidence, contentment, self-control, and willingness to make sacrifices. Henry Wadsworth Longfellow said,

"*He looks the whole world in the face, for he owes not any man.*"

I aspire towards the simplicity and lightness of being that comes with a debt-free lifestyle. These are hard learnt lessons, and I wish the next generation learns from our follies rather than by experience. Start considering a debt-free life and then then, chalk out a plan to get there. It is the new 1% club.

ᚦᚦᚦ

TWENTY-ONE

HOMEMAKER: THE MOST IMPORTANT CAREER IN THE WORLD

The Oxford English Dictionary defines a homemaker as a person who manages a home and takes care of the house and family. The key responsibility of this role is building the family. The famous British writer and theologian C.S. Lewis called homemaking the most important job in the world and argued interestingly in its favour. He once wrote a letter to a friend encouraging her to take up homemaking. He wrote stating that to find happiness, to be happy in one's own home, is the ultimate human endeavour. He said, 'We wage war in order to have peace, we work in order to have leisure, we produce food to eat it. So your job (homemaking) is the one for which all others exist.' All other professions like government, transportation, army, manufacturing, banking and so on only exist to feed the people and keep them warm and safe in their homes. So in this way, it all ends with the homemaker.

Sadly, homemaking is seen as drudgery and lowly in our society today and is not even considered a career choice by either men or women. A homemaker often feels like Sisyphus, who has been cursed to roll a massive rock up the hill only to see it roll down and start again. It is seen as a thankless job and unpaid labour at best.

To this, my favourite actor Audrey Hepburn once said:

"'It is sad if people think that's (homemaking) a dull existence, [but] you can't just buy an apartment and furnish it and walk away. It is the flowers you choose, the music you play, and the smile you have waiting. I want it to be gay and cheerful, a haven in this troubled world. I do not want my husband and children to come home and find a rattled woman. Our era is already rattled enough, isn't it?'"

Our modern society devalues and demeans homemakers to such an extent that homemakers find it embarrassing to introduce themselves as homemakers. It is almost unthinkable today that one says,' I just want to be a homemaker.' The truth remains that the homemaker converts a house into a home where you feel you belong, you feel safe and comfortable, and at home. Not just charity but every virtue begins at home, and the seeds of goodness are planted and nourished by the homemaker. It is a challenging career. It demands that one develop skills like meal planning, home decoration, housekeeping, gardening, resilience, value parenting, accounting, budgeting, family health and well-being.

So, what has gone wrong? Why is this role not desirable today? Here is what is missing today in the homemaker's job: empowerment. What was once an empowering job has been turned into an exploited one. To flourish in any career in the world, one needs to be empowered: one needs a certain level of autonomy, access to resources that one can put to work as one sees fit, opportunities and space to grow, develop and care for oneself and the acknowledgement of one's contribution to family and society building.

How can we reinstate the homemaker to the glory that it deserves? Here are three things that we can do to progress in this direction:

1. Credit the homemaker's account each month with a mutually agreed fixed amount or, even better, have a shared bank account with the homemaker. Let the homemaker have complete freedom to prioritise and choose to spend or save the money for home and personal needs. Never question or doubt the homemaker's judgement; support them when they seek your counsel.
2. Ensure the homemaker has enough leisure to spend on grooming, health, friends, hobbies, and self-development. Then, let them be free to take part-time professional engagements if they choose to. With options like 'work from home or 'work from anywhere, this is undoubtedly possible today.

3. Partner with your homemaker to build the family. Please support them in raising value-conscious children and make your home the preferred place for your family's relaxation, celebration, and laughter rather than seeking these things outside.

I have seen my mother as a homemaker. Always at the centre of our homes and hearts, she toiled relentlessly and raised us to be the people we are. Though a woman has traditionally taken it up, today, it can be taken up by any family member: spouse or partner, man or woman, young or old. During months of lockdown last year, I played this role for several months and learned much from it. The breadwinner's and the homemaker's roles are interdependent and complement each other. We need them both, and some people can play both roles. However, the homemaker is the true happiness-maker of the family- the ground on which love, belongingness, security, spirituality, and values grow. If you are a homemaker or planning to be one- be proud of it. As a civilisation, I hope we understand this role's importance and move towards this ideal again and with more openness and clarity. Let us make homemaker the greatest career in the world again.

ᏢᏢᏢ

TWENTY-TWO
MEANING & JOY IN CHORES AND ERRANDS

During the pandemic, for almost two years, my typical day started with doing the dishes, cleaning the kitchen and rewarding myself with a hot cup of masala chai prepared with grated ginger, a whiff of cardamom and lots of love. But, of course, it was not always like this, and I, like many, thought of this as a menial task, not worth my time. I would rather spend time on things that reward me with growth, health, or wealth- on 'real' accomplishments. We consider ourselves active, can-do people who grab opportunities and solve problems. But when it comes to chores and errands, we are different people.

Today most of us do not find joy in doing chores and running errands, and some of us even hate it- be it stay-at-home parents, children, or working parents. I am not saying people are not hard-working. All I am saying is most of us would not work given a choice and would rather have someone else, like a house help or 'maid' as they call it in India, to do our chores.

It is easy to confuse a chore with an errand. A chore is a routine task, especially a household one. It can be a tedious task yet a necessary one. Some examples of chores are doing the dishes, washing clothes, vacuuming, or taking out the garbage. In contrast, an errand is typically a short journey undertaken outside the home to perform a non-routine yet necessary task. Some examples of errands are taking or fetching clothes from the cleaner or filling the car with fuel. A comfortable life requires that chores be performed routinely and errands are run when needed. I find chores and errands like body functions like digestion, circulation, temperature regulation etc. Both are necessary for the sustenance of health and life. But the difference in case chores and errands is that one must voluntarily choose, decide, start and complete them.

While researching for the most hated household chores in the world, I came across a blog that spelt out the following chores as the most hated ones: Cleaning the bathroom/toilet, washing the dishes, cleaning the stovetop & oven, Doing the laundry & ironing, Dusting, Sweeping & Vacuuming, Mopping, Grocery Shopping & Cooking, Cleaning the windows and Gutter cleaning. Without testing the validity of this claim, I am sure most of us can relate to these chores and how we feel about them, irrespective of where we live.

Shying away from chores can be a sign of lethargy."The source of India's troubles has been the people who are thoroughly idle,' said Mahatma Gandhi. Although I do not entirely agree with that, I do agree that lethargy can be associated with reluctance to do chores.

I would not blame our genes but rather our culture for this. This cultural phenomenon has been a more recent development. For centuries living the life for most meant doing chores and running errands. Any achievement, growth or accomplishment was considered a bonus. The marketing age we live in today prods us to achieve, buy and experience only that which is different from our daily routine.

Our attitude towards chores and errands also says something about the kind of people we are. According to DePaul University psychology professor Joseph Ferrari, two distinct types of people have a problem completing household chores promptly: task delayers and chronic procrastinators. He says, 'They delay at home, work, school and in relationships. Chronic procrastinators make up about 20% of the population. This 20% makes procrastination their way of life. The other category is that of task delayers. For them, procrastination is not waiting; it is more than delaying. It is a decision not to act. So, it's lethargy combined with indecisiveness- a double whammy and a recipe for stress and regret.

Mahatma Gandhi preached and practised sharing housework between men and women of the family. He encouraged women to do intellectual work and men to help in cooking, cleaning and caring, conventionally, women's chores.

Here are more reasons why each of you needs to pick and own certain chores at home:

1. It gives you independence, the dignity of work and the joy of labour.
2. You control your day and your time better
3. You start appreciating the little things that make you happy
4. Chores train you to focus better, make you more mindful
5. Chores are humbling and help size your inflated egos.

In conclusion, chores and errands are the backbones of our lives and necessary for the healthy functioning of our daily lives. They are the canvas we can paint with colours of noteworthy accomplishments and rewards. How one performs one's chores reflects in everything else that the person does in one's personal and professional life. It mirrors one's commitment to one's values and ideals. Doing chores and running errands efficiently and joyfully is a skill that needs to be cultivated with love. For those who shy away from chores, I urge you to review your perspective and reasons and give it another shot.

ppp

TWENTY-THREE

LIVE ONE LIFE. LIVE WITH INTEGRITY

———•♡•———

There are countless ways to live life: some of us believe in living for the day, some want to make the best of the day, some want to live for an afterlife, some want to live many lives in the same one and so on. There are various schools of life we can find, and each has a cult of its own.

I have my proposition on this topic: Live One Life. Whoever you are, wherever you are, and whatever role you play, it is important to realise that you are each still the same person in them. I may be a father, a marketer, a blogger, a son, a husband, a friend, and so on at different times, yet I am the same person playing all these roles. So let us not be a person with multiple faces, leading secret lives.

Living with one face means we live with integrity. But what does it mean to live with integrity? Frank Sonnenberg described it best in the form of 12 characteristics of a life of integrity. Here they are:

Value integrity

Recognise who you are and the values that you aspire to. Provide others with the confidence that your intentions and actions are always genuine. Be prepared to compromise your viewpoint but never your principles.

Be true to yourself

In staying true to your beliefs, be sure to do right by others and always take the high ground. Trust your instincts rather than seek validation from others. You have to live with yourself for the rest of your life.

Keep good company

Surround yourself with honourable people. Support each other. Allow them to serve as role models and sounding boards that inspire you to become a better you. And look for ways to help others grow in honour and integrity.

Be confident

Don't let your behaviour be influenced by others who do not share your values; hold yourself to a much higher standard — your conscience. Your character is on display every moment of every day. Make sure it reflects well on you and causes people to feel proud to call you a friend.

Do what's right

Make good choices. Follow the spirit as well as the letter of the law. At the centre of the United States Military Academy is the Cadet Honour Code, which states, "A Cadet will not lie, cheat, steal, or tolerate those who do." Care about where life is taking you and how you're getting there.

Be honest and transparent

When you stand for honesty, everything you say carries the voice of credibility. But when you're dishonest, your reputation will speak for you. The fact is, honest people never fear the truth.

Honour your word

Every time you make a promise, you put your honour and integrity on the line. Keeping that promise should be as important to you as it is to the recipient.

Be loyal

Meaningful relationships don't happen by chance. When you live with honour, people know your behaviour is reliable, your heart is in the right place, and your word is as good as gold.

Accept personal responsibility

Be prepared to accept the consequences of your actions. Knowing what's right isn't as important as doing what's right. Be aware that you may not be taking the most popular road travelled.

Be resilient

Hard work and sacrifice build character, contribute to success, and promote happiness. This reality moved former baseball player Sam Ewing to observe, "Hard work spotlights the character of people: some turn up their sleeves, some turn up their noses, and some don't turn up at all."

Make a difference

Be a positive force in people's lives. Make people feel special; bring out the best in them; help them without expecting something in return; be genuinely happy for their achievements. The more you do for others, the happier you'll be.

Live for a cause greater than yourself

Find your life's purpose. It will inspire you, keep you grounded, and provide stability regardless of the turbulence in your life. Most of all, living life purposefully will motivate you to get up in the morning and make your life better.

ᏢᏢᏢ

LOVE: Nurture Relationships and Grow with Companionship

TWENTY-FOUR

WHAT IS LOVE?

---·♡·---

The spectrum of love

To love is

To care, protect, hold
To remember, miss, to wish well
To hug, caress, kiss
To understand, be understood, to listen
To counsel, coach, to mentor
To play with, cry with, laugh with
To nourish, support, to invest in
To share, give, to surprise
To trust, respect, to set free

To Love is to Value

Love has become the most versatile word in today's day-to-day lexicon. People love to use the word love in the context of absolutely anything one can think of: shopping, food, celebrities, travel, toys, writers, sleep, recreation, and the list can go on and on. But unfortunately, love has been commoditised to such an extent that it is hard for most of us to explain what love means and why we use it the way we do.

It was Ayn Rand who I first read saying, 'To love is to value.' Does it not simplify how we understand the meaning of love? She said, "Love is the expression of one's values, the greatest reward you can earn for the moral qualities you have achieved in your character and person, the emotional

THINK BETTER AND THRIVE

price paid by one man for the joy he receives from the virtues of another."

'Love, friendship, respect, admiration is the emotional response of one man to the virtues of another, the spiritual payment given in exchange for the personal, selfish pleasure which one man derives from the virtues of another man's character.'

Romantic love is no different, although it takes this appreciation to another level. 'Love is a response to values. It is with a person's sense of life that one falls in love—with that essential sum, that fundamental stand or way of facing existence, which is the essence of a personality.'. This sense of life should have consistency in quality and persistence. 'One falls in love with the embodiment of the values that formed a person's character, which is reflected in his widest goals or smallest gestures, which create the *style* of his soul—the individual style of a unique, unrepeatable, irreplaceable consciousness.'

Any affirmation of love calls for an evaluation regarding who to love and to accept love from. If we are clear about what we value, we can know whom to love and with whom to stay in love.

All love is Self-Love.

We all have, at some point in life, experienced love. It may be the love of people, animals or even plant forms, things, activities, etc. The message of this essay is that there is essentially only one form of love, and that is self-love, and it is this self-love that is reflected by the external world and feels like 'love' to us.

Let me share some examples to illustrate this:

1. A parent's love for the child is one of the highest emotions of love experienced. Why does one feel this love so intensely in one's child and not another? This is so because a parent sees their own image in the child. The child reflects your own likeness, giving the impression that it is very much part of yourself who has come from you. This is parental love.

2. Our love for our partners is also similar. When we see the expression of values we hold dear in our partner, we feel love. Even in love at first sight, you hit a chord that feels familiar and yours. As if the two souls have always been one, as the expression goes. Our partners become our better halves.

3. Our love for things: We all love some things more than others. Some people love their home, cars, bikes, wealth, wardrobe, and property simply because it enhances their self-image.

4. Our love for recognition is also a form of self-love. When we get promoted at work, awarded for our contribution, rewarded for our performance, or applauded for any reason, we feel good about ourselves. It gives us self-confidence and jacks up our self-respect.

In all these examples, we see how externally directed love is essentially a seeking of our internal self. Moreover, these examples show that we can see our reflection of ourselves in others, which makes us happy under certain circumstances or conditions. We see in others an extension of ourselves. We see ourselves in others and others as part of ourselves. And doesn't it bring immense happiness? Even tears of joy at times?

Unfortunately, this way of finding love outside is fraught with uncertainty and frustration too. Why? Because we get hooked on this way of seeking love. We become attached to this reflection and expect it to last all the time, even forever. When circumstances change, we can no longer see ourselves reflected in another; hence, there is no acknowledgement of love. As a result, our children feel alienated. They disrespect and misbehave with us. Our partners feel despicable when they cheat on us, our friends feel like strangers when they work against our values, and our work feels like drudgery and status like a burden when they stop rewarding us.

Our yearning for love is legitimate and a privilege. But when we do not understand that, in reality, it originates in us, that it resides in us, a vicious cycle of seeking, finding, controlling, and frustration begins.

Like the musk deer that carries the mysterious fragrance in its own glands and yet looks everywhere for it, we seek to love and want to somehow find, possess, control and manipulate it to serve us. Yet, the truth is that, like a lamp in the darkness, our own self lights up the world around us, the objects we experience merely reflecting our own light.

This does not mean we should not have children, partners, professions or comforts. We only need to have the maturity of understanding that they merely reflect what we already are. We are happy in pursuit. If we think we are pursuing happiness outside, we must contend with occasional, circumstantial, reflected happiness. Once we understand that all the seeking of love is essentially seeking self-love, we can feel love even when we are not seeking it and in places where we are not looking.

A word of warning here: do not mistake self-love for narcissism. A narcissist makes an object of themselves, treating themselves as an outside person or object. A narcissist has a distorted self-image based on a false reality, where they see one's qualities in an amplified form, feeding on the admiration of others. Narcissists feed on praise and recognition from others and have no real achievement or quality of value. They project a fake image of themselves, turning a blind eye to their flaws and shortcomings. Their self-love is shallow, making them incapable of loving others.

True self-love is grounded, not in social media likes or praise. In Self-love, one takes full responsibility for one's well-being. This self-love can be discovered through self-inquiry alone: by looking within and witnessing the play of our emotions, motivations, and actions, by finding a place of rest within us where nothing can hurt us or disturb us. Understanding that all love of the external world is transient and incidental and that it reflects our self, which remains hidden, like the light in a cloud of smoke or the sun behind clouds. This sunshine allows us to love others and share happiness honestly.

Thus, only one love is reflected in various colours, shapes, and flavours of our desires. Find people who have already found themselves in this manner and ask them to help you find it yourself. This is the only way. The light that can reflect love, bringing ultimate happiness, security and peace, is within you. Discover that light. Seek yourself. Once it is found, the seeking itself ends. Leaving you radiating the love that you already are. This love then follows you wherever you can go, rubbing itself onto all the lives you touch.

Love is hard

It is easy to confess to someone, 'I love you. But, 'Doing' love is the hardest.

For most practical purposes, 'to love' means 'to enjoy another person and lets ourselves 'be enjoyed by them. Even the Oxford dictionary agrees with this practical definition: a strong feeling you have when you like somebody/something very much or a strong feeling of interest in or enjoyment of something. Love is seen as an animal instinct- like a mother's love for a child or attraction to the opposite sex. Love is seen as a mutual exchange of pleasure. Depending on the context, we say we give love or make love. Love is seen as something that comes easily to us- naturally, as if it is hard-wired into us by design. 'Love is blind', we say.

If life has taught me anything about love, it is this: Love is the hardest thing to do.

To love another person means accepting another person with their flaws, quirks, and conditions. To love is to walk on eggshells sometimes and, at times, garland the same person with admiration and adoration. To love is to be with another through their depression, mood swings, irritability, and outbursts, protecting them through the phase. To love is to accommodate. To love is to forgive, at times, even if with a heavy heart. To love is to apologise and make amends when you are wrong.

To love another person means to reveal your insecurities to another person. Even at the risk of being offended, hurt or disappointed. To love is to have uncomfortable conversations.

To love is to commit to another person's well-being and for life. To love another person means to lend a helping hand. To love shows strength and courage that you never knew you had. To love is to invest time, money, and attention in another when you can use them for your enjoyment.

To love is to lend a shoulder to cry on when another needs it, pat and motivate them to grow. To love is to attend to the pain and suffering of another and provide comfort, even if that means spending sleepless nights or moving without rest. To love is to put the other person first.

To love is to participate in pastimes that may not fascinate you, doing things that are not on your priority list. To love is to make compromises for the greater good of yourself and those you say you love. Finally, to love is to be the lubricant through the friction of another person's life.

To love is to protect yourself from exploitation, abuse, disrespect, and harm- even if it means letting go of those you promised to love forever. To love is to experience loss, to grieve. To love is to have to move on when you clearly cannot. To love is to let go.

Matthew Kelly, in his book *The Seven Levels of Intimacy: The Art of Loving and the Joy of Being Loved*, sums it up beautifully:

> "*Love is the wanting, and the having, and the choosing, and the becoming. Love is the desire to see the person we love be and become all he or she is capable of being and becoming. Love is a willingness to lay down our own personal plans, desires, and agenda for the good of the relationship. Love is delayed gratification, pleasure, and pain. Love is being able to live and thrive apart, but choosing to be together.*"

Do not go easy on love. It is the hardest thing to do in the entire universe. Yet, it is anything but blind. It must be cultivated with deliberate, conscious effort. To love is a privilege. It is a celebration of the best in us.

ᎮᎮᎮ

TWENTY-FIVE

THRIVING AT LOVE

---◆♭◆---

Love Flourishes when expressed right

Here are five lessons about love that life has taught me so far. I think of love in a certain way, and I share the same here.

Love flourishes in an environment which has five essential nutrients:

1. When love is expressed unconditionally, i.e., without setting expectations on what you get back in return
2. When love is expressed in a form that is received joyfully by the other
3. When love is expressed at an affordable cost
4. When love is expressed for the sake of love
5. When love is expressed without clinging to it

My first biggest discovery was that each person prefers to be loved in some ways more than others. In his book 'The Five Love Languages: How to Express Heartfelt Commitment to Your Mate ', Gary Chapman outlines five general ways romantic partners express and experience love. Chapman calls these the love languages. They are words of affirmation, quality time, receiving gifts, acts of service and physical touch. Chapman's thesis is that each person has one primary and one secondary love language in which they express and receive love. An example of acts of service can be that your partner loves to do things to help, like cooking, laundry, joining you for shopping, helping with your office work and so on. This can be one's primary language of expressing love or preferred way of receiving love.

Chapman suggests that to discover another person's love language, one must observe how they express love to others and analyse what they complain about most often and what they request from their significant other. I know now from experience that this is quite how it works, so it is crucial to choose suitable languages to express love.

The next lesson I learned was about expectations. I observed that when I love someone, I set expectations for the person and lay certain conditions. The more the love, the higher the expectations and the more the conditions. This expectation from the other person could be in the form of gratitude, loyalty, commitment, appreciation or simply that they think well of me or see me in a better light. However, very soon, I realised this did not work. With higher and higher expectations comes the risk of higher and higher disappointment, too, because love is very subjective and is received and expressed differently by different people. In addition to that, I also start setting higher expectations for myself, wanting to raise the bar every time. So the next time, I tried to make a more grand, refined, more emotionally elevating expression of love, even to the extent that I may not be genuinely expressing it. So, you see? Setting expectations in return for love and loving another with conditions is like a double-edged sword, and it can cause damage either way. And so, I am learning to separate love from expectations.

Sometimes, I have been to lengths that I cannot afford to express love. This is unnecessary and causes more pain in retrospect. It is better to give what you can and can afford than to make gifts or promises you do not have the means to fulfil or can only fulfil with compromises in other areas of life.

The Recipe for a Great Partnership

I have challenged the institution of marriage, even criticised it at times for how it has morphed into a legal, gender-biased, religious and political institution and believed that it requires some reinvention or at least needs to be reviewed. But when I look at marriage as a partnership, or perhaps the greatest partnership of our life, it all starts making sense. A great marriage or partnership needs certain ingredients to make it great and successful. What does it take to make it a great partnership? Many say it is love. It is all about love for each other's company. But Love, like God, is over-used, ambiguous, and abstract and can mean many things to many people. We know that great partnerships will not just happen. To fully describe the building blocks of a great partnership, we need 'actionable' and 'tactile' words.

I work for a company that believes in developing a strengths-based workplace and culture. In a strengths-based culture, leaders, managers, and employees continually develop each person's potential, resulting in an engaged workforce and organic business growth. We once did a workshop on how to create strengths-based partnerships at work. It discussed the *Eight Elements of a Powerful Partnership* identified by Gallup and how we can nourish them in the workplace. However, I could not stop and wonder how they would apply in our personal lives, especially to our love relationships.

Here are the Eight Ingredients that make a powerful partnership that I learnt from our strengths workshop :

Complementary Strengths

Everyone has weaknesses and blind spots that create obstacles to reaching a goal. One of the most potent reasons for teaming up is so that you can work with someone who is strong in areas where you may be weak and vice versa. Individuals are not well-rounded, but pairs can be. Individuals in a partnership can complement each other, team up, reinforce each other's strengths and cover and compensate for the other's weaknesses and blind spots.

A Common Mission

When a partnership fails, the root cause is often the two people pursuing separate agendas. When partners want the same thing badly enough, they will make the personal sacrifices necessary to see it through. As partners, do you have the same vision for your life, a common purpose, and overarching goals?

Fairness

Humans have an instinctive need for fairness. Because the need for fairness runs deep, it is an essential quality of a strong partnership. Fairness reflects in how you treat your partner, share your resources with them and celebrate the results of your collaboration. Boundaries that apply to one also apply to another.

Trust

This is the cornerstone of relationships. Working with someone means taking risks. You are likely to contribute your best work if you trust that your partner will do their best. Without trust, it is easier to work alone. Also, once this trust is broken, it is hard, sometimes impossible, to build it again.

Acceptance

We see the world through our own set of lenses. Whenever two disparate personalities come together, there is bound to be some friction from their differences. This can be a recipe for conflict unless both learn to accept the idiosyncrasies of the other. It is not the same as tolerating another person's misdoings. Any rough edges that can come in the way of achieving common goals must be acknowledged, discussed, and smoothened over time.

Forgiveness

People are imperfect. They make mistakes. They sometimes do the wrong thing. But, without forgiveness, the natural revenge motives that stem from friend-or-foe instincts will overpower all the reasons to continue a partnership, and it will eventually dissolve.

Communicating

In the early stages of a partnership, communicating helps to prevent misunderstandings; later in the relationship, a continuous flow of information makes the work more efficient by keeping the two people synchronized. All the above blocks require clear communication to build.

Unselfishness

In the best working relationships, the natural concern for your welfare transforms into gratification in seeing your comrade succeed. Those who have reached this level say such collaborations become among the most fulfilling aspects of their lives. Each of us needs to genuinely think in the best long-term interest of the other and support the partner to become a better self, into becoming our true better half.

Do these make sense to you? Can you relate to them? Can you see your relationships in the light of these key ingredients? Please reflect on these and review your relationships in light of these elements. Check where you stand and where you can improve and build upon. I hope you find these useful and use this to start/build/strengthen your relationships.

Love and Walk Along

Love knows no taking, only to give, seeks no reward here or hereafter; Seeks no treasure at the end of life's rainbow, so love and walk along.

Love springs from within, not from the other; It comes out of our own nature; like the sun shines and the flowers bloom, it can't be held back, so love and walk along.

Share a smile and break bread; everyone is a fellow traveller here; hold on to no one and do nothing; everyone we know will soon be gone, so love and walk along.

There is no time to build your castle here, but rest a while and create a memory; You owe the world nothing, and it owes you nothing, so love and walk along.

We crawl out of this world; likewise, we sink back into its womb; none of those who cross our ways, we may ever know again, so love and walk along.

Set no expectations, seek no dependents, string no attachments, and carry no baggage; Travel light and you will go far, so love and walk along.

Do what needs doing, and with righteousness shining through; Peace and sound sleep are rewards enough, so love and walk along.

Like a candle to another, pass your light along; burning out, you move from one life to the next, yet your light will always remain, so love and walk along.

Love and Walk Along.

Enjoy everything about loving and being loved, but do not cling too hard to it. Understand the real reason why we love. We love because it is in our nature to want to love. It makes us happy, and it is normal and human to do so. Love comes naturally to us. To love is a privilege, and so is to be loved. So, learn to be grateful for whatever love comes your way. Do not crave it, do not cling to it. Learn to let go when it is time. Do not get stuck in your life journey for lack of love. While it is an important need, it is not the only need. It is more important to have a direction and a purpose for living. Love to the best of your capacity, and keep moving forward.

So here are my five lessons on how to love:

1. When you choose to love, love unconditionally.
Do not withhold. Give wholeheartedly. Be generous in love.

2. Express love in a way that gives joy to another person
Not everyone may get your love. You may express it, but they may understand or accept it. Not because your love is weak but because they did not receive it in a way that brought them joy.

3. Express love in a way you can afford to.
Always act within your means. Do not go overboard or get into debt for love.

4. Love because you love to love.
We love because it is in our nature to love. Loving brings joy. It is an end in itself, not a means to security, a bright future, or anything else.

5. Do not cling to love. Instead, let go and keep moving.
Love cannot be enforced, and it cannot be put into a locker. Let it flow freely like a fresh breeze and of its own accord. Do not try to hold on to it. Appreciate while it lingers, and then move on.

Consummate Love: The Pinnacle of Romantic Love

What is the highest form of romantic love? Robert Sternberg developed the triangular theory of love to describe Consummate Love– a state of perfection in love. He says it comprises three building blocks- an intimacy component, a passion component, and a decision/commitment component.

Passion

Passion is the physical and emotional attraction felt towards a romantic partner. All love stories begin as passion- sometimes beginning as one-sided and sometimes mutually experienced. However, withholding one's emotions, physical distance, and lack of physical bonding kill passion.

Once we get to know our partners well, when there is openness to speaking our hearts out and showing our vulnerability, we develop intimacy.

Intimacy

Intimacy is described as the feelings of closeness and attachment to one another. It is also described as having a sense of ease with one another. We know things about one another that no one really knows. Intimacy is always mutual and a step deeper into love. Secrecy and persistent lying in a relationship destroy intimacy.

Then comes commitment.

Commitment

Unlike the other two blocks, commitment involves a conscious decision to stick with one another. The decision to remain committed is mainly determined by the level of satisfaction a partner derives from the relationship. A commitment normally takes the form of exchanging vows between partners and could be solemnised by a church or a legal institution. A commitment promises loyalty to someone despite challenges, distractions, or options. Breach of trust weakens commitment.

When a relationship climbs through each step, building on the foundation of each previous block, they reach consummate love, the perfection of love. Of course, one need not always follow this logical progression, but irrespective of which route one takes, one can move towards the ideal of consummate love.

Many of us never reach consummate love because we give up halfway, taking any one building block as an end. As a result, some get stuck with passionate love, some with intimacy and some with commitment. Without healthy amounts of all three, the soup of love gets too hot, sour or bitter. To enjoy the soup of love over a lifetime, one needs to grow to the state of consummate love; otherwise, one will always feel a sense of lacking and crave attention, intimacy, or commitment from different partners.

At any point in time, one can either have one, two or all three components in a relationship:

1. **Liking,** in this case, is not used in a trivial sense. Sternberg says that this intimate liking characterises true friendships, in which a person feels a bondedness, warmth, and closeness with another but not intense passion or long-term commitment.

2. **Infatuated love** is what is felt as "love at first sight." But without the intimacy and the commitment components of love, infatuated love may disappear suddenly.

3. **Empty love:** Sometimes, a stronger love deteriorates into empty love, in which the commitment remains, but the intimacy and passion have died. In cultures where arranged marriages are common, relationships often begin as empty love.

4. **Romantic love:** Romantic lovers are bonded emotionally (as in liking) and physically through passionate arousal.

5. **Companionate love** is often found in marriages where the passion has gone out of the relationship, but a deep affection and commitment remain. Companionate love is generally a personal relationship and shares your life with but with no sexual or physical desire. It is stronger than friendship because of the extra element of commitment. The love ideally shared between family members is a form of companionate love, as is the love between deep friends or those who spend a lot of time together in any asexual but friendly relationship.

6. **Fatuous love** can be exemplified by a whirlwind courtship and marriage in which a commitment is motivated largely by passion without the stabilising influence of intimacy.

7. **Consummate love** is the most complete form of love, representing the ideal relationship toward which many people strive but which few achieve. Sternberg cautions that maintaining a consummate love may be harder than achieving it. He stresses the importance of translating the components of love into action. "Without expression," he warns, "even the greatest of loves can die". Consummate love may not be permanent. For example, if passion is lost over time, it may change into companionate love.

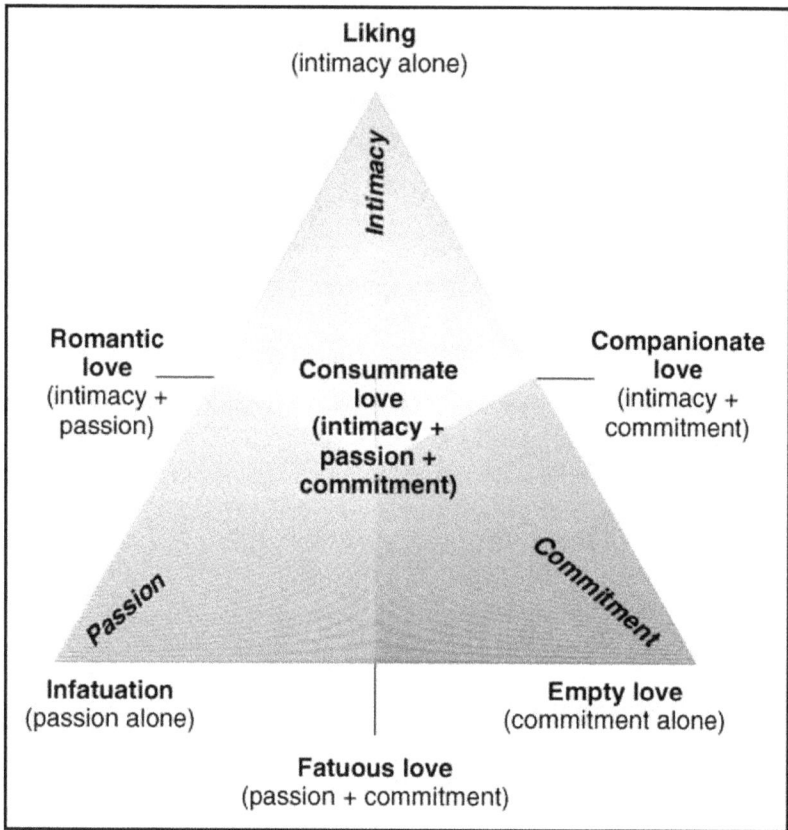

There are all kinds of love.

The balance between Sternberg's three aspects of love is likely to shift throughout a relationship. A strong dose of all three components in consummate love typifies an ideal relationship for many of us. However, time alone does not cause intimacy, passion, and commitment to occur and grow. Knowing about these components of love may help couples avoid pitfalls in their relationship, work on the areas that need improvement or help them recognise when it might be time for a relationship to end.

ᐅᐅᐅ

TWENTY-SIX

THE FAMILY LIFECYCLE MODEL

———◆♭◆———

Everything that lives follows a lifecycle. I learnt recently how even our family lives trace a lifecycle. A family life cycle is the set of predictable steps and patterns families experience over time. It is a set of emotional and intellectual experiences that one has to go through in a family from childhood to old age. A typical modern family may have a lifespan of about 50 years.

Paul Glick developed one of the first designs of the family life cycle in 1955. In Glick's original design, he asserted that most people would grow up, establish families, rear and launch their children, experience an "empty nest" period, and come to the end of their lives. This cycle will then continue with each subsequent generation (Glick 1989). Mastering the skills and milestones of each stage allows you to move successfully from one stage of development to the next. If you don't master the skills, you may move on to the next phase of the cycle, but you are more likely to have difficulty with relationships and future transitions. Family life cycle theory suggests successful transitioning may help prevent disease and emotional or stress-related disorders.

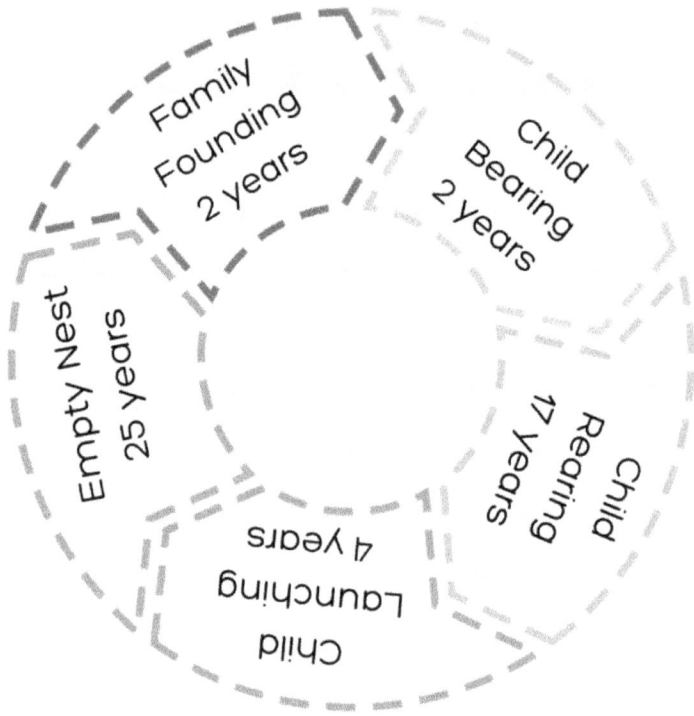

The Family Lifecycle Model

Glick's colleague, Evelyn Duvall, elaborated on the family life cycle by developing these classic stages of a family (Strong and DeVault 1992).

The Family Lifecycle

The family life cycle begins with marriage and ends with the death of both partners. But a family never ends—it goes on through the generations. So each family sends out its satellites during the launching stage to ensure continuity.

The typical young couple starting marriage today can predict about a two-year interval before the birth of the first child. The last baby will typically be born about six years after marriage. This youngest child will be married shortly after the parent's 25th wedding anniversary. More than half of the married years will be spent after the children are grown and away from home. Out of 50 years of married life, you will spend 25 years with each other without your children around. During these 25 years, the couple depends on each other for emotional support. So, when searching for your soul mate, please factor this in. Also, note that this phase comes towards the end of your life, not the beginning of your youth!

The husband will likely precede his wife in death, leaving the wife a widow for approximately 16 years of the family cycle. So, when you plan financially for retirement, consider this.

This way, one stage follows when the previous stage has reached completion. Each stage has a beginning in the stages which have gone before and its fulfilment in the future. Wherever an individual is now, he has his roots in the past and is moving toward the next stage of life.

At each stage of development, families need to complete certain milestones, just like individuals.

Here are the developmental tasks needed at each stage:
1. Family founding

- Establish a home.
- Become emotionally dependent on one another; emotionally independent of parents.
- Work out ways of handling differences.
- Learn homemaking skills.

2. Childbearing

- Learn about pregnancy, childbirth, and children.
- Gain an understanding of the new husband-wife relationship.
- Develop a philosophy of child-rearing. Accept the responsibilities of parenthood.
- Understand the role of grandparents.

3. Child rearing

- Continue to learn about children.
- Adjust financial plans and housing to meet the needs of children.
- Assume responsibility for school and community betterment.
- Become alert to the particular needs of children at different ages.

4. Child launching

- Discard folklore about love and marriage; gain insight and knowledge to help children.
- Enlarge the child's vocational choice by learning about new opportunities.
- Give emotional support to children as they leave home for work, military service, school, or marriage.
- Release children to live their own lives.

5. Empty nest

- Adjust to life as a couple after years as parents.
- Accept the reality of your life's accomplishments.
- Learn about modern methods of child-rearing to improve skills as grandparents.
- Prepare for and adjust to retirement.
- Prepare for living alone.

No two families will follow the same pattern, but the family life cycle concept offers a helpful approach to managing family resources. Your life partner's choice will heavily influence your family's health. Understanding the various stages and the approximate time couples can expect to spend in each stage helps us understand what we are getting into when we are planning to start a family. It helps us foresee the challenges and developmental milestones and helps us take proactive decisions on housing, recreation, insurance, career, retirement and so on.

Family Life Cycle Stage	Emotional Process of Transition: Key Principles	Second-Order Changes in Family Status Required to Proceed Developmentally
Leaving home: Single young adults	Accepting emotional and financial responsibility for self	Differentiation of self in relation to the family of origin
		Development of intimate peer relationships
		Establishment of self rework and financial independence
The joining of families through marriage: The	Commitment to new system	Formation of marital system
		Realignment of relationships with extended families and friends to include spouse
Families with young children	Accepting new members into the system	Adjusting the marital system to make space for child(ren)
		Joining in childrearing, financial, and household tasks
		Realignment of relationships with extended family to include parenting and grandparenting roles
Families with adolescents	Increasing flexibility of family boundaries to include children's independence and grandparent's frailties	Shifting of parent-child relationships to permit adolescents to move in and out of the system
		Refocus on midlife marital and career issues
		The beginning shift toward joint caring for the older generation
Launching children and moving on	Accepting a multitude of exits from and entries into the family system	Renegotiation of the marital system as a dyad
		Development of adult-to-adult relationships between grown children and their parents
		Realignment of relationships to include in-laws and grandchildren
		Dealing with disabilities and the death of parents (grandparents)
Families in later life	Accepting the shifting of generational roles	Maintaining own and/or couple functioning and interests in face of physiological decline; exploration of new familial and social role options
		Support for a more central role of middle generation
		Making room in the system for the wisdom and experience of the elderly, supporting the older generation without over-functioning for them
		Dealing with loss of spouse, siblings, and other peers and preparation for own death. Life review and integration
Source: From Betty Carter and Monica McGoldrick, The Changing Family Life Cycle: A Framework for Family Therapy, 2nd ed. Copyright 1989 by Altyn and Bacon.		

The Changing Family Lifecycle

ᗡᗡᗡ

TWENTY-SEVEN

MARRIAGE: WHY, WHAT, WHO AND HOW

———•ᗞ•———

Should we marry for love?

One day my daughter will find herself at the crossroads where she must choose to take a step toward marriage. I may or may not be around to guide her, or she may not seek my counsel. In any case, I put it down for her here, hoping she may find it helpful someday.

A commonly accepted and encompassing definition of marriage is that it is a formal union - a social and legal contract between two individuals that legally, economically, and emotionally unites their lives.

Today marriage is a legal, social, and religious institution. It is a contract policed by society, religious bodies, and courts of law. It is policed by your friends, family, relatives and even peers at work. As the laws regulating marriage and separation have evolved, they have increasingly become based on compliance, threat, and fear, not trust, mutual respect and love. Many relationships begin with mutual love, trust and freedom, but within a few years of marriage, they become obligation, insecurity and fear. Is it still a relevant institution? Does it still make sense to marry? Should we marry for love? Let us explore some of these facets.

In a Huffington Post article, Susan Pease Godoua gives us three reasons why we should never marry for love:

1. Love is an emotion, and like all emotions is fluid and changing.

2. Love does not make for a strong foundation because it is a changing emotion.

3. Love is not enough to survive, thrive and flourish.

Love is one of the many emotions we feel and is transient and changing depending on circumstances and other physiological factors. So, when the emotion vanes, the relationship feels empty. Sentimental love, being fluid, cannot make a strong foundation. What we need is to have a solid and committed partnership toward common goals.

Does that mean one should not marry? No, it only means one should not marry for love *alone*. And does that mean one should adopt co-living without getting into the legal hassle of marriage? The answer to that is also 'no'. It may make more sense to look at marriage as a contract rather than co-living. Here are some reasons why:

1. Long-term Stability

Strong emotions like love make us vulnerable, and they make us impulsive. This impulsiveness leads to some decisions we might regret, some we cannot even undo. That's why this impulsiveness needs to be regulated to have the necessary stability to grow and prosper by putting our energy and attention where needed. Marrying for stability means that you want your marriage, your partnership to be the foundation on which you can build a stable future, a canvas on which you can paint your aspirations and dreams. But before you get your canvas, you need clarity about what you want to paint. Before we build the home of our dreams, we must know that the foundation can support it.

2. Sacred Companionship

It takes years for people to grow and mature, and you want a companion with whom you can take this journey. We need someone who can at the same time teach us and learn with us. However, this companion should be one with whom you share values, goals, and aspirations. Also, a companion with complementary strengths makes for a better partner. It is rare to find such a companion when you use the lens of love to find them. It requires objectivity and clarity to match such people in matrimony. It must be a sacred contract- for a purpose higher than meeting one another's carnal needs. It needs the sanction of a commonly revered sacred being, faith or institution. We cannot be companions when our journeys and our goals are different. When the marriage is held together by an institution, goal, or a purpose larger and considered more important than individual preferences and priorities, the chances that the marriage holds in rough times are better.

Marrying merely to find a companion to dispel your loneliness is another recipe for disaster. Anton Chekhov once suggested, "If you're afraid of loneliness, don't marry." The sociologists Natalia Sarkisian of Boston College and Naomi Gerstel of the University of Massachusetts at Amherst found that marriage weakens other social ties. Compared with those who stay single, married folks are less likely to visit or call parents and siblings—and less inclined to offer them emotional support or pragmatic help with chores and transportation. They are also less likely to hang out with friends and neighbours.

3. *Value Parenting*

This is the last sensible reason why upgrading from being committed to being married may make sense. Marriage as a contract should be considered when the couple's pregnant. It is the start of a long investment journey to bring a new individual into this world, nourish and protect it and guide it to grow into an educated, cultured, independent and resilient adult. Any such investment requires commitment & security, and the legal contract of marriage, to some extent, provides for it. It is not enough for parents to partner in parenting but, with their example, show their children how to conduct themselves and grow.

We may make many mistakes in life, learn from them, and grow out of them. But marriage is one such act, which is not easy to undo. Although the legal institutions provide for it, one may never fully recover from a marriage or fully undo the damage it may have done to one. And that makes it the most important decision of one's life- more important than choosing a career, your next holiday destination, or the stock you want to invest in.

I am not saying one may not find great stability, companionship and parenthood in marriage based on love, only that it is highly unlikely. It is more likely to find love in a great marriage.

If you are marrying on your spiritual path

I look up to Paul Brunton as one of many spiritual teachers who influenced and taught me. Paul Brunton was a British philosopher, researcher, mystic, and adventurer. He left a journalistic career to live among yogis, mystics, and holy men and studied various Eastern and Western esoteric teachings. With his entire life dedicated to the spiritual quest, he felt charged with communicating his knowledge and experiences in layperson's terms. His greatest contribution, I think, is 'The Wisdom of the Overself', which establishes the highest teachings of Vedanta from first principles without using any oriental training or language background.

Paul jotted down the insights I share today in his notebook, which were made available freely to the public after his death. Although these notes were addressed to men, we can read them to apply to both men and women equally and from both perspectives. I have curated ten insights and arranged them for easy reading. I cannot improve on these notes by rephrasing them, so I am producing them as it is. I think these insights on Marriage that can help any spiritual seeker on the path of Moksha:

"*Each of us being individually complete in his inmost godlike self, no other person is needed for self-fulfilment, no mate or affinity is required to bring him to the realization of life's goal. But each of us being incomplete in his outer self, the longing for such a mate or affinity is human, natural, and pardonable. There is nothing wrong nor contrary to the Quest in seeking to satisfy this longing, although unless this is done with wisdom and after prudent consideration, rather than with ignorance and in impulse, the result may bring more unhappiness rather than more happiness. Nor must such a longing ever be allowed to obscure the great truth of individual completeness on the spiritual level.*

The aspirant who seeks to live spiritually in the world should marry for something more than physical enjoyment and comfort, more even than intellectual and social companionship. He must find a woman whose inner being is polarized to the same ideals as his own, who will walk by his side through every vicissitude as a fellow pilgrim and a wholehearted seeker.

Marriage multiplies burdens, entanglements, anxieties, difficulties, and worldly preoccupations. The single man has a better chance to wed his life to a single undistracted aim. Nevertheless, philosophy does not condemn marriage but leaves it to individual choice. Indeed, when two persons are temperamentally harmonious and spiritually suitable, it definitely approves of marriage.

Marriage is a risky affair when one of the two belongs in every way–spiritual, intellectual, and social–to a class higher than the other. If they cannot meet on these levels, where can they? The bad in both is brought out and made worse; the good is diminished. This was one of the original reasons why the caste system got established in some form or other among the Orientals as if it were an essential part of religion.

One general guiding principle as to whether or not a young aspirant on the quest should enter into marriage is that it is necessary that there should be spiritual harmony. Both must pursue the same ideal, for if disharmony enters this would lead to disaster. Both must stand within measurable distance of each other on the spiritual path. In addition to that, it is advisable that there should be physical, magnetic, and temperamental suitability to each other. In any case, this decision is a matter which should not be rushed and it will be well to take enough time for consideration. It would be well also to ponder the opinions of wise friends who have met the other person. A decision about marriage should not be made on the basis of emotion alone, but checks of critical reason and outside judgement should also be introduced.

Committing oneself to a life-partnership in marriage is not only of vital importance to worldly life but also to spiritual life. It may either help inner progress or else lead to spiritual disaster. It is necessary, therefore, that a man, for example, should explain his views to the lady that he is interested in, and if she is unable to accept them sincerely within a reasonable period then he may face the fact that he would be headed for a stoppage on his spiritual journey if he married her. To make a mistake in marriage will bring both pain and trouble to his wife as well as to himself. He should resolve to choose correctly or else to wait patiently until the right girl appears.

It is not necessary that he remain married in order to pay a karmic debt, nor on the other hand is he free to follow personal desires in the matter. It is a mistake to think that such a debt must continue to be paid until the end of one's life. Yet, it must be paid off if one's inner life and path are not to be obstructed. Only the voice of his own deeper conscience may decide this point.

Marriage is a risky affair when one of the two belongs in every way–spiritual, intellectual, and social–to a class higher than the other. If they cannot meet on these levels, where can they? The bad in both is brought out and made worse; the good is diminished. This was one of the original reasons why the caste system got established in some form or other among the Orientals as if it were an essential part of religion.

If he could find a companion who had the character and capacity to help, and not to hinder, his own inner pilgrimage, then it might be useful for him to marry; but if she were to fall short of this ideal then greater inner misery would descend upon him. There is a certain fate about such matters and if she has to come, she will come into his life of her own accord. In any case it will be advisable to wait to make sure that the inner harmony does really exist.

An individual may keep the ideal of a true mate but understand that one can't be absolutely certain to meet him or her on this earth. The spiritual path is a call to renunciation of personal attachments, inwardly at least, and to a renunciation of the animal nature also. Both have to be overcome if inner peace is to be obtained. But once overcome, the world can be enjoyed without danger because his happiness no longer depends on it. If he lets the natural desire for a mate be included in but transcended by the higher desire for spiritual realization, he stands a chance to get both. But if he feels that the first is wholly indispensable, he may miss the chance to get either. The truth is that the Soul will not give itself to you unless you love It more than anything or anyone else. He may have great capacity for love in his nature, which properly directed by wisdom, may lead him to great spiritual heights and human satisfactions. But directed by impulse, unchecked by reason, it can bring him into situations productive of much misery to himself and others. He must therefore make it a part of his spiritual discipline to secure this balance. Until he has secured it, he should not commit himself to any decision without consulting with a spiritually mature person. Much harm has been done by the pseudo-romantic nonsense and false suggestions put out by cinema, magazines, and novels."

I hope these insights made some sense for those of you who are seeking companionship in life while treading on the part of spirituality. Marriage is a deeply personal and emotional decision for most and also probably the most important decision of one's life and so I think wisdom from any quarter should be welcome. I want to conclude with one final entry on this topic from his notebook, 'Some questions asked about marriage problems ought not to be answered by anyone other than the individual's own higher self. Let him hear the voice of the Overself, which concerns itself neither with conventional contemporary attitudes, outdated Oriental teachings, nor merely personal reactions. Let him listen mentally in profoundest meditation to hear this voice.'

What kind of a wedding to have

The pain of parting with the daughter

'Save the girl child' ads are a common sight in India, and seeing them, my daughter, Aanya, asked me once, 'who do we have to save the girl child from?' After dodging the question a couple of times, I finally could help make the connection for her.

Having a grand wedding ceremony with their chosen partner is a dream for many brides and bridegrooms in India. On this occasion of their life, they become the cynosure of all eyes and enjoy praise, blessings, best wishes, and gifts from many. Music, dance, lights, colours, photographers, decorations, trumpet playing bands, followed by a horse procession and endless delicacies that tantalise every tastebud. The bride and bridegroom glitter and sparkle under the brilliant spotlights. In every sense, an Indian wedding is a grand celebration, and hundreds and thousands of guests participate and enjoy them. The two or three days are like a dream come true for many. Many of us have been there and done that.

In these two or three days of festivities, millions are spent. Not just grownups like us but also children have a gala time. I took my daughter to one such grand wedding. I used the occasion to talk to her and explain what goes *behind* the making of such a wedding.

Without further ado, here are the lessons I tried to pass on to my daughter:

1. Financial hardships of the bride's family

What does it take to throw such a grand wedding? Money. Lots and lots of it. And where does it come from? The bride's parents fund most marriage ceremonies in India, and the millions spent come from the life savings of the bride's parents. That money parents could use to secure them in their old age is squandered on appeasing and entertaining hundreds and thousands of people the bride and bridegroom may meet once in their entire lifetime. It's all done for 'social obligation' and upholding 'respect' for the family. Many brides' families fund the wedding through loans for which they must make huge compromises in lifestyle and undergo emotional and financial stress to repay. It is not just unfair and unjust. It is outright cruel to do so and expect this as a social norm.

2. Waste generated from a single wedding

The wastefulness of a wedding in India is simply ginormous! First, a huge amount of food is wasted, which could feed the millions starving in India. For example, large amounts of rice grains which is potential food showered on the wedding couple as blessings, also go to waste.

Do we even know each person we shook hands with at our wedding?

3. Environmental cost of a wedding

The wedding also generates enormous amounts of waste in the form of paper, plastic and other non-biodegradable decoration material. Blaring sound systems blast out high-wattage 'noise' and disturbs everything living in the locality. The wedding processions also cause traffic congestion, and the power generators which run on diesel-kerosene blend pollute the air irritating the eyes and lungs.

4. Tearing away daughters from their parents

This is probably the worst outcome of many Indian weddings: daughters are expected to be given away as a charity in a ritual and expected to *leave* the parents to take on a *new* family. This new family not just lays claim over their newly *acquired* member but also over her prospects. First, there is an entire ceremony where a bride mourns the loss of her home and parents! Then, as the father, who the daughter considered her hero, and her mother, who she considered her best friend weep helplessly, the daughter is *helped* into the vehicle and taken away. At a wedding I attended with my daughter, I did not want her to witness this last part as I thought she was too young to empathise with that pain, and we had to excuse ourselves politely.

Be it, sons or daughters, if they have been parented well, they owe their parents the most and will always belong to them even if they have a new partner and start a new family. No ritual in this world can break away a child from its parents.

How a wedding should be, with just close family & best friends around

I explained to my daughter, Aanya, that when she grows up, she need not feel any social pressure in such a private matter. I hope she understands now that a typical Indian wedding is a luxury only a few can afford, and it should be socially perceived as such. As a result, most Indian weddings are expensive, wasteful, environmentally costly, and psychologically stressful.

I hope she gets married one day and sees marriage as the start of a beautiful journey of friendship, commitment, companionship, love and parenting. Of course, the lavish Indian wedding is something else. But, if you can get the idea of marriage right, I think we can get the idea of a beautiful wedding right, too: a simple, private and blissful ceremony where new bonds are formed on the foundation of old ones.

So, coming back to the 'save the girl child' question, our daughter now knows the girl child needs to be protected from the exploitative wedding. It is this exorbitant future cost that forces many families in rural India to abort the girl child. Hence the campaign to save the girl child.

Watch how one treats their enemy.

Before getting into a relationship with a person, it makes sense to run this simple check: Watch how the person treats their enemy.

This will tell you how you will be treated if, by chance, you are to be tagged as an enemy one day. You will get to feel that behaviour. Compassion or kindness should be one of the most important criteria to look for in a relationship. They should be a nice person first. Because if, in a particular context, you are reclassified from friend to enemy, you should know the boundaries of someone's ethics. If you see someone being bad to a server, engaging in unethical behaviour, suing other people, or fighting other people all the time, it is only a matter of time before they fight you. Just stay away from these high-conflict people. Everyone has conflict, and no one is clean, but some people engage in conflict and do it regularly and then make it a part of their lifestyle. Just walk away. It is not worth it.

Kindness and compassion should not be categorised: if one is a considerate person, then everyone, irrespective of whether you like them or not, is a recipient of that behaviour. This kindness extends to all beings- plants, animals, birds, and people. Kindness has no race, colour, religion, gender, or income class. A simple acknowledgement that everyone is fighting their own small or large battles goes a long way in making a person 'nice'. We have all met people who are low conflict and easy to get along with. We know they exist. Just stick to those.

It takes deliberate effort to get a marriage to work

Romantic marriage is everyone's ideal. Romantic reasons for marriage include

· Mutual sympathy and tenderness
· We like the same kind of furniture/house design
· Soulmates: they grasp the poetry of our hearts

- We have similar attitudes to childraising
- They understand our sadness
- They finish our sentences
- We will have status among our social group
- The same music touches us both.

So, one may develop love after marriage too. So romantic marriage is possible even for those who did not marry for love. However, a sound marriage requires a blend of romantic flavour and practical harmony. The School of Life website says,

> "'A marriage is a deeply practical project. It is akin to an attempt to run a small business together, which involves dealing with property and household management, serving meals, planning holidays, entertaining friends, and raising children. Suppose we see our partner's organisational skills, financial acumen, or prowess as a host as simply 'low'. In that case, we will not recognise the very genuine contributions these are making to our existence. So it is strategically useful to get more explicit about identifying the most pragmatic reasons why we have picked our partner – and perhaps sum these up in a (secret) list we keep in a bedside drawer. Ideally, we would return to it at points of crisis for reminders of why we ended up choosing as we did – until we succeed in the always tricky task of recovering admiration for, and connection to, our partner's soul.'"

So, if you still need a better understanding of why you are still married or what is working and not working in a marriage, here is a little help. Here is a simple checklist that can help you look at the big picture of marriage and, at the same time, identify areas that need to be improved with mutual effort.

Place a check (✓) on the line under the phrase that best describes the degree of satisfaction you have in relation to the item. If an item does not apply to you, put NA next to the item.	Very Satisfied	Mostly Satisfied	Mostly Dissatisfied	Very Dissatisfied
The way we make decisions				
The way we divide up responsibility for child care				
The way we handle and budget money				
The amount of money we earn				
The way we resolve conflict				
The way we divide up housework and other home-related jobs				
The way we get along with our children				
The way we discipline our children				
The way we get along with in-laws and other relatives				
The way we use our free time				
The way we talk to each other				
The way we care for our home				
The amount of time we have together				
The amount of alcohol used				
The way we give each other emotional support				
The amount of privacy we have				
The way we handle birth control				
The sexual part of our relationship				
The way we plan for our future				
The way we get along with the neighbors				
The way we deal with moral or religious concerns				
The way we handle anger and frustration				

A simple checklist to evaluate the husband-wife relationship

Even if one finds each other 'mostly satisfied' in most of these different areas, one can have an adequately happy married life. Given the statistics on marriage, you would still be among the minority. A good enough marriage is a blessing.

ᕈᕈᕈ

TWENTY-EIGHT
HOW MARRIAGES FALL APART

———◦♡◦———

Instant Messaging's war on marriage

The title may sound like an exaggeration. It is not. Some people may argue in favour of social media usage for sustaining friendships, but it's a sure destroyer when it comes to marriages. The average couple will find it difficult to sustain a healthy relationship while leading independent social media lives. Even the idea of marriage and its relevance in today's times has come to be challenged and questioned.

WhatsApp, Instagram, Snapchat and other such media allow for the first time in human history an opportunity and triggers for flirtatious behaviour, jealousy, envy, inadequacy, emotional intimacy and chances of infidelity that we have not seen in history so far. And all this comes at an unprecedented scale.

Today's world is divided into libertarians who believe in the essential human weakness that leads to infidelity and loyalists who believe in the soulmate ideal or emotional & sexual loyalty to only one partner. Each has its reasons to profess its respective ideology. The reality, on the other hand, swings between these two extremes.

Many people want to be married, have children and then go on to have emotional or sexual flings with one or more of their other partners. They want the best of both worlds for themselves. The security of a home and family to go back to at the end of the day and, at other times, the adventure of emotional & sexual flirting with another person. They want to have secret

Snapchat or Instagram accounts that can stage their adventures and a real family & home to enjoy social respect and status. This balancing act brings a lot of stress, dissonance and turmoil in day to day life of the players. How to come out of it? Does one not have the right to do whatever makes one happy? Why shouldn't one have the best of both worlds?

What is the solution to this? Here is my take on this topic.

- First, a couple must agree to a common marriage definition or partnership. Then, what is this marriage expected to achieve for both? It could be one or more goals like parenting, growth, security, companionship, stability, love, etc.
- Secondly, they need to clarify to each other if they expect emotional & sexual loyalty from each other and if any of them will tolerate straying from this. What does such 'straying' look like?
- Thirdly, draw the boundaries which cannot be crossed without annulling the marriage/ partnership.

Once the couple is on the same page regarding these questions, they are free to put their trust in their partner and lead their lives. These three questions must be discussed before tying the marriage knot. Unfortunately, many marriages today are an act of passion rather than clear, intentional and mutually well-understood decisions.

Like many other institutions, marriage still has its place in our lives and the future of our planet. All that is needed is a clear understanding of it.

Infidelity: Should we live with it in Marriage?

Infidelity is breaking a promise to remain faithful to a romantic partner, whether that promise was a part of marriage vows, a privately uttered agreement between lovers, or an unspoken assumption. As unthinkable as the notion of breaking such promises may be at the time they are made, infidelity is common.

I have come across several examples among people I know. Initially, I believed it was an individual choice and should not bother me even if my friend was involved. But lately, I feel differently about it, and it was best to flesh out what I think about it.

Here are some examples of married people I know:

- A person whose spouse is away for work for most of the year has started a relationship with a distant relative.
- A happily married person sponsors someone who lives alone for leisure pastimes.
- A person is in an extra-marital relationship purely for pleasure, with no strings attached.
- A person seeks multiple partners to love and be loved by while enjoying the benefits of marriage and family.
- A person secretly pursues a long-distance relationship with an unrequited love partner while being 'happily' married.

And there are more. These are all seemingly ordinary married people that you and I may know, who lead ordinary lives, but they display this strange behaviour- they live a second life in parallel. They live in two universes at once, and one hand does not know what the other is up to.

All this passes today as normal behaviour. Craving attention, company, and 'love' of someone outside the committed relationship seems like a 'normal' desire, and many are 'ok' entertaining and even discussing it casually with friends.

There is a fundamental disconnect in understanding the institution of marriage or the basics of a committed relationship. Being in a committed relationship has become more of a social, financial, and practical necessity-something that one must have, like an insurance policy on the foundation of which one can, later, plan one's 'real' love adventures. This is a recipe for disaster!

Research published in Scientific American identified eight main reasons why partners cheat, viz. anger, self-esteem, lack of love, low commitment, need for variety, neglect, sexual desire, and situation or circumstance. Surprisingly, it also revealed that only 1 out of 10 affairs lead to a committed relationship. This clearly shows that those who cheat do not have an appetite for commitment. Therefore, they do not dare to confess or commit to it.

What goes on in the mind of the person who cheats? As per the theory of evolution, it is a sheer animal instinct that makes females seek resources and men seek mothers- both trying to maximise the chances of survival of their progeny to ensure their DNA lives on. This is nature, and inevitably it also comes to humans. The educated amongst us also use this as a justification to rationalise our illicit adventures. But this nature is not what makes us human- it is the ability to rise above this nature that makes us special as humans.

If love is an expression of our values, then marriage is an expression of our highest human values of trust, respect, admiration, commitment, and companionship. One falls in love with the sense of life of a person, seeing the other person as an embodiment of the values one admires most. Then alone, one should commit to a person in marriage. It is your highest achievement in relating, not a compromise. If you have got the marriage wrong, take the courage to dissolve it. Take a stand. If one has self-esteem, one must walk out of the institution of marriage. Any democratic constitution gives you that freedom. Avoid choosing to lead parallel lives.

To cheat on our partners after we have committed is neither wise nor sustainable in the long term. Sometimes, it is important to step back and see the relationship as it is. If there is something you can do to improve or fix it, try it first. And if you think continuing in a relationship does not make sense, there is no future to it- dare to fold your cards and move out. If you find out about your partner's infidelity, your partner confesses and vows to make things right and if you have a big heart, give them another chance. (It only helps in some cases).

Infidelity is easy- all you must do is reply to a text, date that stranger on your Instagram follower list or have that one nightstand. This love has no future. As I have written elsewhere in this book, love is hard. It takes attention, focus and energy to nurture it. Love is not for the weak of the heart.

So, to conclude: infidelity in marriage is absolutely a no-no and should not be entertained or tolerated by anyone with any self-esteem. If you are a parent, teach your children to stand for your values with your own example. The best course, I believe, is to forgive and move on- separately.

ppp

TWENTY-NINE
OUR BIGGEST ASSETS AND LIABILITIES ARE RELATIONSHIPS

We can't own people, but we own relationships. And while we own them, like any property, a relationship can either become an asset or a liability. Be it work or one's private life, one of the biggest influences on the happiness and misery in our lives are the people we live, work and transact with; our relationships impact our personal happiness and misery.

One of my favourite writers Matthew Kelly in his book, The Rhythm of Life: Living Every Day with Passion and Purpose, says

> "The people we surround ourselves with either raise or lower our standards. They either help us to become the best version of ourselves or encourage us to become lesser versions of ourselves. We become like our friends. No man becomes great on his own. No woman becomes great on her own. The people around them help to make them great. We all need people in our lives who raise our standards, remind us of our essential purpose and challenge us to become the best version of ourselves."

Happiness ensues from a relationship when your attitude is to be of value to the other to the same extent as you derive value from the other. That's when a relationship is an asset, a great investment. You may feel burned out and exploited if you give more than you receive. It clearly means the other person is taking advantage of you. It means you are dealing with a parasite that lives off you and sucks your resources out. This kind of relationship is a liability.

Guard against parasitic relationships. One way to do this is to share responsibilities in a relationship. Talk about it, agree on it and commit to it. Another way is to create distance between you and them- emotional and physical distance. Though not better than confronting, emotional distancing is a natural defence mechanism most of us have – it's about losing that empathetic connection with a person.

Without reciprocity, the best relationships can turn toxic.

For example, in the context of parenting, most people believe that parents have to give and oblige all the time to the whims and fancies of their children. Teach children to be helpful to the family. Assign some responsibilities and set clear expectations for them. This can include following a daily routine, adhering to sleep timings, iPad usage and homework commitments. Then there is at least the hope that they would grow up to be assets- if not for you, at least for someone else. In a relationship like parenting, which involves lots of giving on the part of parents, it's ok to set expectations and demand compliance. They will be grateful one day.

So now, let's take a test. Think of one of the important relationships you are in and see how many boxes the relationship ticks. The judgement of whether your relationship is an asset or a liability, I leave it to you.

1. Is the person better off with you in their life than they were before?
2. Are you making the other person learn and grow as a person?
3. Is the other person financially better off with you in their life than otherwise?
4. Are you in any way contributing to the better emotional and physical health of the other person?
5. Do you let the other person manage their time more efficiently and effectively?
6. Is the energy of the other person more positive when around you?

A 'No' to one or more of these questions should make us rethink our role in the relationship. Here are some ways of approaching such a situation:

- If we are a 'no' in one area of the relationship, we should try to be resourceful and a 'Yes' in another area.
- While we continue to improve the value we bring to a relationship, we can clearly communicate our intentions and plans to the other persons in the relationship.
- If I receive value in one area, think about how I can return value in another.
- At least think of ways you can not be a liability; thinks of simple things you can do to reduce the pain of the other person.

A more honourable way to live is to be an asset to your spouse, boss, peers, customers, friends, community, or nation. Work to bring symbiosis in relationships- exchanging value for value is the best way to keep any relationship healthy and thriving.

As Ralph Waldo Emerson rightly said,

> "*The purpose of life is not to be happy. It is to be useful, to be honourable, to be compassionate, to have it make some difference that you have lived and lived well.*"

Try to be useful. Try to be of value.

Make a difference. If you can't, then stay out of relationships.

Can family relationships turn toxic?

We have been conditioned to believe that relationships in the family are always beautiful and full of love and fulfilment. But, like all other things, it is not always so. I have seen how toxicity starts showing in relationships. When left unchecked, these relationships take a toll on our physical and mental health and erode our sense of self-worth and self-esteem.

Here are five signs that indicate its time to reevaluate the worthiness of a relationship:

The relationship has become parasitic

In this case, one person constantly enjoys it at the expense of the other. For any relationship to thrive, there needs to be a healthy exchange of tangible or intangible value in the form of love, care, support, motivation, and handholding.

Invasion of personal space

For example, it is not very rare for some of your folks to invade your privacy and take over your home and workspace under the guise of family visits. If you feel entirely drained instead of happy after spending the day with them, that is a sign that something is not right.

Disrespect

You are belittled and disrespected despite bringing good to the family. The use of foul and abusive language in family conversations is another sign of mutual disrespect.

Lying

There is persistent lying to conceal facts and represent them in a different form altogether. Not just facts but also honest thoughts, emotions and feelings are faked or covered to protect one's selfish interests.

Breaking trust

Every relationship is founded on unwritten rules, many of which are sacred. Without trust, life can become a nightmare and relationships dysfunctional. It is almost impossible for a relationship to thrive. Trust encompasses several values like loyalty, emotional fidelity, confidence and reliability. It is the most fundamental thread holding a relationship together.

We can warn against imminent pitfalls and emotional agonies if we watch for these signs. Some relationships can get toxic. Like a tumour in the body, depending on the threat it poses, it needs to be managed or taken out of our lives.

Some relationships can be like sunk costs, and just because we are invested in them, we torture ourselves to continue living in them. In contrast, the right approach is to exit at the first sign and protect ourselves from unnecessary pain.

THIRTY

BREAKING OUT OF THE DREADED DRAMA TRIANGLE

———◦♭◦———

Every once in a while, we all find ourselves entangled in negative and destructive interactions. We refer to these kinds of conflicts as the Dreaded Drama Triangle. In any relationship conflict, there are three roles and each person involved dons one of these three roles most of the time. You play one of these three roles: the persecutor, the victim or the rescuer. Many parents can relate to the three roles from their parenting experience. Once you understand this triangle, you will immediately be able to connect most of the dramas in your personal and professional life to this model. That is the first step we need to take to resolve the dramas we unnecessarily get ourselves caught up in our day-to-day life. Like they say, to solve a problem, one must first understand it.

Steven Karpman placed these three roles at each of the three corners of an inverted triangle and called them the faces of drama. Let us understand these roles better:

The Victim

The Victim thinks, "Poor me!" The victim feels victimised, oppressed, helpless, hopeless, powerless, and ashamed and seems unable to make decisions, solve problems, take pleasure in life, or achieve insight. If not being persecuted, the victim will seek a Persecutor and a Rescuer who will save the day and perpetuate the victim's negative feelings. E.g. A child being threatened or admonished by a parent may think 'Why does it have to be me who compromises every time?" 'Why is the world so unfair?' 'Why does it happen with only me?!'

DRAMA TRIANGLE
(Steven Karpman)

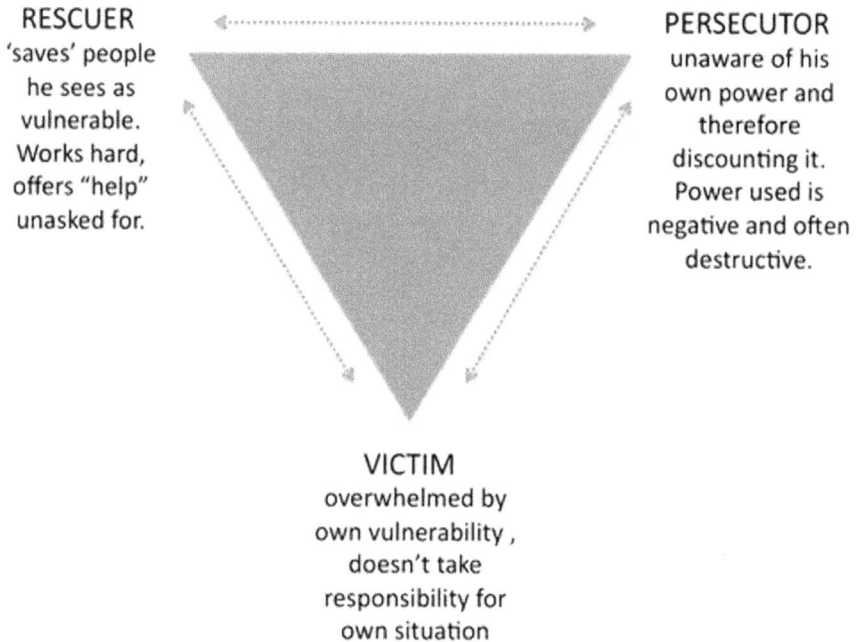

RESCUER
'saves' people
he sees as
vulnerable.
Works hard,
offers "help"
unasked for.

PERSECUTOR
unaware of his
own power and
therefore
discounting it.
Power used is
negative and often
destructive.

VICTIM
overwhelmed by
own vulnerability ,
doesn't take
responsibility for
own situation

Steven Karpman's Drama Triangle

The Persecutor

(a.k.a. Villain) The Persecutor insists, "It's all your fault." The persecutor is controlling, blaming, critical, angry, authoritarian, rigid, and superior. E.g., A parent telling the child that 'You cannot go out to play, or you cannot have Maggi today' or 'You do this every time! How many times do I have to teach you? Can you not follow such a simple instruction!'

The Rescuer

The rescuer's attitude is, "Let me help you." The rescuer feels guilty if they don't go to rescue the victim. Yet their rescuing has adverse effects: It keeps the victim dependent and gives the victim permission to fail. This rescuer's role is also pivotal because their primary interest is an avoidance of their own problems disguised as concern for the victim's needs. A most common example is one parent trying to rescue the child while being prosecuted by another, saying, 'Give the child a break! She has been busy with school for hours. She is tired.'

In a drama, you don't just play one of the three roles, but you also change roles going from Rescuer to Prosecutor and from Victim to Rescuer and from Prosecutor to Victim. So, a father trying to rescue a child from a prosecuting mother may turn in the next moment into a prosecutor and make the mother a victim. The child again goes clinging to her mother, trying to rescue her. And the drama goes on and on. That is why it is a closed triangle- indicating that the actors keep shifting roles endlessly, keeping the drama alive. But, as we all may already know, no one wins in a drama triangle. Everyone is stuck, stressed and a loser.

We can easily cite examples from personal and professional lives where this drama triangle has played out daily. Fortunately, there is a way to learn to break out or, as I say, 'resolve' the drama triangle. The first step we have already seen – it is to understand the drama triangle and relate the drama in your life to the faces of the drama triangle. In the next step, you have a choice between two possible methods to resolve the drama triangle:

Approach 1: Winner's Triangle

The first approach is called the Winner's triangle. In this approach, the victim should understand that they are vulnerable and caring, the prosecutor should adopt an assertive posture, and anyone recruited to be a rescuer should react by being "caring".

Vulnerable – a victim should be encouraged to accept their vulnerability and problem solve and be more self-aware.

Assertive – a persecutor should be encouraged to ask for what they want, be assertive, but not be punishing.

Caring – a rescuer should be encouraged to show concern and be caring, but not over-reach and problem-solve for others.

Assertive

Accepts others' value and integrity

- Knows own feelings, needs and wants
- Non-judgemental
- Uses 'I' messages

Nurturing

Accepts others' ability to think for themselves

- Gives help when asked
- Cares and understands
- Doesn'tneed to be needed by others

Vulnerable

Accepts Self
- Shares real feelings

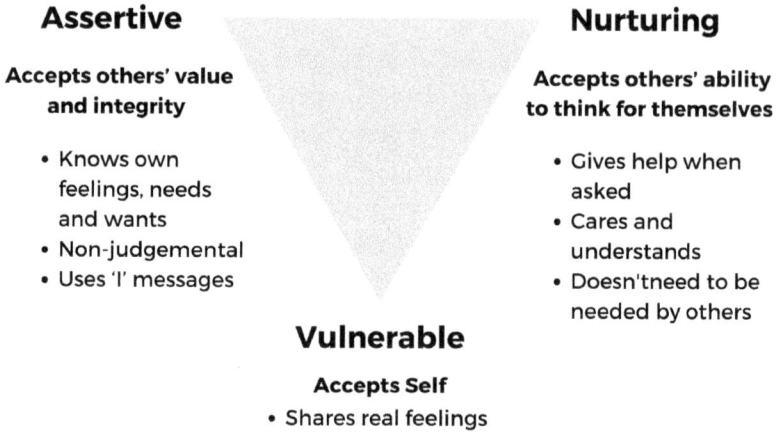

Approach 1: The Winner's Triangle

Approach 2: The Power of TED

The second method is called the power of TED. It recommends that the "victim" adopts the alternative role of creator, view the persecutor as a challenger, and enlist a coach instead of a rescuer.

Creator: Victims are encouraged to be outcome-oriented instead of problem-oriented and take responsibility for choosing their response to life challenges. They should focus on resolving "dynamic tension". Dynamic tension is the difference between the current reality and the envisioned goal or outcome. Resolving dynamic tension means taking incremental steps toward the outcomes they are trying to achieve. The victim must first acknowledge their strengths and capabilities. The victim should think I can function productively and get independent of the prosecutor. E.g. 'I will simply complete my homework every day. It takes just a few minutes, and I can easily do it. Then I am free to play.'

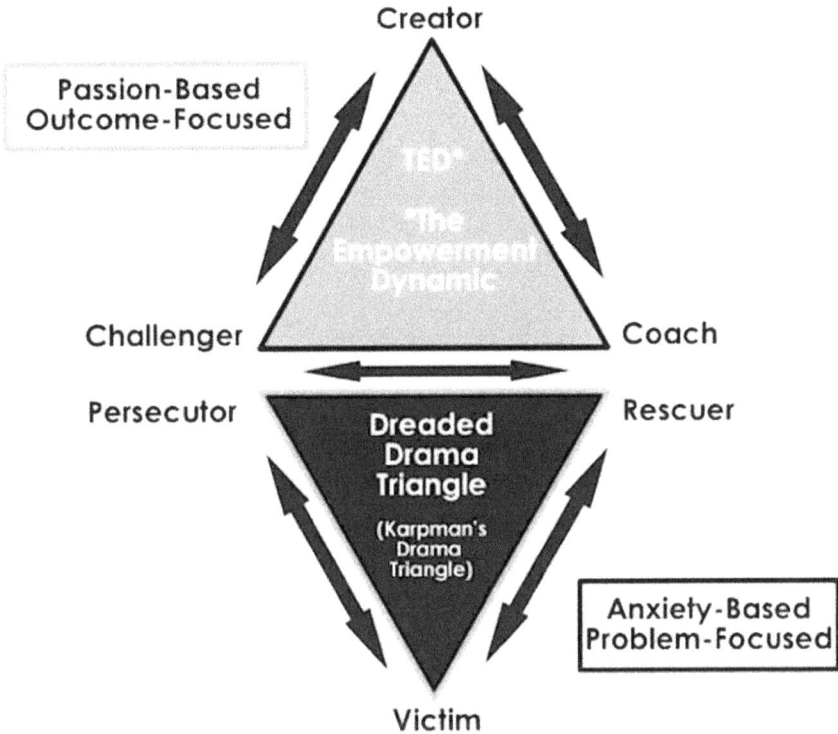

Approach 2: The Power of TED

Challenger: A victim is encouraged to see a persecutor as a person (or situation) that forces the creator to clarify their needs and focus on learning and growth. The prosecutor should first become a good listener- hear out the victim. Then, they can set clear expectations upfront, like 'you can have Maggi once a week, any day of your choice but not every day or 'you can play once you finish your homework.

Coach: A rescuer should be encouraged to ask questions intended to help the individual make informed choices. Their good intentions need to be channelised into the coach's role. The critical difference between a rescuer and a coach is that the coach sees the creator as capable of making choices and solving their problems. A coach asks questions that enable the creator to see the possibilities for positive action and to focus on what they want instead of what they do not want. For example, a coach can say,' I will hear you out or ' I can suggest possible solutions but will not engage with the prosecutor'.

We can adopt one or both approaches to solve the dreaded drama triangle. It is also a skill one must practice and develop over time. Where living in a drama triangle comes naturally to us, breaking out is not easy. I am far from mastering it myself. But it's never late to start. At least let's start by seeing the play of the drama triangle in our own lives and the lives around us; then, we can choose whether or not to try breaking out of it. It's a skill that deserves to be on our must-learn life skills list and also one that each parent should try to pass on to their children.

Is an apology enough?

Children and adults are used to saying the words 'Sorry and 'it's alright. But unfortunately, these phrases have become commodities and seldom *mean* anything in daily usage. It seems an apology cancels out forgiveness, but it is not true.

Let us look at what it means to forgive first. Forgive is a verb, and the dictionary meaning is 'to stop feeling angry or resentful towards (someone) for an offence, flaw, or mistake.' However, if you understand the meaning correctly, you will notice that this kind of forgiveness cannot be voluntary. Feeling angry or resentful is a reaction, something that happens by itself. And for the same reason, 'stopping to be resentful or angry' is also involuntary. So if this is so, can we forgive anyone at will?

That is why we need to understand 'forgiving' in a new light- as an act of understanding. To forgive means to acknowledge the hurt and process it emotionally and intellectually. Forgiveness requires that we reach a level of maturity in understanding the other person, the law of causality and, more importantly, the hurt itself. It is meant to reduce the pain of the hurt and not undo the hurt or wrongdoings altogether. Forgiving doesn't and cannot acquit the other person of his misdeeds.

Let us look at what it means to apologise now. To apologise, as per the dictionary, means to express regret for something that one has done wrong. 'I am sorry.' Or, at best, saying, 'I am deeply sorry.'

When we hurt someone with our words or deeds and apologise for it, we do not undo the hurt. The damage is done. The person may forgive us, but as we have seen above, the person has only protected themself from more pain and not simply forgotten the hurt and moved on as if nothing happened.

So, what is the proper apology? It offers an expression of regret and an offer to redress the hurt by some means. 'How can I help overcome this hurt? How can I be of help?'

A commitment to help the person heal is needed. Making this commitment is the best we can do. Actions have consequences, and words alone cannot restore the damage. Words can only express regret and intent to help the person heal.

Committing takes a lot of work. We are all in a hurry to move on and start afresh. And in this hurry, we leave behind a trail of hurts. And we teach our children the same way of transacting with the world. Is it any wonder that we think the world is harsh and ruthless?

People won't care about hurting others if they only need to say 'sorry' to undo it. It is not a natural behaviour to apologise and help a person heal. When you hurt someone, point out the damage you might have done and ask how you can help restore or heal it. Make a commitment and try to fulfil it.

ᐁᐁᐁ

PARENTING: Raise Children to be
Confident, Kind and Resilient

THIRTY-ONE
GENDER BIAS IN PARENTING

———◆♭◆———

Before we embark on our discussion on parenting, I must get this one topic out of the way first: gender bias that plagues developing nations like India. The Indian constitution today treats women and men alike and bestows upon them the same rights and duties. There are also many initiatives promoting the welfare of the girl child in India. However, most religious communities of India, hence societies, continue to place higher importance on a male child over a female one. As a result, many parents consider a girl child a liability while considering a male child an asset. To any rational person, this may seem silly at the least and appalling at the most. I fall towards the latter side of the spectrum.

I believe that societal design rather than nature is responsible for making the girl child a liability. Let me explain how. When women marry in India, society expects them to leave their parents' homes and enter their spouse's homes. And here, she is expected to adopt her in-laws as her parents and is made responsible for their well-being, health and prosperity. She can be an independent working woman but is obligated to serve her husband and in-laws first and foremost, sometimes even at the cost of the well-being of her parents.

Until recent times, parents needed to save up for the dowry of the girl child, which many parents start saving for while putting their own retirement needs at stake. This brings tremendous expectation anxiety to the girl's parents. Fortunately, this practice is now made criminal in the country. However, although the dowry system has taken a back seat, a new demon has taken its place, viz., the bridegroom's expectations that the bride has educational credentials that can sufficiently supplement the family income. So now brides are assets for the groom's family that provide payback through professional earnings to grow the family fortune in the years to come.

Society makes a girl child look like an ungrateful child by design. Parents in India treat male children as an investment and insurance for their old age. As a result, women, although emotionally attached to their parents, are financially barricaded from them. Men, on the contrary, can be emotionally attached and financially obligated to support their parents. Unfortunately, today even many educated women have bought into this idea and have internalised it. No sooner a girl child is born than the parents are flooded with investment schemes to plan for the girl child's wedding expenses. That girl child thus becomes a liability and is almost institutionalised. People with a girl child are encouraged to have more children in the hope of bearing a more 'useful' male child. The system is biased against the girl child.

The most popular TV soaps in India are the ones that show the conflict between the mother-in-law and the daughter-in-law. Now I can see one reason why. Their conflict is simply an outward expression of an inner conflict. Both have been separated from their parents, uprooted from their culture and their loved ones, to start a new life in a new culture, among new people, with new responsibilities, in a new place they must call home where both do not belong. The new home becomes a cockpit where only one can survive or thrive. So moving out to become a nuclear family becomes the only solution- another compromise for both women. Soon, they become bitter, insecure, anxious, and nagging. But it does not have to be like this.

The fact is that it is a hard life for women in India, from education to opportunities, empowerment, financial independence, to finding inner peace: it is a long and arduous journey. Very few indeed make it to the end. Many families believe in this age-old societal design, and I suggest you not subscribe to it. This status quo can change- starting with you, your family, and your girl child. Raise your girls to be strong, independent, resilient women who can stand for themselves, stand for what they love and can choose life and a lifestyle that works best for them. Someone once said if you educate a man, you educate an individual, but if you educate a woman, you educate a family. Raising a happy girl child today is equivalent to raising a happy family in the future. Celebrate the girl child!

☙☙☙

THIRTY-TWO

ADOPTING THE VALUE-BASED PARENTING APPROACH

———◦♡◦———

Parenting is about nurturing the child's mind.

The Oxford dictionary defines parenting as caring for your child or children. Most see parenting as providing a child with nourishing food, security, care, shelter, discipline, and education. However, in the light of Values, parenting goes deeper and aims to build, shape, and fine-tune the mind, the inner instrument of a child. Seeing your child as a mind that interprets, analyses, and transacts with the world, changes the overall approach to parenting.

The mind is the only place where knowledge takes place; for those on a spiritual path, it is also the only place where liberation can occur. It is also the only place where ignorance is found and removed. The primary content of the mind is thoughts & thought patterns containing a sense of identity, motivations, desire, judgements, decisions, memories, habits, and biases. The term 'values' encases all these, and so it is in the mind that values take shape and influence behaviour. If we prepare the mind well, we have laid a strong foundation for the child's future, where the child is independent and thriving in this world. In a value parenting approach, we nourish different capacities of this mind, which include knowing and desiring, decision-making, memory-forming, and identity. This way, a parent attends to, nourishes and protects all four aspects of the mind.

The value parenting approach entails instilling values in the child's mind and teaching them how to live them. By one's example, a parent teaches primary personal values like non-injury, truthfulness, non-stealing, hygiene and self-restraint or self-control. There are several other values like self-study, always keeping a higher power in one's heart, contentment and so on, which parents and teachers can introduce at different stages of growing up, step by step. Like any fine instrument, the mind needs to be sensitised and calibrated- the right action should feel right and wrong should feel wrong. Conscience cannot be forced simply by laying rules or following the carrot & stick approach. Children see the reasons and the causal chain that results from their thoughts and decisions. Parenting thus builds a moral sense that helps discriminate well-being from pleasure, moral from immoral, appropriate from inappropriate, and lasting from fleeting. Parents must keenly observe and provide measured appreciation, correction or guidance where needed without micro-managing, demotivating and hurting the child. While doing this, parents should respect children's individuality and nourish their capacity to grow mature and self-reliant.

Parenting can be one of the most rewarding and joyful experiences in life. In the light of values, it can flourish and forge emotionally intelligent, resilient minds. To such minds, ethical, appropriate, and righteous behaviour comes naturally. Value parenting lays the foundation for the child's future, where they will be resilient, independent, and dynamic.

What is Value-based Parenting?

Value parenting is a parenting approach based on values that you, as parents, hold most dear. Value parenting is thus a universal approach because parents from any nationality, background or society can adopt it and orient it around their core values.

Values are principles or standards of behaviour that you deem necessary in life. To talk about values is to talk about what kind of person you want your child to be. Our values define us in so many ways – what we aspire for, how we choose, what we celebrate and what we mourn.

I always believed that the values we choose should be universal and apply to all humans, not just one community, creed, or religion. You should be able to arrive at these values from first principles, and once you know them, you must put them into practice to live them. As we are creatures of habit, it may take a deliberate effort to practice the values until they become second nature and embedded in our conscience.

Parents want children to understand what is good and the long-term consequences of their actions. Therefore, children need to develop an intuition for good, to value this goodness over immediate rewards.

An idealist value-based mind clearly understands the difference between the immediate and long-term good and chooses to do the *right* thing rather than the most *convenient* or *advantageous* thing. Such a mind may go through *hardships* and *inconveniences* in the short run and be mocked by others sometimes, but they choose what is good in the long term.

A child with an idealist mindset will seek a cure, not a fix. It will seek a solution, not a workaround; a confrontation, not a retreat; strength and not sympathy; respect and not praise; responsibilities, not tasks; career, not jobs; joy, not just fun; journey and not ride.

From Learning to Knowing

With children, we usually associate 'learning' with representing all activities of acquiring new understanding, knowledge, behaviours, skills, values, attitudes, and preferences. It essentially means conditioning, and I am not discussing how to condition children. Instead, I am trying to illuminate how knowing takes place in the mind. Conditioning is easy- be authoritative, set rewards and punishments for desired and undesired behaviours and train them. Learning can be lost as quickly as it can be gained. 'Knowing' is different.

The pursuit of truth or knowledge comes to some of us naturally and to some not so naturally. It is an inner drive and an intrinsic motivation to discover the truth or reality of this world. It is a relentless pursuit, and one finds solace and contentment in gaining knowledge.

Interestingly, knowing, although it sounds like a verb, is something one does, but it is not. On the contrary, it happens when the conditions are right. Knowing is not the same as downloading a book in one's mind or committing a text to memory. That could be learning.

Suppose we understand knowledge as the phenomenon occurring in the mind rather than words that abound on the web and in texts. In that case, we will have a different quality of education altogether- one oriented towards knowing, not learning.

It needs three prerequisites: a desire to know, the right mindset, exposure to the correct object of knowledge and the employment of suitable means.

It cannot be forced like learning. We need to let it happen by itself in our minds. It also happens at its own pace, with the person actively listening, resolving conflicts, filling gaps in understanding, and finally reflecting on the knowledge gained.

Knowing sticks. All we can do is allow it to take place by exposing children to a healthy environment where they can explore, doubt, question and seek answers. Such a place will enable them to reflect. We must remove the impediments and distractions that can detract them from this process.

Lao Tzu said,

"*Knowing others is wisdom; knowing yourself is Enlightenment.*"

It is this 'knowing' that leads to wisdom and enlightenment.

How can we teach values to our children?

The best way to imbibe values in our children is by modelling them. Leading by example is the most essential and effective way to teach values to children. Parents are a child's best friends as well as role models. What they see in us, they emulate. Unfortunately, getting children to wholeheartedly do what we, as parents, do not believe and follow is almost impossible. So, whatever your family and cultural values, you model them first.

Bob Keeshan once said,

"*Parents are the ultimate role models for children. Every word, movement and action have an effect. No other person or outside force influences a child more than the parent.*"

When you model behaviour, it still needs to be made clear to the children why you do what you do. Therefore, it is crucial to have a conversation regularly on the importance of values. Let us call it the **reason method**. Without understanding, it simply becomes psychological conditioning. Therefore, we must complement our actions with clear words or concepts to encapsulate the value.

We can take a specific value like non-violence and discuss its various facets with children. We can debate its different forms, like not hurting others in thought, speech, or behaviour—the consequence of it and how it is hard to undo. We can also discuss its various causes. We can discuss examples from real life that they can relate to easily. And finally, we can ask them to summarise their understanding of it. I sometimes use my evening walks with my daughter to discuss values, and it is amazing how interesting the questions and conversations can get. You end up learning many new things too.

The second method is the **auto-suggestion method**. It is a psychological technique where individuals guide their thoughts, feelings, or behaviour. You can do this in a couple of ways. One way is to get children to say *positive affirmations.* Then, when they repeatedly suggest to themselves, the values behind the affirmations get reinforced.

I choose to move FORWARD everyday. growing and learning as I Go!

I can Learn Anything!
I can Know Anything!
I can Be Anything!

I have Amazing POTENTIAL AND I CAN Make GOOD choices

Today I will treat others with Kindness and I will be a friend to someone in Need

Example of a Pin-up chart of your affirmations

You can also print these and pin them up at home.

These affirmations can evolve as they grow. So, for example, you can change or upgrade them each year as your child grows. They can also recite affirmations when they start the day or retire to bed. The other way is getting your children to make resolutions or set targets for the day or a week and, at the end of it, evaluate and say for themselves how they did.

Affirmations also help them learn introspection.

The third method is called the **community method**. This method does not mean you send your children to attend religious discourses. Instead, you make occasions for them to be in an environment or amongst people who also model these values. Children have a sharp sense of awkwardness, so anything we tell them that may feel socially awkward is not welcome.

The fourth method is that of **deliberate practice**, and it involves neutralising negative values by deliberately practising the corresponding positive value. This method is more of a last resort or, say, a second last resort. It is especially applicable for adults with much prior negative conditioning that needs to be reversed. In this method, children can address anger by practising patience; miserliness can be countered by practising acts of generosity; they can counter arrogance by practising humility; jealousy by deliberate appreciation; and so on. It follows the policy of *fake it till you make it.*

The last and final method I suggest here is our ultimate last resort. It is that of using **prayers**. First, we pray when we find it impossible to teach them ourselves. Then, whichever higher power we believe in, we pray to it that these virtues grace us.

All these methods are not my invention, and I have learnt from my spiritual teacher, who taught me the importance of nurturing and learning values.

Feel free to use one or more of these methods to complement the primary one, for which there is no alternative. Let us first live the values that we expect our children to value. That is the best way to teach them the importance of values.

Wrong must first feel wrong.

'We all make mistakes' goes the modern thinking, giving acceptance and justification to many things we do wrong – knowingly and consciously.

If you consider something wrong rationally but do not feel wrong, there is little hope that you could ever be stopped from doing it. Our strongest defence against doing something we consider wrong is our intuitive feeling that it is wrong. This inner force holds us back and keeps us on the right path. This feeling comes from developing a sensitivity that takes years to build.

We think our ability to reason is our biggest defence, but it is not. Even the voice of reason can be suppressed by rationalisation. We can always say to our reasoning mind, 'one last time and I will give it up or 'one last cigarette', and we can create a chain of exceptions that soon become our habit and our addiction.

That person for whom lying, stealing, breaking, hurting others, or cheating does not *feel* wrong cannot be improved, helped, or rehabilitated easily. Treating and fixing such a mind may take years or even a lifetime. Without an inner sense of right and wrong, good and bad, a person is set off on a one-way journey to self-destruction and destruction of lives and families dependent on such a person.

Our strongest defence is the intuition that guides us through the thick and thin of life. It acts as our inner compass while we navigate the rough seas of choices and decisions. However, intuition may not always be right unless it comes from a cultivated mind. Einstein rightly said that (right) intuition does not come to an unprepared mind.

This inner compass develops and takes shape during our formative years-childhood and teenage. Good parenting is key in calibrating this compass to help it always point in the true north. The formative years of a child are crucial. If we fail to build this sensitivity in a child at a young age, it may take years and many hard lessons to learn. Making mistakes is the hardest way to learn life lessons. Good parenting can ease this for a child. If we can help develop an inner sensitivity in a child to the dos and *don't*s of life while they are still young, we can save them from mistakes that may hurt and scar them and may take years to heal and undo.

Human beings are rationalising animals. We reason in favour of our intuitions. So realising that intuition is our strongest defence and compass in life is the first step in getting parenting right. Once intuition is rightly calibrated in children, right reasoning will automatically find its place in their thinking and reinforce their defences.

I think, at the end of the day, it is this intuition that we want our children to inherit and pass on to the next generation. It will truly be an achievement on our part as parents if we can ensure that the compass we pass on is more accurate and more finely tuned than the one we received from our parents.

11 Values to value by age 11

Here is a curated list of the eleven most important values I would like my daughter to appreciate by the time she turns 11.

1. Time

Most regrets we have later in our lives are about how we used our time in the past. It is the most limited resource each of us has. An appreciation of time, its practical use cultivated earlier in life, gives the child a headstart over many others.

Time is also the greatest destroyer, a ravenous mouth consuming everything, including pain. That is why we must give time the respect and treatment it deserves. We need to learn not to fritter it away ourselves and then set an example for our children. Teach children to become a master of time and not its victim.

2. Non-injury

Non-injury in thought, word and, of course, action. It is relatively easier to practice physical non-injury, and exclusive focus on it amounts to denying subtle acts of injury. By our example, we can teach children to think carefully about the impact of their words on others. It is said that the way we, as parents, speak with our children, that tone becomes their inner voice. So, before you snap at your child in anger, think again. This voice may stay will them for the rest of their lives.

3. Simplicity

In our strange complex world, simplicity can come naturally to us if we want it. Simplicity is beautiful, is relaxing. Simplicity is staying in the present and not making things complicated. It is about enjoying a simple mind and intellect which is free from excess. It is permission to simply *be*. Simplicity is appreciating the small things in life. Simplicity helps create sustainable development. Simplicity teaches us economy — how to use our resources wisely, keeping future generations in mind. Simplicity avoids waste and value clashes complicated by greed, fear, peer pressure, and a false sense of identity.

4. Love

Understanding love's value means to realise that 'I am loveable and I can love. I have love inside.' Love is caring, sharing, being kind and being close. Love makes us feel safe and needed. When there is lots of love inside, anger runs away.

5. Cooperation

Nobody in this world today can be truly independent. I believe true independence is impossible, and it has always been. Mere survival today requires that we depend on farmers to grow food, traders to supply it to the market, and shops to distribute it to us. Same with water and many other things we deem essential for survival, health, and security. Understanding that one can achieve so much more by cooperating than by striving alone is the key to learning. Most of the human achievements in the arts, science, technology, and commerce are products of cooperation on a larger scale.

6. Hygiene

This involves cultivating an appreciation and preference for cleanliness and orderliness. Parents and children must practise hygiene at four levels: our surroundings, personal hygiene, mental and sensory hygiene, and intellectual hygiene.

One of my spiritual teachers once said, "Even every day while I do my business, a little dust settles on my skin, some dirt smudges my clothes, my desk becomes littered, and my mind gathers dust in my transactions with people. Smudges of envy settle, a spot of exasperation lands, streaks of possessiveness appear, and overall fine dust of self-criticism, guilt and self-condemnation spread. Each day, until my false identification with the mind dissolves and self-knowledge arises, I must clean the mind. What is the detergent for the mind? It is applying the opposite thought. It should be applied even though my negative attitude seems justified by circumstances." This skill of internal hygiene comes through training and discipline.

7. Self-control

Self-control is the ability to regulate one's emotions, thoughts, and behaviour in the face of temptations and impulses. Self-control is necessary for regulating one's behaviour to achieve specific goals. For example, it is the ability to give up on small, short gains to reap larger, long-term benefits. Or it can also mean tolerating short-term discomfort to attain comfort in the longer term. It can apply to all areas of achievement like health, diet, exercise, hard work, savings and so on.

8. Persistence

It is an age-old adage that when the going gets tough, the tough get going. Aphorisms like try till you succeed or never give up reinforce the value of persisting in our endeavours till we meet a certain level of success that we can be content with.

9. Rectitude / Congruence

It means cultivating uprightness or straightness in behaviour. It requires bringing an alignment between thought, word and deed. Only a mind free from cognitive dissonance or inner conflict can cultivate rectitude. We can also include the value of truthfulness under this value. It means being able to freely speak and stand by the truth as far as possible and in a way that does not cause mental injury to another person who does not deserve it.

10. Respect for teachers

This involves developing a sense of respect and deep gratitude for the teachers contributing to our inner growth. This respect is elevated to even reverence for our spiritual teachers or guru.

11. Responsibility

This is one of the hardest-to-learn values in life. Being responsible means, you do what you are expected to, irrespective of whether you are in the mood for it and accept the consequences of your actions. For children, responsibility can mean caring, taking care of things, helping others as per capacity, doing their share of work, and doing their bit to improve this world.

In the end, remember that the best way to teach values is through your example. Nothing beats that one!

Is Meat right for Children?

Here, I express my stand on the topic based on my experience. My intention here is not to offend meat eaters and meat lovers. Meat is a dietary choice and something that each of us must reason with ourselves about.

Many children are raised consuming meat- parents encourage and serve meat as 'normal', healthy, culturally natural, and rather 'good' to eat. However, I believe it is *not the best approach* parents can take, and I present my reasons here. As parents, we have a fiduciary responsibility towards our children to keep them from any action they may regret. Withholding serving them meat until they can choose to consume it, for whatever reason, falls into one such responsibility. (A fiduciary responsibility is a commitment to act in another person's best interests.) More than at any other time in history, today, meat-based diets are known to have far-reaching health and ethical implications. It's not something we can brush aside, saying I do it because I like it, or it's a way of life.

It is more than well-established that animals are intelligent, sentient creatures who not only feel pain like humans but also have the will to live, memories, family connections and connections with other humans and ecosystems. There is a lot of research that shows why meat-eating is environmentally non-sustainable and highly inefficient, given the human population on earth. We also know that livestock contributes most to CO_2 emissions and global warming. There is mounting evidence not just for ethical plant-based diets but also for healthier choices. Nowadays, plant-based eating is recognised as not only nutritionally sufficient but also to reduce the risk of many chronic illnesses. According to the American Dietetic Association, "appropriately planned vegetarian diets, including total vegetarian or vegan diets, are healthful, nutritionally adequate, and may provide health benefits in the prevention and treatment of certain diseases."

We may have lived on earth as hunter-gatherers for thousands of years, but we have come far from that life. Therefore, humans need to take a moral high ground on several topics like meat eating than justify existing questionable moralities.

So, here is the point: Let us suppose some children, when they grow up, may come to endorse some variant of ethical vegetarianism, which holds that eating meat, or more broadly acting in a way that leads to increased demand for meat, is morally wrong. If they come to this conclusion, and if they have eaten meat up to this point, it follows that their parents' actions in feeding them meat are likely to have corrupted their moral integrity. And such actions by parents could have been easily avoidable.

The best approach would be for parents to withhold (or limit) meat from children until they are old enough to make their own decisions about consumption. Most meat-eaters are meat-eaters simply due to childhood and social conditioning and not by choice. So, I strongly believe that we, as parents, should acknowledge that there are moral costs to choosing to give meat to a child. Just like we withhold serving alcohol, cigarettes, adult entertainment or driving a car (even in limited amounts), we can withhold meat too.

Today we have enough awareness of nutritional substitutes for meat, and we can afford to choose from them for our children. I followed this approach for our daughter. As a result, she has never been served meat or eggs. She is eleven now and healthy. And guess what? She chooses to be an ethical vegetarian; she reasoned her way to it; she understands it and advocates it. And she thanked me for bringing her up as a vegetarian.

So coming back to the question, 'Is meat right for children?' Let us give children freedom and a fair chance to think and decide for themselves.

Setting rules or teaching values

As parents, we expect our children to develop good character and virtues to grow into responsible adults and good citizens. But, while our expectations are clear, what seems like it could be clearer is the effective method.

Most of us set rules to steer our children in the right direction to build character. We set rules like 'never lie to parents or anyone, 'do not steal, 'do not use abusive words, 'do not hit other children, 'wash your feet before getting on the bed', 'homework first, play later', 'do not touch my mobile' and so on. The list can go on and on. We either set a rule for *doing* or *not doing* something. But the question is, does this build character?

Let us look at the adult world. We live in a world of rules and policies- travel policies, incentive policies, traffic rules, tax rules, customs rules, investment rules, gender equality, fair play, equal opportunity and so on. Do these rules make us any better as a person or help build/improve character?

An alternative approach is to focus on teaching values or virtues and making them see their beauty and realise their importance. This means that we adopt a *virtue-based ethics* method to build character. Virtues are internally applied, while rules are externally applied. They are opposite approaches. It requires us to work on our children's inner world and not their external world.

As a parent, I believe that only *virtue-based ethics* can build lasting character, not *rule-based* ones. We can only *enforce* rule-based ethics externally on the child, and it doesn't do much to change the child internally. It is very easy to set rules and reward/punish children based on whether they followed/disobeyed the rule. It may help get the desired behaviour temporarily, but it will not make a mark on their character.

How will they act if we take this reward-punishment system away? And most importantly, how will they act when they do not know the rules of something? Think about it.

So then, if you see how I see, new questions arise: 'How do we adopt virtue-based ethics? 'Can values be taught?' And 'How can we teach them virtues like non-violence, courage, temperance, justice and wisdom?

ᐅᐅᐅ

THIRTY-THREE
CHOOSING THE RIGHT PARENTING STYLE

———•ᑭ•———

Practical parenting: the misguiding philosophy of our time

Apparently, pragmatism, or being practical, is the guiding philosophy of this age. Simply put, everyone wants to be *pragmatic* about most things in life, and many expect their children to be *practical* too.

So, what exactly does it mean to be a pragmatist or practical? Pragmatism means we adopt an approach/belief that works to our advantage. If it works for me, I believe it. Simple. And this attitude guides choices and decisions in work, play, love, and health.

On the surface, this seems so harmless, but its impact is more far-reaching than we know. A Pragmatist normally does not think beyond the immediate consequences of beliefs/choices/ actions. He does not go far enough to define 'what is good and 'what are the long-term consequences of my belief, choice or action on my character'. This thinking separates such a *practical* person from an 'idealist.'

For a parent, teaching children what is good and the long-term consequences of their actions is essential. Children need to develop an intuition for good, to value this goodness over immediate experience. This approach stands contrary to pragmatism and is called idealism.

An idealist clearly understands the immediate and long-term good and chooses to do the *right* thing rather than the most *convenient* or *advantageous* thing. An idealist may be required to go through *hardships* and *inconveniences* in the short run and be mocked by many sometimes, but they choose what is good in the long term.

A child with an idealist mindset will seek a cure, not a fix, a solution, not a workaround, a confrontation, not a retreat. A child with an idealist upbringing will seek strength and not sympathy, respect and not praise, responsibilities, not tasks, career, not jobs, joy, not just fun, journey and not ride.

Suppose we merely teach kids how to take the path of least resistance, of choosing convenient experiences over journeys. In that case, they will live a shallow life whose meaning is always contextual, relative, and changing. They will constantly seek variety as the spice of life and think life is a series of meals to be enjoyed, not realising that we must eat for nourishment and growth.

Pragmatism is the race of a moth into the fire, which cannot distinguish between the nourishing sun and the consuming fire. Idealism is the growth of a seed into a tree, rooted firmly in values and reaching for the sun braving storms and winters. Let us encourage our children to lead a life of purpose and meaning and let values and ideals of goodness guide them.

The Four Parenting styles Model

We all want to raise intelligent, confident and successful kids. But where to begin? And what's the best parenting style to go with? Parenting styles fall under four main categories. Depending on the situation and context, you might use one or more of these different styles at different times. Look at these four parenting styles in the matrix on the next page.

Research tells us that authoritative parenting is ranked highly in several ways: Academic, social-emotional and behavioural.

What is authoritative parenting?

Authoritative parents are supportive and often in tune with their children's needs. They guide their kids through open and honest discussions to teach values and reasoning. Like authoritarian parents, they set limits and enforce standards. But unlike authoritarian parents, they're much more nurturing. Some common traits of authoritative parents:

- Responsive to their child's emotional needs while having high standards

- Communicate frequently and take into consideration their child's thoughts, feelings and opinions
- Allow natural consequences to occur, but use those opportunities to help their child reflect and learn
- Foster independence and reasoning
- Highly involved in their child's progress and growth

The 4 Parenting Styles

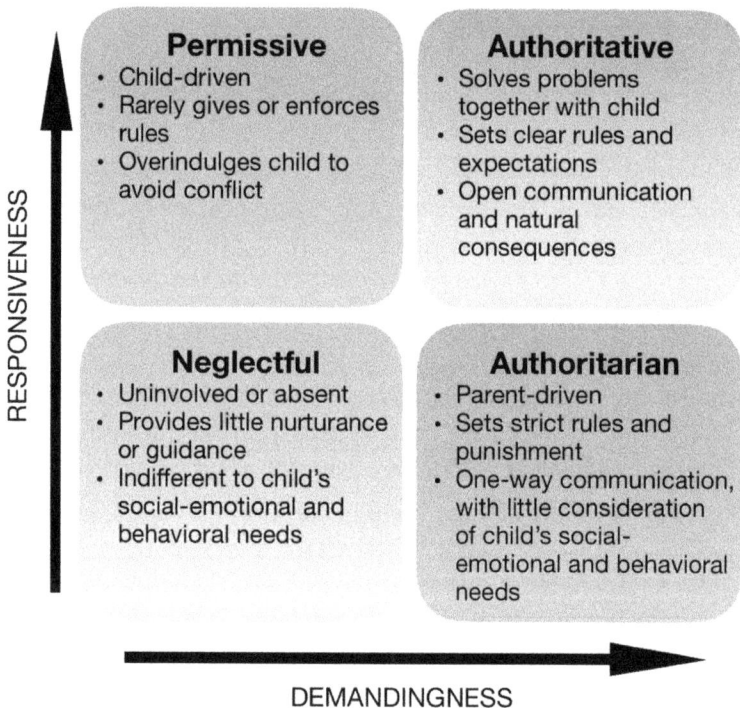

The 4 Parenting Styles (Source: Francyne Zeltser, CNBC Make It)

Why experts agree authoritative parenting is the most effective style

Studies have found that authoritative parents are more likely to raise confident kids who achieve academic success, have better social skills and are more capable of problem-solving. Instead of always coming to their kid's rescue, which is more typical among permissive parents, authoritative parents allow their kids to make mistakes. This permission to fail offers kids the opportunity to learn while also letting them know that their parents will be there to support them.

Authoritative parenting is beneficial when dealing with conflict because how we learn to deal with conflict at a young age plays a significant role in how we handle our losses or how resilient we are in our adult lives. With permissive parents, solutions to conflicts are generally up to the child. The child "wins", and the parent "loses." I've seen this approach lead to kids becoming more self-centred and less able to self-regulate. Of course, there are times when punishment is necessary. But the problem with constant punishment is that it doesn't teach your kid anything helpful. Instead, in most cases, it teaches them that the person with the most power wins, fair or not.

Let's say your 10-year-old son begs not to go to soccer practice: "I don't want to because I don't think I'm good at it."

In response,

- A permissive parent might say, "It's up to you."
- A neglectful parent might say, "Whatever you want ... it's your life."
- An authoritarian parent might say, "You have to. I don't want to hear another word from you."
- An authoritative parent might say, "I understand that you don't want to go. But sometimes, you get better by fighting the urge to avoid doing something hard!"

While authoritative parents do set limits and expect their kids to behave responsibly, they don't just demand blind obedience. Instead, they communicate and reason with the child, which can help inspire cooperation and teach kids the reason behind the rules.

Authoritative parenting doesn't guarantee success.

While experts praise authoritative parenting, it's important to note that using just one method does not always guarantee positive outcomes. Parenting isn't an exact science. In many ways, it's more like an art. My advice is to be loving and understanding and create structure and boundaries.

Don't simply focus on punishment. Instead, be supportive and listen to your child. Ask them questions and try to understand things from their point of view. Allow them to use a decision-making process so they can grow and learn things independently.

ᵱᵱᵱ

THIRTY-FOUR
DISCIPLINING THE CHILD

————◦♡◦————

It is Wrong to Hit Children. Period.

One of the biggest evils plaguing the lives of the children of the world today is violent discipline practices. Spanking, whooping, beating- it all means hitting, a big, powerful person hitting a smaller, less powerful person. It also goes by the word corporal punishment. In most countries, more than 2 in 3 children are subjected to violent discipline by caregivers. While teaching children self-control and acceptable behaviour is an integral part of child-rearing in all cultures, and many caregivers rely on violent physical and psychological methods to punish unwanted behaviours and encourage desired ones. It is not just a widespread practice at educational institutions but also in the very homes of children.

Before you think I misunderstood the meaning of violent discipline or what it includes, let me resort to some authoritative definitions. According to UNICEF, *violent discipline*, also known as 'corporal punishment ', is any punishment in which physical force is used to cause pain or discomfort. It includes, for example, pinching, spanking, hitting children with a hand, or forcing them to ingest something. However, violent discipline need not merely be physical but also psychological. *Violent psychological discipline* involves "verbal aggression, threats, intimidation, denigration, ridicule, guilt, humiliation, withdrawal of love or emotional manipulation to control children".

Violent discipline violates a child's right to protection from all forms of violence while in the care of their parents or other caregivers, as summarised in the United Nations Convention on the Rights of the Child.

Percentage of children who experience violent discipline at home

Percentage of children aged 2–14 who according to self-reports by caregivers, experienced any violent discipline at home in the past month.

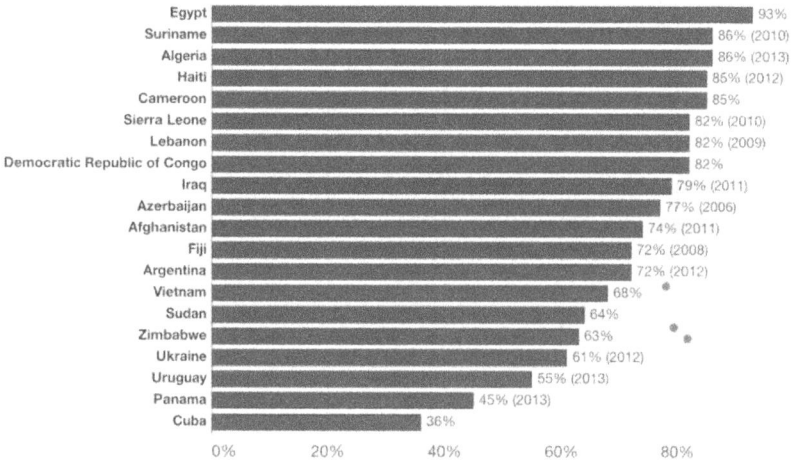

Country	Percentage
Egypt	93%
Suriname	86% (2010)
Algeria	86% (2013)
Haiti	85% (2012)
Cameroon	85%
Sierra Leone	82% (2010)
Lebanon	82% (2009)
Democratic Republic of Congo	82%
Iraq	79% (2011)
Azerbaijan	77% (2006)
Afghanistan	74% (2011)
Fiji	72% (2008)
Argentina	72% (2012)
Vietnam	68%
Sudan	64%
Zimbabwe	63%
Ukraine	61% (2012)
Uruguay	55% (2013)
Panama	45% (2013)
Cuba	36%

Source: Violent Discipline - UNICEF Global Databases (2016) OurWorldInData.org/violence-against-rights-for-children · CC BY
Note: In some instances observations refer to only part of a country. See sources for more details.

Unicef Statistics on Violent Discipling Cultures (Source: https://ourworldindata.org)

Fortunately, or unfortunately, this chart may not show data for your country, so I would leave that to you to check the numbers for your country. In India, this number is over 50%. Indian Parents use 30 Different Ways of Abuse, according to a UNICEF report. These range from shouting and slapping to denying food. Most parents would be embarrassed to read the list. In India, it is quite common for parents to reprimand children by slapping them, pinching them on their arms, or even throwing things at them. Hurling, physical abuse and yelling are commonplace too.

Overall, in the last couple of decades, several research studies have been conducted to study the impact of violent discipline on children's growth and development. In addition, a new APA (American Psychological Association) resolution cites evidence that physical punishment can cause lasting harm to children and that physical discipline is ineffective. Not just that it is ineffective, but it also harms children's mental health, as well as their cognitive, behavioural, social, and emotional development.

As parents, there is a huge misconception that children learn by suffering pain, humiliation, guilt and overpowering. "Children do not need the pain to learn," says Gershoff, a University of Texas at Austin professor, "We do not allow aggression among adults. It is a sad double standard that we don't give children the same protection against violence." **Children learnt most and best by modelling the behaviour of their parents.** I know most parents do not get this or that it is hard to understand this: children learn to behave by seeing and emulating how you, as parents, behave, with each other, with them and with others. Using physical force on a helpless child talks more about the parent than the child's state of mind. I am not saying that we paint parents black or white based on their ways of disciplining. I am sure most parents have their children's best intentions in mind and do not have a deliberate intention of causing harm or injury to the child. Rather, it sometimes stems from anger and frustration, a lack of understanding of the harm it can cause or limited familiarity with non-violent methods. I understand this. No one is perfect, true, but that does not mean one cannot get better. The point is if we learn from what our parents do well, we are also influenced by what they do not do well. And both can have a lasting effect on children's minds.

Parents and teachers in India continue the practice of physically punishing children regardless of thinking whether it is right or if it is even effective in discipline enforcement. People want to believe in the age-old dictum, "Spare the rod and spoil the child". In contrast, there is no proof of beaten and bruised children growing up into responsible citizens any more than those who were spared the rod and brought up in a loving and nurturing environment. A rod cannot be a substitute for conversation. There is no point in a conversation where words need to become abuse and abuse into physical violence or pain. For a mature person, there are innumerable ways to illustrate the difference between appropriate and inappropriate behaviour toward children. Resorting to inappropriate behaviour cannot be one way of doing it. Physical abuse only hardens the children, and they harbour resentment towards the disciplining authority for punishing them. Children grow up to resent and rebel against their Parents for practising this, allowing this and the institution for facilitating it. They may also look for an opportunity to settle scores and resort to violent means of retribution. Sometimes their impressionable minds may mistakenly accept it as the right way, and they may grow up as abusive adults believing in the power of violence. Either of these is wrong.

Violent ways of disciplining children at home and corporal punishments by institutions are tantamount to child abuse. They both need to stop. There are already laws against corporal punishment, which we need to create more awareness about. But most importantly, as parents, we need to change our mindset and adopt a zero-tolerance approach towards violence against children in our own homes and by ourselves. **Children (like parents) have a right to be treated with respect and dignity.** Discipline them but with love. That takes actual skill, creativity and maturity.

Non-violent Ways of Disciplining Children

We have already discussed the topic of the violent disciplining of children. Here, I wish to share solutions as we have already discussed the problem enough. I understand that parents often resort to violent discipline tactics simply out of frustration and inability to communicate their point through conversation. Here are various alternatives to violent discipline methods compiled by Pam Kemp from the Suzuki (music) Association of Americas.

1. Ignore the problem behaviour if it is not dangerous. Paying attention reinforces it, so it will likely happen again.

2. Redirect the child's attention to another activity.

3. Restructure the environment to remove or cut down on temptations for misbehaviour. This type of restructuring is commonly called "child-proofing the environment" and is especially appropriate for young children.

4. Pay attention to the positives. Try to reward constructive behaviour while ignoring troublesome behaviour.

5. Re-examine your expectations. Is it possible that the child's behaviour is age appropriate after all? Sometimes behaviours that frustrate parents—such as crying or wanting to "do it myself"—are a normal part of the learning process at a particular stage of development.

6. Use a time-out procedure. Calmly remove the out-of-control child to a dull but safe location. Briefly tell the child why the offending behaviour is unacceptable and that he must sit, doing nothing, in the time-out location until you say he may leave. One minute for each year of a child's age is a frequently recommended guideline in deciding how long to leave a child in time-out. Any yelling, arguing or tantrums results in the timer being restarted. After a time-out, let the matter drop-no nagging, lecturing, or recrimination. Expect to be tested at first. Remaining firm and calm are essential.

7. Examine your behaviour. Is the child possibly responding to your unclear expectations, confusing communication, threatening attitude, or inconsistency? If so, a change in parental behaviour is probably the quickest route to a change in the child's behaviour.

8. Less is more. When children become disruptive, it is tempting for the parent or caregiver to respond in kind, with a loud voice, aggressive language and non-verbal signs of physical tension. Unfortunately, this often makes matters worse. Instead, find your calm centre, establish eye contact, and lower your voice. Calm has a wonderful way of breeding calm.

9. Touch. Many kinds of touch can help children restore order to their lives-a gentle hand on the shoulder, a stroke of the hair, or a back rub. Yet, gentle touch carries a largely overlooked power in our low-touch, fearful society.

10. Name the unacceptable behaviour. Although this seems obvious, sometimes parents assume that the child knows what she did wrong or that an admonition like "be nice" will provide enough direction. Do not assume. Instead, expressly state what is wrong and why. For example, a parent might say, "I will not allow you to stab your brother with your bow. That hurts."

11. Examine the environment for unacceptable behaviour models the child may imitate. For example, did he hear that kind of foul language from Dad, from TV, or from a friend? Does Mom pout and slam doors when she gets mad, too? With embarrassing accuracy, our children have a knack for emulating our most negative behaviours. Perhaps the child's role models will need to change so that the child may change more quickly.

12. Permit logical consequences. Forgetting a homework assignment logically leads to a poor grade on that assignment. Spending the allowance now leads to not having money to buy something the child may need or want later in the week. Do not rescue the child. Let her learn from the consequences, with no "I-told-you-so's."

13. Reward positive behaviour with a tangible reinforcer, like a sticker or a favourite snack. We, adults, work for reinforcers (money), and children will do too.

14. Give a choice but be sure both alternatives are acceptable. "You may practice now or wait until after dinner. Which do you prefer? Not practising is not an option.

15. Invite the child to help figure out how to deal with the negative behaviour. Sometimes children, especially older ones, have surprisingly wise suggestions. Explain the problem and "Katie, for the last two or three weeks, and you have been putting off doing your homework and then wanting to stay up past your bedtime to finish it. Now you are starting to complain about being tired all the time. How would you suggest dealing with this problem of procrastinating on homework?"

16. Hold a family meeting if other members are involved in or affected by the problem. Brainstorm solutions and, in consultation with the child, pick a helpful approach.

17. Remove a privilege consequent to the behaviour. Offer the child privileges that are meaningful and have some logical connection to the behaviour. For example, "If you do not get your homework done by 10:00 P.M., you will not be permitted to watch TV the following night because you haven't used your time wisely."

18. Tell the child directly what you observe, think, feel, and want, using "I" statements. For example, "When I see you abuse your instrument like that, I feel angry and worried about what damage you might do. However, I think you are old enough to find a better way of expressing your frustration. What ideas do you have?"

19. Use gentle—not criticising—humour to put the situation in a new perspective for the child and yourself. Well-timed humour can turn a raging bull of a child into a laughing hyena faster than ten minutes of reasoning together.

20. Develop a nonverbal warning system for repetitive bad habits that the child may do without being aware of them. For example, when Mom tugs her earlobe (like Carol Burnett used to do), that might mean, "Oops! You are biting your nails again." Scratching the head with two fingers crossed might mean, "Did you know that you're chewing with your mouth open?" Children who hate nagging will often accept nonverbal reminders as a replacement.

21. Keep a behaviour count of the problem behaviour and let the child establish a goal of how much to decrease that behaviour that week. Decide together on a treat, such as a special activity together, if the goal is met.

22. Help the child substitute acceptable behaviour for unacceptable behaviour. This strategy is built on the principle that it is unwise to take a behaviour away without providing a substitute.

23. Try to establish physical links to emotional states and specific behaviours. For example, you can teach pre-schoolers that a particular piece of music means it is time to get quiet and calm. The lullaby and bedtime story routine means it is time to rest. Ringing a bell might mean it is time to come practice.

24. As a family, establish a list of rules and consequences. Don't make too many; renegotiate them as the children get older. Making rules and consequences together helps children feel a sense of ownership and assures parents that children truly know the rules and consequences since they helped make them.

25. Look for causes and deal with them. For example, consider the context of a child having a tantrum when asked to practice. Has his play been interrupted with no opportunity for a transition? If so, you might prevent the tantrum next time by giving the child a five-minute warning.

Isn't it refreshing to know there are so many alternatives to discipline the child? So, the next time you lose your cool with your child, please read through these and pick a better alternative.

Working with the Child using the SCARF Model

We discussed how we could employ the SCARF model for effectively collaborating in the workplace in the Work Section. The same model can also be applied to working with children. Here is how you can apply this to parenting (I am trying too):

Status: Do not compare your child to other children trying to prove her to be better or inferior to them. Tweens especially are very conscious of 'status'. They love to be appreciated for the good things they do when their efforts are appreciated in a social group or even on your social media page. I try to reframe criticism as room for improvement but always try to add ideas or hacks to do the same.

Certainty: Share a clear understanding of the boundaries they cannot cross: for example, I tell my daughter never to go to the basement or outside the premises of our gated community on her own or with her friends. I have also asked her to avoid interactions or divulging personal or family information with strangers. When you share advice with them, make sure to clarify the reasons why you suggest so. Let them have long-term goals and milestones to achieve and review them regularly.

Autonomy: Give them the freedom to think and act in a way that is natural and spontaneous. When they have autonomy, they can better express themselves and are more creative and original. These are really the first steps towards appreciating the value of freedom and independence. Once they have the task and goal, let them figure out how best they can reach them.

Relatedness: One of parenting's biggest achievements would be to be best friends with your children. If you are able to reach a level of confidence and trust with them where they can proudly refer to you as their best friend, you're already a super successful parent.

Fairness: Always be fair when you treat your children - not just with respect to other children but also with respect to grownups. Keep your promises and be candid with them in all interactions. We always treated our daughter as an equal and never shushed her away when she participated in a conversation with older adults and peers.

ᑭᑭᑭ

THIRTY-FIVE

TRANSFORMING BOREDOM

The great philosopher Arthur Schopenhauer once said, 'The Two enemies of human happiness are pain and boredom.' The associations with boredom have invariably been negative, and most see it as undesirable. Another great philosopher Soren Kierkegaard confirms the same when he says, 'There is something more terrible than a hell of suffering: a hell of boredom. '

A question that I pondered is whether boredom is a quality of our surroundings or our minds. Is boredom induced in mind by a dull environment, or does boredom comes from a boredom-inducing mind? I am trying to address this question in this chapter.

Psychology and philosophy seem to differ in their understanding of boredom. Psychology looks at boredom as an emotional and psychological state of experience that makes its appearance when we are left without anything to do and are not interested in our surroundings.

On the other hand, philosophy looks at boredom as a particular type of perception. Boredom is a condition characterised by perceiving one's environment as dull, tedious, and lacking in stimulation. This can result either from leisure or a lack of aesthetic interest. That is why Leo Tolstoy defined boredom as the desire for desires. Which definition do we accept as more accurate? I would go with the philosophers here.

I believe boredom is more a product of one's mind than one's surroundings. When people are bored, it is primarily with their selves that they are bored, said American Social Philosopher Eric Hoffer. Some of the greatest works of creativity, invention and discovery occur in a state of boredom. The novelist Robert Pirsig says boredom always precedes a period of great creativity.

How a child or a teen, or a young adult handles boredom can become a key differentiator in the person's growth and development. The default reaction to boredom is that you tend to get into a mode of restlessness and blind consumption. Blind consumption can mean indulging in passive entertainment like watching web series, taking to substance abuse, reckless spending, mindless eating or ruminating on negative thoughts.

So, how does one transition from boredom to creativity rather than boredom to consumption? Here is my thesis as to how we can pull this trick off. It takes the help of one of these three agents, viz. Purpose, Meaning or Inspiration.

Purpose

If you have an overarching purpose for living and an orientation towards a long-term goal, it can jolt you out of your slumber and get you into action mode.

Inspiration

Or you need inspiration, an ideal, a vision of something so beautiful, majestic and awesome that it gets you to pick that pen and paper or that hat and umbrella and get you going.

Meaning

The last trick under your sleeve could be to seek meaning in boredom. Viktor E. Frankl, in his bestselling book Man's Search for Meaning, said, 'Those who have a 'why' to live, can bear with almost any 'how'.' He says, 'Everything can be taken from a man but one thing: the last of the human freedoms—to choose one's attitude in any given set of circumstances, to choose one's own way.'

Understand that none of this comes naturally, and it takes immense power of the mind to actuate. Handling boredom is a skill, a life skill, rather than that only a few ever master in their lifetime.

Some psychologists believe that boredom has an evolutionary basis and encourages humans to seek new challenges. It also seems to influence human learning and ingenuity. Here is a word of caution, though. Although for most of us, boredom can be routine, for some, it can also be an indicator of an underlying mental disease, and one can tell this by observing when one's feelings become excessive and all-consuming and start interfering with daily living.

Be it an honest day's labour or an intricate work of art, it seems we have a choice whether to become passive and alienated towards our work or get immersed in the tedium before passively reacting to boredom, first attempting to acknowledge the state of boredom. Become mindful of it. The Zen master Jean Kabat-Zinn said, 'When you pay attention to boredom, it becomes very interesting.' And then find a rope of purpose, inspiration or meaning, throw it across new horizons and peaks, and pull yourself out to reach newer heights.

And if nothing works, think of these words of Friedrich Nietzsche: '*Is life, not a thousand times too short for us to bore ourselves?*'

Create a Nourishing Space for Children to Learn and Grow

One of the most beautiful gifts that Goa (on the West coast of India) bestows on its inhabitants is space- colourful, creative, and cultural space. During the pandemic months when I lived in Goa, I used to bring my daughter to this beautiful place called the Museum of Goa- a gallery and community of contemporary art founded by one of India's most respected contemporary artists, installers and sculptors, Subodh Kerkar. Besides being home to his art, it is also an incubation centre for creative artists. It offers its community and visitors that much-needed creative space in the form of a beautiful cafeteria, gift shop, and art workshops for all ages. It also hosts several events where they invite all kinds of artists, from Chefs, classical dancers, actors, and many other artists, each week to tell us their stories and their journey to success.

You may wonder why I am talking about this while discussing parenting. Because – for me, parenting is all about creating this space- where one is free to explore, think, create, learn and grow without the fear of deadlines, exams and judgement of any kind. I feel most schools stifle and suppress this in children. No one is more vulnerable to negativity, fear and threat as much as children. Unfortunately, many schools thrive by exploiting this vulnerability and beating kids to submission, conformance and control in the name of discipline, education and careers.

Art Workshop at the Museum of Goa

The first time I visited this place, the Museum of Goa, I knew there was something special about this place. It felt different and made us think differently. So when I brought Aanya to the art workshop on Saturday, the receptionist told me that they had cancelled the workshop on the day because no children had registered online for the same. And then I bumped into the great Subodh Kerkar himself. He looked at Aanya, and he immediately arranged for someone to attend to Aanya's art craving. Then he simply left her free - to creatively express herself on the canvas for the next two hours. Watching my daughter get into the flow of creative expression was a joy to watch.

Can we create such space in our homes and our schools- a space where children can give their talents the freedom to express themselves in a safe, friendly, fearless manner and learn?

If the answer to that is Yes, then there are three essential ingredients such a space would need: the right environment, experiences and conversations.

1. Expose children to the "right environment."

- Strive to learn more about how children learn by reading articles, books or watching informational videos.
- Take advantage of every opportunity to engage children in learning.
- Create an environment at home that is conducive to learning.
- Inspire in children a desire for learning.
- Allow children to interact actively with the environment and explore and ask questions.
- Do not restrict children to experiences that focus only on one set of skills or to experiences that only interest the parents.
- Show love for all your children equally. (Do not be partial to some of your children.)
- Celebrate the uniqueness of each child.
- Model respect for other's beliefs and values and expect children to respect others' beliefs and values.
- Do not criticise or demean children for their actions, beliefs and behaviours.
- Do not impose your will without an explanation for your action.
- Plan the home's physical environment with children's needs and desires in mind.
- Purchase toys that are specifically designed to stimulate children's thinking and creativity.

2. Expose children to the "right experiences."

- Turn as many everyday life experiences as possible into learning opportunities.
- Model learning from everyday experiences.
- Talk about the importance of learning as a self-initiated activity.
- Expose children to experiences that teach social, academic and motor skills.
- Capitalize on children's interest in selecting learning experiences.
- Provide opportunities for children to excel and experience positive feelings about themselves.
- Provide children opportunities to learn and problem-solving by using all the senses.
- Teach children that some questions do not have a right or wrong answer.
- Provide children with opportunities to role-play.

- Avoid teaching children to learn only by reading and memorising materials.
- Avoid teaching children that one way of learning is better than another.
- Provide opportunities for children to appreciate art and music.
- Do not leave children's learning to chance.

3. Expose children to the "right conversations."

- Talk to children as often as possible.
- Engage children in conversations.
- Ask for their views about specific topics of interest.
- Increase children's vocabulary on different topics through conversations.
- Don't criticise children for the way they say words or express themselves.
- Do not turn down an opportunity to explain or respond to a question.
- Do not expect children to listen passively.
- Do not dominate a conversation with children.
- Take advantage of children's questions to extend learning.
- Always interact with children when they ask questions (Do not say, "I don't have time to talk").
- Respect children's views of the world.
- Ask and value children's opinions.
- Provide opportunities for children to communicate ideas through speech or writing.
- Show children ways they can communicate ideas.
- Encourage children to use acceptable behaviour and redirect unacceptable behaviour.
- Do not criticise or demean cultures or languages that are different from theirs.
- Do not teach children to react or respond in one specific way.

These are some ideas that I put together after researching a bit online. Of course, there is a lot that I need to learn and put into practice, but educating myself on the topic is a significant first step. Like marriage, parenting can be one of life's most rewarding and important commitments. So let us give it our best.

ᐅᐅᐅ

THIRTY-SIX

PARENT AS THE ROLE MODEL

———◦♡◦———

Inspire responsibility in children

Try defining 'responsibility' to yourself simply, and you will see that it's not as easy as it sounds. Teaching and inculcating children with it is even more challenging. Even the dictionary meanings of the term are very circular. For instance, it's a state of being responsible, accountable, and answerable.

This difficulty arises because 'responsibility' is a complex value made up of several independent values. It means we keep our word and do what we say. It also means we make our own choices. It can mean that we need to accept the consequences of our actions. And it also means that we think of consequences before we act. Finally, it means we should do the 'right' thing in any situation. So, you see, it is a complex value.

So, when I was looking this up, I found an interesting article on mbaresearch.org that explained how responsibility is made of five essential elements. Once we know these, we can better teach them to children. The five elements of *responsibility* are *honesty*, *compassion* or *respect*, *fairness*, *accountability* and *courage*.

- Being honest means that you speak and value the truth, base decisions based on facts and not emotions, and finally, acknowledge that aspects of us need to change for the better.
- To be compassionate and respectful is to treat everyone with the kindness that we expect from others and be tolerant of the differences

you may have with them.

- To be fair means to balance our own needs with those of others.
- To be accountable is to acknowledge the consequences of your actions, decisions and mistakes and keep your promises.
- Finally, to show courage is to do the right thing even in the face of challenges or difficulties.

So how do we teach responsibility? We do it first by demonstrating responsible behaviour and then explaining the importance of it.

As a start, we can model ourselves to act responsibly and teach children to emulate us to:

- *Follow the rules*
- *Tell the truth* (out of trust & without fear of punishment)
- *Admit our mistakes*
- *Finish tasks with care and on time* (household chores, homework, project etc.)
- *Always act appropriately* (wherever we may be, be kind and respectful in all interactions)

This is how I have gone about this. However, we should also realise that it is hard to be responsible, and it is not always possible to do the right thing all the time. Even adults find it hard. So, make allowance for children to make mistakes and falter. Responsibility is as much an expectation from ourselves as it is from our children.

Let children see the good and bad in you.

As parents, we need to allow children to see the good in us and the bad in us. Do not make it look like you are perfect and everything you do or do not do is the right thing.

Children emulate by default. They learn by mirroring the people around them. They even speak with the same tone and accent that they are talked to. Their vocabulary is made up of the words you speak with them. Your expressions influence their expressions. They even mirror your value system. That is why if, at times, your behaviour or language or thinking is improper, point it out to them. Tell them that it is not proper, and they must know it. Also, assure them that it is something that you are aware of and that you are working on it and are trying to be a better person.

Otherwise, they will never learn the difference between right and wrong, proper and improper, and appropriate and inappropriate. At least they will not be able to learn this from you. The teaching from the books will appear to conflict with the world outside their curriculum and school, and they may choose then to take neither seriously.

When you occasionally point out the flaws and weaknesses in your thinking and behaving to children, even they will start stepping out of their picture and learn to introspect and look at themselves objectively. This ability to objectively introspect is a life skill that will serve them well in the long run. Love grows and blossoms where there is honesty. And do not think that they will not understand it or will judge or hate you. On the contrary, they will respect you even more.

Minding our swear words and gestures

Every language in the world has cuss words. And there are as many excuses for swearing as there are languages worldwide. Some say they swear because they don't find a better word, some say it feels good to say them, and some say it's just cool and swearing can make you an in-group member of a gang.

In The Stuff of Thought, Steven Pinker lists five ways we can swear: descriptively, idiomatically, abusively, emphatically, and cathartically. I am sure you can think of an example for each of these. However, none of these functions *requires* swearwords.

I know a lot of parents who causally swear when among adults or friends but become very conscious of them when around their children. Yet, they somehow find it inappropriate to swear in the presence of kids and convenient among adults. It is not hard to see hypocrisy or double standards here.

If we see value in our children not using swear words or gestures, we must model that behaviour for them. So let us erase them from our diction first. It is not easy as it has years of conditioning behind it, and any good habit will take its time to build by conscious and deliberate practice.

The words and gestures we use reveal our culture, character and maturity. One of the oldest languages in India, Sanskrit, also means 'cultured'. I believe that any language is generous enough to give us a wide variety of words to grade and express our feelings, emotions, and intentions.

Let our dialogue, conversation, and conduct reflect the values we have drawn from our rich culture and tradition.

I believe there is another very important role language plays in our lives- it helps us process emotions. Using words properly can help children process emotions appropriately. When we are subjected to extreme emotions like passion, embarrassment, anger or anxiety, how we talk to ourselves is as critical as how we respond to others. Both require the use of words. All proven powerful motivation techniques, like gratitude journaling, affirmations, goal setting and future-self exercise, are all about how we use language to uplift us. Our senses connect us to the external world, but our words help us relate. And that is why our choice of words for expressing anger and disappointment is as important as it is for expressing love, devotion and wonder. Our words reflect our minds. Hence the expression 'mind your language'.

So, let's *mind* our language, kick swear words and gestures out of our diction and body language and let our next generation inherit a rich lexicon of emotions.

OUR FAMILY
Rules & Values

WE RESPECT EACH OTHER

WE DON'T YELL

WE USE KIND AND
    POLITE WORDS

WE TELL THE TRUTH

WE TAKE CARE OF
    OUR BODIES

WE LISTEN TO EACH
    OTHER WITHOUT INTERRUPTING

WE TRY TO MAKE GOOD CHOICES
EVERY TIME & WE ALWAYS
CHOOSE LOVE

WE ARE RESPONSIBLE FOR
OUR ACTIONS

WE KEEP OUR HOUSE
    CLEAN & HAPPY

WE KEEP OUR PROMISE'S

WE LAUGH AND
HAVE FUN.

WE FORGIVE
EACHOTHER

WE PUT FAMILY
FIRST

WE HELP EACH
OTHER

WE ARE GRATEFUL
FOR EVERYTHING

WE GIVE MANY
HUGS AND KISSES

WE CHASE OUR
DREAMS AND
NEVER GIVE UP

WE LOVE EACH
OTHER
UNCONDITIONALLY

Family Values Poster

THIRTY-SEVEN

ON TEACHING MONEY, SOCIAL MEDIA AND NATIONALISM

Teaching children about money management

Money management is everything about earning, saving, spending, borrowing and repaying the money. To manage money well, you need financial literacy. Financial literacy is the ability to manage money in ways that help you achieve your goals in life. Money management and financial literacy are essential life skills that even young children can start learning. You, the parent, have a significant role in helping your child build these important skills. Financial literacy at a young age can help children develop healthy money-related habits and attitudes later and give your children an edge in their adult life where they will be sucked into the money-driven world.

Basic money management concepts for young children start with learning what money looks like and where the money comes from. As they grow older, it is about learning more complex concepts like what money is for – needs and wants, how to use money wisely – budgeting and saving and how to get value for money.

One of the most effective ways of helping children learn about these concepts is by talking, role-modelling, playing and practising money-related skills together. For example, you can explain to them how money is earned through jobs and how banks receive deposits and lend money; you can also show them your bank statement, how money gets accounted for there, and how the money is used to buy necessities and fulfil dreams. A great way to employ role-modelling play can be making shopping lists and going through the shopping experience together, which involves comparing brands, and prices and picking the best deals. And then there is the classic 'pocket money' practice that you can employ to help them pay for non-essentials each month. In my daughter's school, the teachers organised a supermarket play where children sold and bought items from a store using model currency notes and coins. They learnt how to exchange goods for money, return change and spend within a given budget. The idea is to pick a suitable method for the child's age and learning needs.

Here are some key lessons to pass on to children gradually:

- Importance of saving
- Power of compounding
- The two sides of debt - its destructive and beneficial powers
- Needs always come before wants, and wants before desires.
- Showing that mom and dad are not banks of unlimited money.
- Letting children make their own money mistakes and learn.
- Earning comes before spending.
- Learn to give back to the community.
- Learn from experience that what goes around comes around.
- Guiding children to make decisions. Do not make decisions for them or dictate to them.
- Understand how the credit card industry works and how it is not free money.
- Reward kids for extraordinary acts, not what they are supposed to do anyways, not for their routines.

Several activity books are available online that you can download on this topic of money management for children. Here is one example of a simple activity book on money management for children that you can use: google *Yes You Can - Understanding Money Kids Activity Book (octo-capital.com)*

Here are some essential but not exhaustive milestones for teaching kids about money:

Age 3-5 years:

- Identify coins, notes and value
- Identify items that cost money
- People earn by working
- The idea of having to wait to get something you want
- Understanding the difference between wants and needs

Age 6-10 years:

- Allowance discussion
- Choices for how to spend money
- Comparing prices
- Open a savings account

Age 11-13 years:

- Save at least 10% of the allowance
- Goal setting
- Value of hard work
- Don't spend money that you don't have
- Importance of privacy and security

Age 14-18 years:

- Creating a budget
- How to write checks
- Importance of avoiding credit card debt
- Understand what taxes are and how it affects jobs and life
- Get a job

Young Adult:

- Understanding Credit score and how to build a good credit score
- Saving three months' worth of expenses for emergency
- How to rent an apartment
- How to balance a chequebook
- Basics of Investing
- How to buy a car
- How health insurance works and how to buy one

There are also several courses on financial literacy for children readily available on youtube and MOOC platforms like Udemy that you can get them enrolled in.

The key takeaway is that financial literacy needs to begin early for children at home, and it has to be age-appropriate. Most adults get financial education late in life, while others never get it. Most learn it the hard way; that need not be the case for the next generation.

Protect adolescents and teens from social media

I once read the news of a famous social media teen star committing suicide. It shook me up and made me think about the evils of social media and inspired this article.

What kind of influence can cause a sixteen-year-old to end her life? When I was looking up this topic, I could see innumerable research studies that have consistently shown a direct correlation between social media usage by teens and anxiety, depression, attention deficit, sleep deprivation and mood-related issues.

This essay applies as much to adults as it applies to teens. I believe more and more adults today have still not outgrown the teenage mindset. Many of us are far from intellectual maturity in the race to stay young at heart. This discussion attempts to persuade parents to think again about how they should approach the topic of social media for themselves and their children.

While it puts the people we want to connect to at our fingertips, social media also has its dark side. Following are some of the evils that can plague you and your children if you take social media to be a harmless pastime:

Anxiety

Adults and teens feel emotionally invested in their social media accounts. There is a constant impatience to look at notifications and to respond to messages and posts. Besides, social media images constantly reinforce the illusion that they are incomplete, imperfect and inadequate, and they need to constantly strive to improve their acceptance and status in the circle. This impatience causes stress.

Not only do they feel pressure to respond quickly online, but they also feel pressure to have perfect photos and well-written posts. All of which can cause a great deal of anxiety. Some studies have found that the larger a teen's social circle online, the more anxiety they feel about keeping up with everything online. It takes a lot of time and effort to keep up with each social media platform's unspoken rules and culture. As a result, this puts additional pressure on teens, which can cause feelings of anxiety.

Sleep Deprivation

The mobile and tablet screens do not let the transition from day to night-time happen. Glaring screens trick the mind into thinking there is still so much more I am missing out on and yet to do on social media. As a result, sleep time takes a beating, and the body cannot fully rest and restore health in the morning.

Sleep deprivation causes low immunity, mood disorders, ADHD, and mindless eating. Research also shows girls are more prone to sleep deprivation due to the use of social media on phones than boys. So it is no wonder many children constantly complain of boredom and tiredness.

Envy

Jealousy and envy are the most fundamental emotions that social media constantly stirs in adults and teens alike. Moreover, the selective display of positive moments and evading of negative emotions and experiences makes one feel that the grass is always greener on the other side. And unfortunately, this greener side seems forever out of one's reach.

I believe these three reasons are good enough to dissuade any sensible parent from encouraging the use of social media for themselves and their children. So what can we do as parents? Here are some suggestions I could gather to help us wean ourselves and our children away from social media.

This 4 Ds framework was introduced to me by one of my spiritual teachers to help manage the mind. I am applying the same to managing social media:

1. **Discrimination**: Educate children on how social media works, why it exists and how people make money. It's all visible and verifiable, and they are smart enough to understand. At the same time, listen to them and try to understand their motivations and concerns. Never humiliate them among their peers- it will have the exact opposite impact.

2. **Discipline**: Draw clear boundaries on what children are allowed and not allowed to do on digital media. They must clearly understand where the boundary is. Boundaries can be setting screen time limits, applying child settings to media platforms and knowing what they do on digital platforms.

3. **Desire**: Our ability to desire in thousands of ways is one factor that makes us unique as humans. And desire needs to be cultivated and tended to from a young age. It is important to direct the minds of our young ones towards positive, healthy, and fulfilling pursuits. For example, nudge them to desire actual playtime with friends, to learn activities that engage their body-mind-intelligence together or do a course that stretches over a few weeks to give them a specific skill and certification.

4. **Dispassion**: This does not mean we teach ourselves and our children to be detached and become disinterested in things. Teaching dispassion means that we teach them to recognise when something becomes a binding attachment- that demands engagement, even at the cost of their well-being and growth. Seeing that an activity controls us and not the other way around will deter them from addictions even when we are no longer around as parents to guide them.

These are some pointers we can use ourselves to deal with the risks of social media and screen addiction. But, of course, the best way is to set an example for our children by following what we teach.

Teach Healthy Nationalism

One of my favourite writers Jared Diamond, Professor of Geography at the University of California, LA, says that asking whether nationalism is good or bad is like asking a person whether self-confidence and ego strength are good or bad. Having too much of it means you are so full of yourself that you ignore other people. If, on the other hand, you lack self-confidence and are too dependent on others for your self-image, then you will lack the courage, sentiment, and identity to deal with your issues. That is why it is better to adopt a healthy level of nationalism. A great example of healthy nationalism, he goes on to say, can be seen in Finland. The Finns speak the Finnish language even though no other country in the world speaks it. It is the root of Finnish national identity. Also, every Finn can recite the Kalevala, a collection of Finnish legends transmitted orally until published in the 19th century and now regarded as the Finnish national epic.

Similarly, an excessive national identity, espoused by the likes of Hitler in the 1930s, would give rise to the discrimination, exploitation, and violence that we are well aware of. Germany today is also a great example of a country with a healthy national identity like Finland. Its identity today is not based on going out and conquering the world and dominating other countries but on recognising that there are wonderful things about Germany that distinguish it from other countries and that it can take pride in.

Where nationalism goes bad and sour is when the love of one's own country is based on hatred of others. When nationalism takes up the agenda of brainwashing an entire nation or generation to hate its neighbours, it becomes evil. The list of horrors of unhealthy nationalism is long and includes world wars, holocausts, pogroms, chauvinism, jingoism and xenophobia, to name a few. At the social level, it fulfils the essential function of consolidating the group and its identity above and beyond individual needs.

A healthy nationalism does not manufacture hatred for others. It only breeds concern for one's fellow citizens. The belief that everyone is a member of one nation fulfils a basic psychological need to belong. It gives people a sense of security and status. At a social level, it helps citizens to endeavour together and value each other's welfare. Healthy nationalism can make people less selfish. Healthy nationalism is good for a nation at a macroeconomic level, just like healthy self-interest is good for economic progress at a micro level. It is no wonder that countries with higher-than-average nationalism are wealthier today. United States, Australia, Germany, Switzerland, and Sweden are to name a few.

India has a rich treasure of culture, traditions, wisdom and values. We have enough to take pride in, identify, and relate with. So, this brings us to the question of how we can teach healthy nationalism. The answer is through developing patriotism. If nationalism is a belief, patriotism is the behaviour that espouses it. Patriotism is the love of your country and the desire to defend it.

And there are four ways to teach patriotism to young and old alike:

1. Respect all cultures and traditions and celebrate them in your capacity: To each his own. The Sanskrit word for religious beliefs is 'matam' which means opinion. So simply respect another person's opinion as you are entitled to your own. Celebrating the festivals of the tradition that we identify with is a great way to promote culture. Invite fellow citizens from another community/tradition to participate in it while respecting their tastes and boundaries. Greeting others and participating in the festivals of other traditions and cultures is a great way to show inclusion and solidarity. And when it comes to national festivals- celebrate and contribute together.

A note on handling traditions: treat your tradition as a living organism- have the openness and courage to adapt them to changing times, keep them relevant and yet take pride in identifying with its evolution. Support those that are trying to adapt and transform for good. Learn to appreciate diversity. Remember that a garden's beauty is in its flowers' diversity, not its homogeneity.

2. Enlist and expound on values that unite all citizens of the nation. Most of these are universal. Spot these values in the lives and achievements of personalities, from the events, from our nation's historical past. Remember and cherish them. Let all schools and colleges teach these values to all children and youngsters. Let us support and contribute to these institutions in our capacity. When asked, 'what are the most important values that make us Indian?' we should be able to answer it easily. We should at least know what we are trying to love and defend.

3. Honour and respect your armed forces. While most of us love our country and our defence forces on national holidays, the defence forces put this love into action daily. So unconditionally support, have faith in and love the protectors of our borders.

4. And finally, it is important to respect the law of the land. All the values are also typically the founding principles of the constitution and take the shape of the law of the land. And so, living in harmony simply means living as law-abiding citizens. Therefore, express support and extend your votes to policies that espouse healthy nationalism.

With healthy patriotism comes healthy nationalism, and with healthy nationalism, we can build a healthy nation and a healthy future for the generations to come. I hope these thoughts resonate with you and make you think. Nationalism, like politics, religion, or food, is neither good nor evil, neither black nor white. It is how we wield it, how we interpret it, and how we impose our biases on it that make it so. And so let us choose to wield it well. Cheers to healthy nationalism!

True Wealth, as per Vedanta

Wealth, by definition, is the abundance of valuable possessions, a plentiful supply of a desirable thing. It is the value sought after by everyone in some form or other. Money is the default form of wealth known to us. Vedanta, the esoteric and ancient science of happiness and fulfilment, discusses real wealth being sixfold, 'shad-sampatti' (Sanskrit).

Just like money is used for external transformation, this sixfold wealth is meant to bring about inner transformation, bringing true freedom and peace.

1. **Objectivity** (śamaḥ): This discipline leads to mastery over one's ways of thinking rather than being at their mercy. Objectivity also helps to resolve or manage the mind and refine it. It prevents one's thoughts, feelings, and impulses from running the show and is achieved by exercising dispassion, i.e., objectivity and right understanding, and keeping our and others' long-term well-being in mind. Only a mature, dispassionate, objective mind has śamaḥ.

2. **Self-restraint** (damaḥ)

It means mastery over the organs (powers) of sense and action. When there is a possibility of inappropriate use, such as in the expression of anger or excessive indulgence, damaḥ is required to channel the emotion appropriately. Damaḥ requires being alert to one's responses and choosing responses such that one's speech and actions are appropriate. When the mature, objective outlook needed for śamaḥ is unavailable (when anger has risen, for example), damaḥ may be needed to ensure appropriate behaviour.

3. **Mindfulness** (uparamaḥ or uparatiḥ)

A calm, steady, quiet mind that, due to being disciplined through śamaḥ and damaḥ, no longer turns habitually or mechanically to outer sensory involvement. The mind becomes alert, poised and available for the task. You live in charge of your life instead of being at the mercy of sense objects.

4. **Forbearance** (titikṣā)

It means cheerful forbearance or endurance. It is our ability to bear with opposites cheerfully and objectively, such as heat and cold, and honour and dishonour with equanimity. Titikṣā is the capacity to deal cheerfully and objectively with external conditions and events that are beyond our control – it does not mean allowing pain to happen and then putting up with it. On the contrary, Titikṣā is developed by willingly undergoing minor difficulties without dwelling on or lamenting them.

5. **Trust** (śraddhā):

Acceptance by firm judgement as true the teaching and spiritual teacher. Śraddhā is often translated as faith or trust, but it is more than that. Initially, a degree of trust, viśvāsaḥ, is necessary for any teaching situation. It allows us to stand apart from our ideas and, for now at least, give the benefit of the doubt to the text and the teacher rather than to our views. It is a form of acceptance that is pending verification. And if what is taught seems incorrect, having śraddhā means I do not reject it but question my understanding until what is being taught is clear. With further knowledge, that acceptance takes the deeper form of a clear, carefully reached understanding or conviction.

6. **Goal-Orientation** (samādhānam):

Simply put, it means focused intent, i.e. being always conscious of the goal of liberation from sorrow without being distracted. Regularly check your progress against where you want to reach. Never lose track of the freedom and peace that you are aiming for.

Anyone who works towards earning these six accomplishments transforms internally to feel complete, free and at peace.

ᚦᚦᚦ

THIRTY-EIGHT

ON BELIEFS, TRUST, CHAINS AND WINGS

———◆♭◆———

Parenting is the mother of Religion and Atheism.

Most of us have seen the security and comfort children derive from the company of their parents. We know the discomfort children find in not seeing their parents around. I believe this longing for security and warmth is something we continue to carry with us as we grow into adults, and it seems this is one of the founding stones of religion and love for God or the Creator. Adults re-live their childhood by taking to their new parents: Gods and Goddesses and holy men. The urge to feel comforted and safe in parents' company is transposed onto religion.

And we must acknowledge that religion does the job for most of us, irrespective of the facts or science. The commonality between parenting and 'religioning' is that they both get work done. Both are meant to help seek psychological comfort and peace of mind and may have nothing to do with facts or reality. That is why whatever we expect from good parenting can be expected out of a 'good' religion too.

We live in a relative world, one that is conditioned by our genetic programming and social conditioning. The fact remains that evolution is blind, and the only purpose, if any, rests with the genes wanting to propagate into the future, wanting to survive, multiply and thrive. We are hardwired as children to seek 'parenting' and as adults to pursue religion. In both cases, we are not simply seeking an individual but all the things the individual stands for and does. What we expect from a great parent is also what we expect from a great God.

In this sense, atheists, too, seek a God. But their God is an abstract one. They seek God through principles, values, laws, institutions, leaders and so on, without needing a personal God. It is like asking for the benefits of parenting without having to engage with parents. It is like growing up in an all-paid boarding school where you don't get to see parents, but many aspects of parenting are delivered via an institutional channel (minus the warmth, of course).

If religion is like re-living childhood, atheism is like re-living teenage years- years when the flesh rebels against the will of society and authority. It rebels. It seeks to mate with someone outside its genetic pool to give rise to a new person with a genetic combination that thinks, feels and behaves differently, even though only slightly.

Have you noticed how similar the lives of religious people are to those of atheists- they feed, breed, grow, thrive and protect and promote their kind? So a difference in the belief system is no real difference at all.

One becomes a grown-up, a real adult when one starts seeing the child in us and its needs. We become adults when we start seeing how nature works. We become adults when we acknowledge the 'nature' in us and, simultaneously, see ourselves as separate from it. When we can see how our minds work, individually and collectively and when we can channel our energies for the individual and common good, we truly grow up.

Parenting is the mother of all religions, including atheism. If we can get parenting right, we will have already set the foundation of a great religion for generations to come. Parenting, religion, or atheism culminate in intellectual maturity, financial independence, individual freedom, fulfilment, and happiness. They are all means to similar ends.

Use beliefs as means rather than end

Most of us are products of societal learning and conditioning. We grow up with different beliefs based on the communities and traditions we grow up in. A belief is accepting that something exists or is true, especially without proof. Most of these beliefs we never question or are allowed to question, and many are unverifiable.

An excellent example of this unverifiable belief is that of a God and an afterlife. Almost every community believes in some version of heaven. In some versions, everyone is a child looking up to a God with a flowing white beard and singing hymns. In some versions of heaven, there are rivers of milk, where God is in the form of a cowherd boy tending cows, where devotees take the form of cows, grass, trees, birds or even cowherd girls. In another version of heaven, one believes in entering a land with greenery, with rivers of alcoholic beverages, where beautiful damsels serve you an unlimited menu of food, drinks, pleasure, and entertainment. These are only some versions, and I am sure you have heard one of your own.

Some believe God creates the universe like a Potter creates pottery from clay. While some believe God spins this world out of himself like a spider spins a web. Some believe God is a male, some believe God is a female, and others believe God is without gender. There is no end to where imagination can lead us with beliefs, and it doesn't take long for beliefs to turn into superstitions.

As parents, the critical question we must ask ourselves is: Is it wise to pass these beliefs on to your children? Even though they come across as childish at the least and downright questionable of one's intelligence at the most.

There are two approaches that I have tried and seem right to me:

1. Until the age of 7 or 8, let children 'believe' in myths and, if needed, explain one myth using another. Indian mythology is full of tales of gods, demons and devotees, even talking beasts and their drama, adventures, battles and lessons – something that can catch the fascination of a child's mind, and they learn some morals from them.

2. After age 8, I do not consider introducing and rationalising mythical tales and adventures wise. I find them impossible and childish to believe in myself, so when my daughter turned 9, I stopped justifying myths as history and reality. I explained to her how myths might start as historical facts and turn into supernatural myths over time. It is more important to focus on the import of the mythological tales than their historicity. This way, I stay true to my conscience too.

Today my approach is to encourage her to ask questions and have the complete freedom to doubt the reality of some of these beliefs. I have conveyed to her that many of these beliefs are simply a means to learn and practice values. When we listen to mythical stories, rather than taking them at their face value, we should only take from them the teaching and see the unreal as props that help us learn some real truths, like the story of the tortoise and the hare. At the end of the story, we do not waste time questioning the plausibility of the tortoise and hare talking to each other and instead focus on what the story is trying to tell us. We pay attention to the lesson we can take from here to apply elsewhere. The same approach can hold for myths and beliefs. I think that is something a 9-year-old or a 10-year-old can understand and may also appreciate our honesty.

I tell my daughter, Aanya, that everything we believe but cannot prove is a means to gain a higher understanding and perspective rather than an end to getting emotionally fixated about. One need not evade one's conscience, suspend one's intelligence or get ready to discriminate, die or kill for one's beliefs. Once you get the learning, you can drop the props and the symbols as they have served their purpose. If we get hung, holding tightly onto the pointing finger that is trying to show us the moon, we will miss the opportunity to locate it and appreciate its beauty. This approach has worked well so far, and if I must revise this approach again, I will surely do so.

I, for one, would not like to pass on the crutches of beliefs to my child. Beliefs cripple the mind. I would instead give her the sails of intelligence and the compass of wisdom to tread life's challenges and treacherous waters. She can have the freedom to choose her beliefs if she must but let her reach her conclusions through self-enquiry, trust and reason.

Trust a better guide than belief.

I define 'trust' as a process of reaching a firm judgement that something is true. Though the dictionary meaning is different, I hope I can convince you by the end of the chapter to favour this definition.

I have already explained my take on beliefs, how it is best to deal with unverifiable beliefs, and how to discuss them with children. Here I want to put light on an alternative to belief, viz. trust.

I think the faculty of trust is a better guide to understanding reality than belief, and here are some of the reasons why:

1. **Trust is dynamic**, while belief is static. Trust takes time to build.

2. **Trust requires an open mind**, while belief requires a closed mind. It requires a certain openness to experience, where it is possible that you temporarily drop your guard down and be willing to listen to multiple points of view and evaluate perspectives by yourself.

3. **Trust requires an exercise of reason**, while belief requires suspension of reason. We must never forget that reason is one of the leading faculties that make us human. Moreover, trust building requires objectivity in thinking rather than subjectivity, like in the case of belief.

4. **Trust can be verified**, but in most cases, a belief is unverifiable. Trust-building is a process in which one may need to set aside one's biases and start with a foundation of trust. Then, if someone breaks that trust or proves it not to work, one can learn from it. So, there is an element of learning in trust.

5. **Trust makes you accountable**. You are accountable, at least partly, for where you choose to put your trust and the consequences thereof. In belief, it is easy to blame your parents, society, religious books or community and wash your hands of the consequences.

These five simple reasons make trust (shraddha in Sanskrit) a better guide to living than belief. Shraddha is the attitude that upholds and nourishes truth. To trust deeply is to truly know deeply. The trust we put in our spouse, parents or best friends to help us in difficult times is not a belief. The trust we put in our pilots when we board the flying machine, or the trust in ourselves, is not a belief. Trust is the knowledge that may take years to develop and turn into a firm judgement.

Here is a simple exercise: list your most deeply rooted beliefs and subject them to their 'trustworthiness' using the above five criteria.

As parents, learn what to trust through your research and experience. Prove it yourself first. Then tell children what they can and cannot trust based on your knowledge and experience. And tell children they can put this trust to test themselves and form their judgement.

The legacy of trust needs to stand the test of time and experience from one generation to the next.

Give children wings, not chains.

Have you ever thought of how much parenting is about setting expectations? Parents expect from children in the name of sacrifices they have made, and children expect from their parents as their right. Does it ever seem that it has become a race towards who gets the best of whom?

Even before our toddlers begin grade school, we want them to grow up to be Engineers or Doctors or whatnot. Wanting them to choose a profession of your liking, marry a person of your choice, believing in your own unverifiable beliefs, is that what love is? Using children to fulfil one's unfulfilled desires is folly.

This kind of desire on the part of parents is simply a binding attachment and an agenda, not love. What we are doing is that we are trying to possess and dominate our children. Some expect kids to be 'obedient' like trained pets, some to be 'faithful' like a servant, and others to be 'slaves' of traditions. Is it any wonder that children develop a bitterness or feel estranged from their parents as they enter adulthood?

The best kind of parenting is that which frees the parent as well as the child from anxiety and guilt. It doesn't bind and allows children to become independent, strong and resilient individuals- intellectually, financially and, as far as possible, emotionally. Attend to children as you attend to a rose plant: keep them safe from weeds and pests, nourish them, give them sunlight, and they will bloom on their own. Do not manipulate to get your choice's colour, fragrance, and texture.

Encourage them to ask questions and let them explore more and more viewpoints as they grow. Let them know the difference between beliefs, facts and unknowns. Do not hesitate to say you do not know when you don't. Let them not be conditioned like the chained elephant, which, despite having the strength, would not dare to leave captivity. Someone once said, 'One who is conceived in a cage yearns for it.' Instead, let us teach them objectivity and how to reason.

As parents, we control very little of what becomes of our lives and our children's; whatever success we see can be attributed to many more factors that we know and do not know of. So, do not get anxious about the future of your little ones.

To love is to accommodate without fault-finding. Love truly begins when we step outside of attachment and allow children the freedom to walk, explore and learn about the world around us. This freedom will eventually bloom into responsibility and responsibility into independence. Leave them universal values as their inner compass, not your rule book and chains. Prepare them for the world and not prepare a world for them. Give them wings, which you may never have grown and not pass on your crutches. Let them spread their wings and find their skies. That is the true joy and fulfilment of parenting.

ppp

THIRTY-NINE

MEETING THE EMOTIONAL NEEDS OF CHILDREN

———•♡•———

Statistics show that 50% of mental health problems are established by age 14 and 75% by age 24. It is easy to identify a child's physical needs: nutritious food, warm, clean clothes, a roof over their heads, routine bedtimes, and medical care when needed. However, a child's mental and emotional needs may not be obvious. Good emotional health helps children develop socially and learn new skills, self-confidence, high self-esteem, and a healthy emotional outlook on life.

Included here is a list of a child's emotional needs by age, from birth to teenage.

Baby's First Year

- **Love:** All the times you feed your baby, give cuddles, and do a myriad of small things to show your love. They want all of it.
- **Touch:** Skin-to-skin contact after birth is extremely powerful. It helps regulate babies' temperature, heart rate, and breathing and helps them cry less. It helps moms too. When mothers cuddle their newborn babies, they get a hit of the cuddle-hormone oxytocin.
- **Safety:** Your baby is new to the world and looks to you to keep her safe. A baby always needs to know that there is someone to care for and

someone to always turn to in need.

- **Attention:** An important emotional milestone for babies is learning to have 'conversations' with parents and caregivers.

Toddlers

- **Praise:** Encourage a growth mindset—a belief that kids can develop basic abilities through dedication and hard work. Kids who are praised for their effort and method instead of their knowledge, or the result, are more likely to develop a growth mindset. This will also positively impact their confidence. Praise them sincerely and honestly. Do not shower false praises. Be specific and descriptive in your praise. Avoid giving conditional or controlling praise like 'Well done! But you can do better!' or 'I want you to do better next time!'. Also, avoid comparisons in praise like 'You are the smartest in your class or 'You are so talented, just like your brother'.
- **Empathy:** Children feel respected and valued when you acknowledge their opinions, feelings, and desires. For instance, telling him/her, "I know it's hard to stop playing with your Legos and take a bath," communicates that what he is doing is essential to you.
- **Safe boundaries:** The world they are exploring is a big place during these years. There is much to learn, much to see, and so much to figure out. Children count on parents to set up limits and guidelines, show them when to stop and let them know they will keep them safe. But, deep inside, they want to know that their parents will not let them go too far.

Child (4 – 11 years old)

- **Unconditional Love & Acceptance:** Children need to know that you accept their feelings and mistakes and love them unconditionally. For example, telling your child, "I know you spilt the milk, but you didn't do it on purpose," or saying, "Crying is OK. You feel sad your friend is moving." Acceptance also means they need to be treated with respect, kindness, and courtesy, just like adults need. Acceptance also means that their feelings, opinions and ideas are valued and their uniqueness is acknowledged.

- **Safety through the familiar routine:** Children, like the rest of us, handle change best if it is expected and occurs in the context of a familiar routine. A predictable routine allows children to feel safe and to develop a sense of mastery in handling their lives.
- **Permission to Fail:** Children are learning and they will make lots and lots of mistakes along the way. Each will teach them something new to help them get things right the next time. When we see our children get into difficulty, it's our instinct to rush in and fix the problem. If we stand back, they often find a way to resolve things independently. Children also need to be treated with respect, kindness and courtesy like adults on failure.

Emotional Needs of a Teenager (12 – 18 years old)

- **Knowing You're Always There**: As your teen interacts with the world, they will pull away from you. It's all part of growing up. But the confidence and security to do so often rely on knowing there is a safe and consistent haven at home. Adolescence is an exhilarating time full of emotional lows and highs. Parents can play an important part in supporting and guiding teens to feel good about themselves as they deal with heightened emotions. Therefore, parents' steady, unwavering presence is critically important.
- **Freedom to make decisions:** Teens need to be independent and make their way in the world. It's hard, as parents, to let them make decisions that we know might be wrong. But giving them the freedom to do so can build their self-esteem and minimise frustration.
- **Forgiveness**: Every teen is expected to make mistakes, some of which can be easily fixed while others can have greater consequences. They will know they have messed up when they see the consequences firsthand. Showing you forgive and love them, even when they have made a mistake, counts for an awful lot. It helps them to want to gather themselves again, get up and get going. It builds resilience.
- **Communication:** If you time how much you communicate with your child each day, you will see that it's hardly in a few minutes. Teenagers need to be listened to and understood. They need a friend so they can

speak their heart and reach out for guidance or help without having a fear of being judged or reprimanded. Be your child's best friend if you can. If you have a busy routine, it is best to set aside at least 20-30 min of uninterrupted and focused conversation time with your teens each day.

Emotional health provides a foundation for success in school, work, marriage and life. Failure to recognise and satisfy these needs jeopardises our children's future and that of succeeding generations. Emotional health contributes to a healthy family environment and strengthens our nation. You are your child's best emotional coach.

ppp

FORTY

EFFECTIVE USE OF PARENTING TIME

As parents, we want to take up the responsibility of raising our children alone and try to do everything we can to contribute to parenting. Juggling work and home turf have become a common central challenge. If not done right, juggling work and home can get stressful and ultimately affect both work and home. Being hard-pressed for time and patience, how can we ensure that we spend our parenting time and energy correctly, especially as our children age and change? Instead of feeling underappreciated or guilty about the time you do or don't spend with your kids, you can proactively allocate your parenting time and energy. How? By prioritizing tasks and responsibilities based on impact and talent.

Begin by asking yourself two questions:

Impact: Which activities I do, tasks I perform, or types of support I provide have the most significant impact on my child's development?

Talent: Which activities, tasks, or types of support give me the most motivation, inspiration, or energy as a parent?

You can take the two criteria above and create a corresponding 2×2 matrix with four quadrants to help guide decisions around parenting time. I call this the Parenting Time Matrix.

Parenting Time Matrix

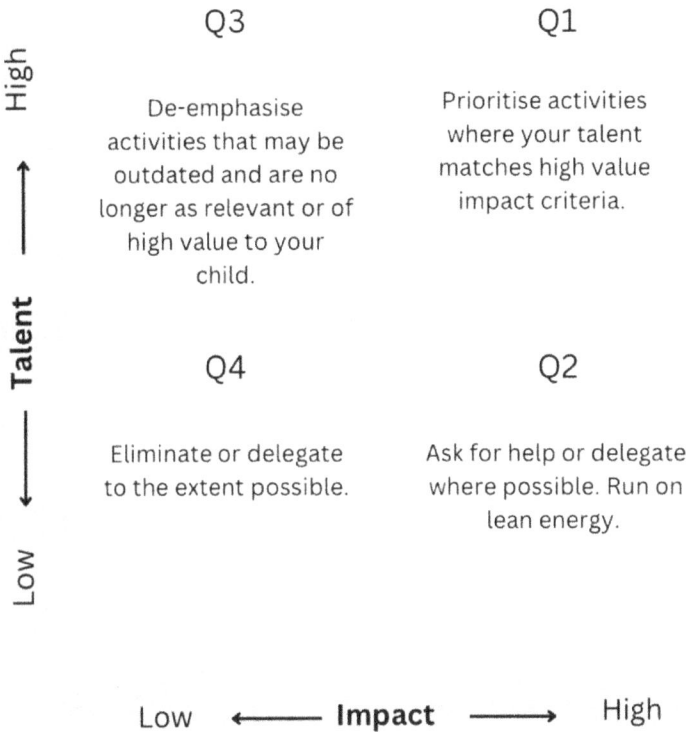

	Q3	Q1
High	De-emphasise activities that may be outdated and are no longer as relevant or of high value to your child.	Prioritise activities where your talent matches high value impact criteria.
Talent	Q4	Q2
Low	Eliminate or delegate to the extent possible.	Ask for help or delegate where possible. Run on lean energy.

Low ←——— **Impact** ——→ High

Parenting Time Matrix

Parenting Time Matrix

Quadrant 1: High Impact/ High Talent

This quadrant is the sweet spot of parenting time, as these activities add value for your child and give you an energy boost because you are good at this yourself. You have a talent for this. These are the activities where parents and children truly bond. Let's say your child is not very good at math yet and needs some coaching. And you love mathematics and have a flair for teaching it. Then you should become your child's math tutor. Make this your priority parenting task. You take this task on yourself. So start prioritising your parenting time for things that fell in quadrant 1.

Quadrant 2: High Impact/ Low Talent

Activities in quadrant two can be tricky as our kids will have needs that may drain our energy. The answer isn't to stop doing them entirely but to minimise their energy impact or identify resources that can help. For example, working parents can have a caregiver to optimise their energy and time. If you think math is necessary for your children but know you're not good at teaching math, you can find a tutor to take that load off you.

Quadrant 3: Low Impact/ High Talent

Our kids' interests and needs are constantly changing. Quadrant 3 is a real danger zone for parents because often, we find ourselves engaging with our kids around activities or interests we love but our kids don't value. Even worse, we risk putting inadvertent pressure on our children to engage in an activity because they know we care about it as parents. Therefore, it is critical to set up regular checkpoints with our kids to understand how they regard our contributions as they age. As a working parent, I make a yearly ritual of sitting down with my child and ask three things that I do best that the child values the most. This sweet spot changes with time and so stay flexible with changing times. For example, I liked driving my daughter to school every day and then to work. But soon, I realised it was not so much worth my time as we could hardly use that time for anything of value. So, I decided to hire the services of the school bus instead. So, ensure staying in quadrant one versus quadrant 3.

Quadrant 4: Low Impact/ Low Talent

When things are busy, or you try to do everything, you can engage on auto-pilot in activities that neither add value nor bring you passion. It is easy for parents to fall into habits and assumptions and continue doing what they have always done without reconsideration. Such patterns and beliefs can lead to frustrating moments. If you find yourself in quadrant 4, it's best to stop doing those activities that are no longer relevant for you or your child and gain back precious time.

Here are some tips to help you put this mental model into practice:

1. **Operationalize into Your Calendar**: Learning the quadrants is only the first step. If you don't plan to put your insights into action, your good intentions to spend time with your kids in the best ways will get swept up in your long list of to-dos. So use your calendar to carve out and protect time for quadrant one activities.

2. **Use pre-blocks**: Pre-block your calendar with significant school events like performances or teacher conferences as soon as that information is available. Of course, it's not perfect, and there will be plenty of weeks where work, travel or deliverables get in the way, but proactively planning will enable you to have an honest discussion ahead of time when you can't be there.

3. **Colour-code**: Color-coding your calendar can help you take a longer view of how you spend your time. For example, mark all parenting tasks in yellow, and office tasks in blue. Colour coding does not make you feel guilty (as working parents often do) but serves as a cue to adapt as needed.

4. **Stay in Active Dialogue**: Even with the best triaging or planning time with your kids, staying in active conversation with them is vital to keep them involved and adapt to changes.

5. **Use look-ahead**: Throughout the year, bring your family together to see what is upcoming on the calendar. For families with older children, you can designate a day and time, such as Sunday morning at breakfast, to have everyone pull up laptops and calendars and scan for the upcoming week. Especially with multiple kids, where sibling rivalry over parents' time and attention can exist, the family look-ahead can help you to ensure that you distribute parenting time fairly. For younger children, use visuals such as wall calendars or large whiteboards with pictures denoting when you have work or other obligations. Often, the uncertainty and inconsistency of when you will or won't be home are what kids struggle with the most.

6. **Talk about it:** Talking to your kids regularly about where and how you spend your time allows you to model good communication and time management practices. If the amount of time you are (or aren't) spending with children is a road bump in your family's progress, have a

conversation rather than avoiding it or letting things fester. Ask your kids to be active problem solvers with you in finding more satisfying ways to spend time together. Let them see you ask for help from other family members, neighbours, or your spouse when you get into a time bind.

Ultimately, you will feel much more in control and effective as you become intentional about your parenting time decisions. My hope for myself and all working parents is that the practices outlined in this article will help us find new confidence in how we spend our time and alleviate guilt about letting go of some things we don't have enough time to do. In addition, these changes can increase our fulfilment at work and help maintain meaningful relationships with our kids as they grow up.

ϼϼϼ

FORTY-ONE
TRACKING A CHILD'S MORAL DEVELOPMENT

Moral development is the process through which children develop proper attitudes and behaviours toward other people in society based on social and cultural norms, rules, and laws. We all want our children to grow up to be morally strong citizens of society. But how do we know how they are developing, where they stand and where they need to grow? This is where some scientific research and a mental model come in handy.

The psychologist Lawrence Kohlberg (1927-87) thought that moral development was a kind of hierarchical ladder with six rungs. He asked children of all ages to reason about problems involving fairness, justice, equality, loyalty, benevolence and various kinds of social welfare. He also looked at how children encouraged each other to cooperate and how they resolved conflicts. He was convinced that children can sense a natural moral order and grow towards a universal and objective morality that we all eventually come to share. He could see moral development as progressing in six stages:

Universal Ethics

Social Contract

Law and Order

Pleasing Others

Self-Interest

Reward/ Punishment

Stages of Moral Development

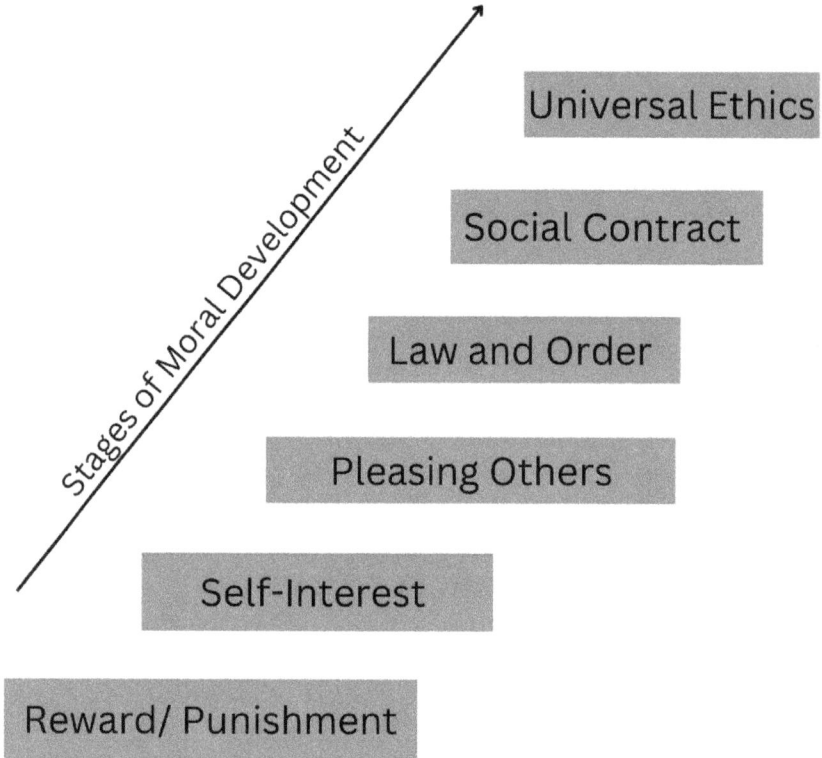

Kohlberg's Stages of Moral Development

Stage One: Obedience and Punishment

Being moral in this early stage means no more than being obedient because of the fear of punishment. This is how most children start. They are moved simply by the consequences of their actions; they choose based on what causes them pleasure or pain.

Stage Two: Individualism and Exchange

Conforming to the norms of a peer group, but for selfish reasons. This is where the seeds of understanding reciprocity are sown in their minds, but only as long as it serves their individual interests. They recognise that others have interests too and that you can make an exchange to serve each other's interests.

Stage Three: Developing Good Interpersonal Relationships

Being moral means being a good boy or a good girl and seeking the approval of others. In this stage, they focus on living up to social expectations and roles. They try to be nice and start seeing how your choices affect relationships.

Stage Four: Maintaining Social Order

Here, being good means being loyal to authorities and social institutions. Doing what is right makes you a good citizen and a member of a group. Here the focus is on recognising the social order and ensuring that it is upheld. At this stage, people start considering society as a whole while making decisions or judgements. Following law and order, doing one's duty, following rules and respecting authority are signs that one has matured to this stage.

Stage Five: Social Contract and Individual Rights

Starting from this stage, people start recognising the abstract principles of morality. They also start acknowledging other people's differing values, opinions, and beliefs. They can see how rules of law are essential to maintaining society, and members of society need to adhere to them. They also start agreeing with Utilitarian views on happiness, the greater good and democracy.

Stage Six: Universal Principles

This is the highest stage of the moral development of a person. The person's belief in certain universal moral principles override all other obligations, even society's laws or empirical observations of 'happiness'. At this stage, people follow these internalised principles of justice, even if they sometimes conflict with laws and rules. Laws are valid only insofar as they are grounded in justice, and a commitment to justice carries with it an obligation to disobey unjust laws. Here, one's action is never a means but always an end in itself; one acts because it is right and not because it is instrumental, expected, legal or previously agreed upon.

So you begin your moral development journey as a selfish brat, and, with time, you end up as Buddha or Immanuel Kant. That's the idea. Kohlberg freely admitted that some adults never get much beyond stage three, and only a few ever reach the giddy Kantian heights of stage six. Research suggests that most of the population resides between the 1st and 4th stages, with only a few making it to stages 5 and 6.

Kohlberg was primarily interested in moral reasoning. His six stages have little to do with the ability to empathise or show compassion. His tests for moral thinking are almost wholly about problem-solving. For value-based parenting, morality may be more about caring, benevolence, dialogue and relationships built over time. Being moral implies negotiation, being tentative, recognising that there are rarely simple solutions in life and being prepared to suspend judgement sometimes. To be fair, Kohlberg never said that the results of his research were conclusive. However, subsequent and more sophisticated experiments seem to show that Kohlberg's conclusions about moral development may well be about right.

It's a complex topic, and parenting in this regard is easier said than done. But models or frameworks like these help build or benchmark a person's moral core. Kohlberg's analysis of moral development can be helpful for parents as well as teachers. Children already have their own relatively simple understanding of morality, so it's best to try to build on that rather than attempt to impose an incomprehensible 'higher' one. Simulation games exploring moral issues are one way of challenging children to think in new ways. You can also use thought experiments and case studies to discuss with children and see how they think and guide them with new ways of thinking. Discussions and lessons that end in disagreement are often more interesting and valuable than those that reach a happy consensus. But modern education is an ambivalent process. We encourage children to compete and then expect them to cooperate. We want them to obey teachers and then think for themselves.

If Aristotle is right, we shouldn't leave moral development to chance. First, lift yourself higher on the moral development ladder and then try to lift your child.

FORTY-TWO

MEASURING THE SUCCESS OF PARENTING

———•♡•———

Knowing Children's Rights

As grownups and adults, I am sure most of you know your rights. You know your basic needs and how you like to be treated while operating as an individual. Social awareness campaigns and school education have educated you enough on the topic. But do you know what the rights of children are?

It is never late to learn, and here is an opportunity to do so. In 1989, world leaders made a historic commitment to the world's children by adopting the United Nations Convention on the Rights of the Child – an international agreement on childhood. It has become the most widely ratified human rights treaty in history and has helped transform children's lives worldwide.

I think all parents and institutions must read through this, understand it and share the understanding with children too. This gives us a good idea about what children need to receive from a parent. The parent's ability and success in providing the children with these essential rights is the first fundamental measure of the success of parenting. So, it is quite clear from this list that parenting comes with a lot of responsibility and accountability. This is one important reason I dedicated a separate section to parenting in this book.

Convention on the rights of the child

Measuring the success of Parenting

The most significant investment of one's lifetime is parenting a child. It is an investment that takes 25-30 years of committed labour, love and resources to show signs of maturity. How can we say if we have succeeded in our parenting endeavour? I am attempting to describe what it means to succeed as a parent.

But before we get into that discussion, it is essential to note the formula for success. Success in any endeavour depends on three critical factors:

1. Your hard work and persistence.
2. Your attitude to work and life.
3. God's grace (some call it luck or timing or chance- it doesn't matter).

The presence of all three is needed to lead any pursuit to success. It is possible to fail despite hard work, commitment and the right attitude because you may not have God's grace. So, now let me share my perspective on successful parenting. First, it all depends on how the children turn out. Successful parenting should translate into successful children.

Here are the **five ways of checking if we have turned out a successful child after 20-30 years of upbringing**:

1. **Education:** This is on the top of my checklist because parents have the most control over this. Sufficient education which is socially respected is a bare minimum that the child needs to complete under the sponsorship of parents.
2. **Ability to earn a livelihood:** Is your son or daughter earning a livelihood enough to support themselves and their family and maintain a decent standard of living? Many parents claim that their sons and daughters are capable, but do they have enough self-respect to fend for themselves? That's the question.
3. **Living family values:** Are your children living the values you claim to have passed on to them? Every family has a particular set of values and commitments to relationships, e.g. loyalty to a spouse, observing traditional rituals and so on.
4. **Growth:** A family can prosper only when each generation tries to be as good as the previous generation and then adds a little over it to improve. If each generation grows the family wealth, standard of living and goodwill in society, taking it a notch higher than where their parents left off, that is true success. This is what makes a proud parent.
5. **Love:** When love given to children finds its way back to parents in different forms of care, support and warmth, it is also a solid indicator of your success as a parent.

All these five measures put together define parenting success. Any other success of the child in the form of achievements or contributions to society is icing on the cake. If it seems too complicated, here is a simpler test. Just try answering, 'Are you really proud of your children?' A simple Yes or No will tell you. If your answer is a definite 'yes', that is a reliable measure of parenting success. I look at how my parents raised my sister and me and how we turned out to be. They have said this one thing more than a few times, 'I am so proud of you!'. So, I can safely conclude they did succeed as parents!

And if you are starting your journey as a parent, think of the three factors I talked about: put in hard work and commitment, keep the right attitude, put in lots of love and always be humble to seek God's grace.

ᑭᑭᑭ

FORTY-THREE

IF YOU ARE A SINGLE PARENT

———◦♥◦———

Being a single parent is never easy. Someone once said being a single parent is twice the work, twice the stress and twice the tears but also twice the hugs, twice the love and twice the pride. Single parenting is a dark cloud with a silver lining. Single parenting requires the same ingredients as regular parenting, if not more, with the main difference being that it requires you to commit yourself twice. In this chapter, I have shared some basic counsel on how to go about single parenting.

Draw up a support system

Always secure this first! As a single parent, there will be occasions when you are not around the child to attend to it personally. A support system is an absolute must to allow a parent peace of mind. Your child needs to be kept safe while you are not around. So, your first challenge should be to build a support system that provides the necessary child care in your absence. This can be in the form of a daycare centre or a many hired for part or full time for her services. This is the easy part. But more importantly, for emergencies, you need a practical three-layered support system: immediate neighbours, friends, and family.

It is ideal to be less than two kilometres away from your nearest good friend. Friends can be most helpful in emergencies; you can always count on them for anything. And the ultimate safety net is family: siblings and parents. You have to be upfront with them, so you can use their support. Anyone planning to be a solo or a single parent must first think of this support system in case of emergency. Like seat belts, while driving a car, this support system is the first thing you need to secure before you begin your single parenting journey.

Setup a daily routine

'The secret of your future is hidden in your daily routine.' – Mike Murdock.

My next job is to understand and set a daily routine. A daily sound sleep of 7-8 hours has to be made sacrosanct if you have to function optimally through the day. So, sleep has to be protected and routinised. Once you secured the sleep hours, you could build the day using the rest of the hours. Apply the Pareto principle of 80/20 to the day. That 20% of items/tasks, which cover 80% of the 16 hours, should be routinised and converted to a simple schedule.

For example, your morning routine, children's school, office, children's tuition and sports coaching, evening snack/glass of milk or evening play with friends and your business calls together could make 12 hours of solid, fixed daily routine. Add to that an hour of dinner & sleep routine, and we have effectively used over 80% of the available 16 hours.

The rest can stay flexible- where you could use the time for driving out to friends, the bookstore, the temple, birthdays, or dinner- keeping it completely flexible. A weekly plan like this helps a lot. As far as possible, keep the weekends completely flexible and use your creativity to design them and spend some quality time together with your children and with friends.

Quality time routines

In many countries, the amount of time parents spend with their kids has been increasing over the last 50 years, despite significant changes in family structure. Single-parenting and women working outside the home have only increased over the years, yet parents spend, on average more time with children each week. Looking carefully at the time parents spend with their kids and the forces that shape this time helps us understand an essential aspect of family life and childhood development.

In 2016, two researchers, Guilia M. Dotti Sani & Judith Treas, published a study in the Journal of Marriage & Family that studied how much time parents spend with their children daily. This study was performed across developing and developed countries in America and Europe. They measured the childcare time in minutes per week. They measured the average change in the daily childcare time from 1965 to 2012 and found that across the board, the childcare time had gone up by almost 400% both in the case of men and women parents. (the only exception was France, where the average childcare time has gone down). In 1965 the average parent spent about 30 minutes per week on child care, while in 2012, the average parent spent about 150 minutes per week.

Based on these statistics, assuming you spend 150 minutes per week with our children in childcare, it amounts to 22 minutes per day. Do you think it is enough? It is best to ask the child. Even if you think it is enough, ask yourself whether you would call it quality time.

Once, when I travelled abroad for over a week on work, I realised how much I missed spending quality time with family, and it got me thinking. I asked myself, 'do I spend quality time with loved ones? Do I understand clearly what quality time means?' This chain of thought led me to explore what quality time meant and how I could incorporate it into my parenting routine.

So, what is quality time? Here is my favourite interpretation. Oxford dictionary defines *quality time* as time in which one's child, partner, or other loved person receives one's undivided attention in such a way as to strengthen the relationship. There are two important criteria to determine whether the time you spent with your loved one was quality time:

1. Did you provide undivided attention to your loved one?
2. Did you deepen the relationship in the process?

Given the digitally distracted world, undivided attention is clearly the scarcest resource we have. The only way we can achieve that is by setting aside dedicated time as 'quality time' This is the time slot of your day or week where you keep away your phones, iPads and TV and engage with your loved ones with all your attention.

So, I realised I needed to spend more time with my daughter, Aanya and needed a healthy routine. And this is the routine I came up with:

1. Post-school catchup (15 min): an informal chat with Aanya to understand her day, what she learnt, what the highlights were and so on.

2. Evening badminton (30 min.): This can be an excellent outdoor engagement where we can learn and, at the same time, spend some quality time together.
3. Homework time (30 min): helping Aanya with her homework and using the time to teach and talk about new things.
4. Post-dinner walk (15 min): The late evenings are pleasant, and a walk with Aanya and chatting with her informally about life sounds like a great idea.

This routine was perfect, and it felt fulfilling when I followed it. I could never make every day perfect, but many for sure. It beats the 22-minute global average, hands down, any day! Weekends, as I have already said, could be more creative. But remember, the idea is to spend quality time together, which can be fun, informal, and a great learning & sharing experience.

FORTY-FOUR

OUTGROWING THE PARENTING INSTINCT

———•ᗡ•———

Children come through us; they do not belong to us

A century ago, in a war-torn world, the Lebanese-American poet, painter, and philosopher Kahlil Gibran wrote *The Prophet* in 1923. In that poem, there is an instance where a young mother with a newborn baby asks for advice on children and parenting. So naturally, the poetic prophet responds to her.

> "*And a woman who held a babe against her bosom said,*
> *Speak to us of Children. And he said:*
> *Your children are not your children.*
> *They are the sons and daughters of life's longing for itself.*
> *They come through you but not from you,*
> *And though they are with you yet, they belong not to you.* "

Birthing a child can feel like playing God. Parents feel that they have created life, a true miracle. Parents feel proud that *they* brought their children into this world. Mothers take pride in carrying children in their wombs for months, while fathers take pride in their contribution as breadwinners and protectors of the family. True roles were played, but the fact remains that children happen to parents. Post-conception, it's an automatic process – all we do is take care of ourselves. It seems like a trivial and commonsensical fact, but it has profound implications. It means that children are, by and large, an act of nature where we, parents, have an instrumental role. We don't know how to choose a child's intelligence, traits, features, or complexion. We bring them into this world. They are nature's gifts to us, an expression of nature's longing to propagate herself. We are asked by nature to parent the child while it needs it. We provide our home's environment, the warmth of our love, and the nutrients of virtues, allowing them to grow. While they remain with us, we serve as their custodians, not owners. They will be masters of their destinies, with the same choices once available to us. We only provide for them and do not control what they become. Choosing a profession, friends, partners or whether to love you back will be solely their decision.

Outgrowing the parenting instinct

One of human life's greatest joys is to become a parent. The sheer happiness of holding your child first time in your hand is magical and indescribable. Anyone who has experienced this will vouch for me on this. Even the mere sight of watching a parent with a child brings so many emotions. Any behaviour from either or both parents that help their offspring survive can be grouped under parental care. A parent holds the child to her bosom, nurses it, and cuddles it. A parent also closely watches over it, protects it, and keeps it comfortable and warm. As the child grows older, the parents try to educate the child, discipline it, and provide for it through its physical, emotional and mental ups and downs.

However, parenting behaviour or Parental care is not unique to humans. In many birds, parental care includes building a nest and feeding the young. Parental care takes the longest time and is the most complex in mammals, which always involves the mother feeding milk to the young, besides holding the child close, warm, and away from danger. Parental care in mammals may also include teaching the young essential skills they will need when they are older and no longer cared for by their parents. For example, meerkat adults instruct their pups how to eat scorpions. They show the pups how to handle poisonous insects safely and remove the stingers.

Conversely, most fish species release the sperm and the eggs in the water, forget about them and let nature do the rest. In multiple ape species, you will also find parental care is provided not just by parents but also by social groups that they live in. The drive to mate and have offspring is not unique to humans, nor is the drive to provide parental care- it is purely out of instinct. The drive is not chosen by independent free will or what we more popularly call love. We carry the instinct for it. An instinct is an innate, typically fixed pattern of animal behaviour in response to certain stimuli.

Let's pause for two questions: Is human parenting behaviour driven by love or instinct? Does it make a difference whether we see it as love or instinct? I think it does. Most psychological problems from adult parenting can be attributed to a lack of understanding or clarity. First and foremost, let us acknowledge that there is nothing wrong or embarrassing in acknowledging that childrearing behaviour is an instinct hardwired in humans. It serves a specific larger evolutionary purpose – of ensuring that our genes are passed on successfully further in time.

Human parenting differs from animal parenting because humans have high expectations from the recipient of the parenting behaviour. We set expectations for our children during childhood, adolescence, teens, and adulthood. We identify with their successes and disappointments. If they do well in life, our hearts swell in pride; if they don't, we shrink in embarrassment. Many parents in India expect their children to care for them in their old age, while children expect their parents to support them in their projects. As a result, both suffer anxiety and despair in the name of love. We do not say that this parenting behaviour is an instinct and instead believe that it is a higher form of the human pursuit of pure love. What we call love is just binding attachment – attachment to the returns one expects from investment in parenting. It is instinct taken to its extremes, causing unease or distress, jealousy, anger, depression, fear, anxiety, and regret too often, resulting in inappropriate behaviour and sorrow. All such unfortunate responses leave a residue of unfinished business that perpetuates the cycle of emotionally driven problems known. This cycle is never-ending until broken by correct knowledge of oneself and the world.

Irrespective of whether we acknowledge it, we are all driven by instinct – for survival, for seeking safety and nourishment, for seeking a mate and to birth and care for offspring. There is nothing wrong with it. What makes humans unique is we can outgrow our instincts. Unlike animals chained to their instincts, we can surf on our waves of instinct to find peace, harmony, and freedom.

The ancient Indian vision of Vedanta shows us a similar path. We can use our instincts and channel them with the help of Karmayoga into the pursuit of the ultimate freedom, Moksha. In Karmayoga, behaviour is aligned with reason, long-term interests, and ethical laws. Karmayoga brings self-

THINK BETTER AND THRIVE

regulation, moderation, balance, and purpose to our instinctual behaviours. The path of Vedanta is not a path of fighting our instincts but using them as material to build a raft that can take us across the sea of Samsara. This way of life purifies the mind in preparation for self-knowledge - it entails mastering one's emotions and ways of thinking, including giving up personal biases, attachments and aversions. It teaches us what love is not- that it is not an instinct, it is not an attachment, it is not fear of loss, it is not a passion, it is not a conditional transaction, it is not binding. Then what is it?

Parenting is a responsibility, duty, and preparatory stage that one undertakes for one's spiritual growth and finding one's peace and freedom without binding oneself with expectations, while at the same time setting an example to the child of how it's accomplished. When it is needed, step in and do your job but also understand when your duties are fulfilled and it is time to move forward. That is one instinct we do not quickly get from our animal nature.

One of my friends and guides is Harold Justice, a retired simulation engineer and rocket scientist. He has achieved what many of us are setting sail to achieve. He and his wife raised three children to have master's degrees. Between their three children, they have eight grandkids. Some of his grandkids have already finished college. On parenting, Harold jokingly advises,

> "The role of a parent is to get rid of their kids. By that, I mean you rear them by properly teaching them to become more and more independent, helping them get a great education that provides them with the tools to move out and establish their own household."

I take Harold's experience-distilled wisdom and counsel to heart, together with his sprinkle of humour. So the key takeaway here is that we need to learn to let go when it is time and continue our voyage towards self-understanding, emotional independence and enlightenment. Parenting requires you to understand while being understood, to listen while being listened to; to counsel, to coach, to mentor, to play, to laugh and cry, to nourish, support, invest; to share, trust, respect, and finally, to set the children free.

 charmsoms

SPIRITUALITY: Discover Your True Self

FORTY-FIVE

THERE IS NO DIFFERENT SPIRITUAL WORLD

———◦♌◦———

Spiritual life is like the process of cleaning a mirror. Most spiritual activities are meant to undo the conditionings, habits, dependencies, beliefs and biases that block us from seeing the truth. As you progress on the spiritual path, the mirror becomes more reflective, clear and truthful. One of the biggest impediments to spiritual progress is the belief that we work for an afterlife. We treat this life as a preparation to gather enough fortune and goodwill to get us entry into a spiritual world after death. The belief that ultimate happiness and freedom lie elsewhere in another realm is a mental model we need to break away from. This will help us understand spirituality better too.

Many religions ultimately try to address the problem of happiness & freedom. They do so by getting you to work towards living the life of a lawful, god-fearing member of society so that you can reap the reward of happiness in an afterlife in a supernatural world not accessible to us as humans today. On the other end, you have the psychic cults that manipulate your brains by ingesting psychedelic substances that promise to open the doors to higher worlds. Alcoholics, drug addicts, and rave party followers all belong to these cults – with differences being in the way and the extent to which they can manipulate your brains. Many of us today believe that salvation or nirvana or svarga or heaven or moksha lies utterly beyond our present life, and this life of earth is merely a preparation to earn the tickets to that place.

Now spirituality also belongs to the category of religions & psychic cults in the sense that it is also trying to solve the same problems, viz., happiness and freedom. But what makes spirituality different is that it talks or promises of no spiritual world or kingdom or realm outside of the world we are living in, the planet we are living on today. Spirituality aims to solve the problem of happiness and freedom in our here-and-now world. It doesn't try to move you from one world to another or one set of senses to another. Instead, it tries to teach you, from experience, skills to live happily, freeing you from emotional bondage. It teaches you that every experience is a spiritual experience – only if we look at it the right way. On the outside, a profoundly spiritual person may appear to live life and fulfil responsibilities just like any other person, but they experience life differently. They share a union with others and this universe like no other.

Alan Watts best describes what spirituality is.

> "It is a deep sense of freedom based on the realisation that one's self is in complete union and harmony with life, God, the Self of the Universe, or whatever that principle may be called. It is the realisation that union has existed for all time, even though one did not know it, and that nothing in all the world nor anything that one can do can destroy it. So it is that the whole might of the universe is at work in one's every thought and action, however trivial and small. In fact, that is true of all men and all things, but only the spiritual man knows it and his realisation gives a subtly different quality to his life.."

And that is why there is no different spiritual world. We are already in it and will always be. This foundational truth must be understood before you begin on any spiritual path.

Everyone belongs to some religion or the other - a religion one subscribes to or simply the faith in which one is raised. Religion influences a majority of people in some way or the other. But only some take to spirituality. The next chapter discussed how you could move up from religion to spirituality.

ᑭᑭᑭ

FORTY-SIX

MOVING FROM RELIGION TO SPIRITUALITY

———•♭•———

As travel opened up after the pandemic, millions of people in India, like in other countries, have thronged tourist destinations. Most of us have experienced the difference between hiring a tour agency to plan our itinerary and the effort it takes to plan a travel on our own. The former is the easiest way to travel: you don't have to take any pains in choosing hotels, plan your day and meals, or arrange for travel or taxis. No thinking is involved. Just pay, sit back and enjoy the vacation. Whereas the latter takes a lot of effort, deliberation and careful decision-making. It also involves taking risks or allowing something to not go as per plan. The former will enable us to rely on the guide to translate the local menu, to learn about the importance of places you visit and to interpret the culture. In contrast, the latter involves making an effort to carefully decode the local signs, gestures, laws, maps, people, food menu, culture and so on.

As travel preferences have changed from backpacking to buying package tours, so have the ways of religion changed. Today, being spiritual or primarily religious means subscribing to a tour agency or a religious organisation and delegating your spiritual journey to them. Each religious outfit follows its branding, flags, values, dress code, customs and tour packages and caters to a specific demographic like youth, upper-middle-class, senior citizens, or the emerging middle class. They tailor everything to their target market's taste, keeping customer experience and comfort in mind.

In both scenarios, one has undertaken a journey, but who has experienced the real country, culture, and people? Who has merely experienced a curated, filtered, translated, manipulated version of reality? Who has a firsthand experience of the natural world?

Today's world largely follows a theocentric religion: someone creates an image of God, ascribes laws, attributes and expectations, and coaxes the world to follow it. While spirituality is humanistic - centred around the individual, any individual; it is centred on you. It's about finding out what it really means to be human, how we suffer and how we can find freedom- irrespective of our significant religion, tribe, caste or race. It is scientific – hence it is uniting in nature, takes people from all walks of life into its stride and shares a universal message. Like any theocentric religion, it is not centred on subjective beliefs that cannot be validated, proven or tested. *Spirituality is about seeking the divine in the human, not human in the divine. And it would help if you did the necessary hard work. You can't simply delegate it or buy your way.*

When applied to daily living, it is about choosing to do what is right in any situation over everything else. It moves us to perform our duty in any station of life – as a student, as a son/daughter, as a parent or spouse, as an employee or employer- with one's utmost devotion. This is the highest form of worship. Spirituality is not about giving up responsibilities, obligations and roles; instead, it teaches the importance and skill of owning them up without getting attached to them. It teaches us to objectively see our human life and its strife and gifts, to celebrate the godly in each of us and keep the demoniac in check. It teaches us to navigate the rough seas of life with courage and clarity, not to escape and flee from it.

Spirituality means embarking on a journey that starts with mastering the body-mind-sense complex and takes us towards preparation for inquiry into the nature of our self, our true nature because this alone leads to freedom. Spirituality is the science of freedom; freedom from being this limited, incomplete and wanting person. It shows us the path that leads to our ultimate well-being and also to our greatest accomplishment.

Interestingly, religion comes from the Latin word Religare which means 'to bind'. Spirituality aims at the contrary, not to bind us but to unbind us, untie our minds and intellect, and free us. Being spiritual is to seek freedom from our vicious cycles.

Seek to be mentored by the realised teachers. Learn about the life journeys of recognised men and women. Be relentless in your quest. The truth is One. It is not sectarian, communal or property of any creed or religion. It is universal. It is in You. It is You.

All spiritual processes are ways of recognising misconceptions in life and discarding them one by one by deliberate practice. The next chapter presents three such great misconceptions.

ᑭᑭᑭ

FORTY-SEVEN

THE THREE GREAT MISCONCEPTIONS

———•ᴘ•———

The great Zen Master Thich Nhat Hanh recently passed away at the ripe age of 95 at the Từ Hiếu Temple in Huế, Vietnam. Although I am a student of Vedanta, I have learnt a lot from this great master. If I have come across an enlightened Buddha, it is this great teacher. Teachers like Thich Nhat Hanh never die. He lived by example; his message is his life itself. His teachings will always live on in his students; he lives on in me.

I am especially reminded of his book 'The Art of Living, which came to me as grace when I needed it the most. It was a time when I had strayed from all things spiritual, turned into a sceptic, and saw purposelessness everywhere, and the pangs of existential angst bit me each day.

One day when I was drifting aimlessly among Amazon's audible library, for some reason, this book caught my attention, and without knowing, I started already listening to it. And there he has, Thich Nhat Hanh, in all his kindness, just pouring his rich life wisdom onto this arid desert of my mind, desperately looking for a single dark cloud. He wasted no time and started addressing my pain right from the introductory chapter. He diagnosed what was bothering me most and articulated it beautifully as the three most fundamentally wrong views that lie at the base of our suffering. In this note, I will quote these three wrong views from his book as I cannot explain them any better.

"*The first wrong view we need to liberate ourselves from is the idea that we are a separate self, cut off from the rest of the world. We tend to have an individual self that is born at one moment and must die at another, which is permanent when we are alive.*

As long as we have this wrong view, we will suffer; we will create suffering for those around us, and we will cause harm to other species and to our precious planet.

The second wrong view that many of us hold is that we are only this body and that we cease to exist when we die. This wrong view blinds us to how we are interconnected with the world around us and how we continue after death.

The third wrong view that many of us have is that what we are looking for–happiness, heaven, or love–can be found only outside us in the distant future. As a result, we may spend our lives chasing after and waiting for these things, not realising they can be found within us right in the present moment."

These three wrong views lay the foundation of my existential angst. Thich Nhat Hanh immediately prescribes three excellent practices to alleviate this suffering, which is discussed in detail in the rest of the book. I was cured of this suffering by reading this book and could see hope again. This launched me onto my spiritual path again, and I have never looked back. The light of wisdom he lit in me burns brightly to this day. If you too can relate to these three views, I recommend this audiobook or the book to you, whichever you prefer best. There are many more books where he has poured his compassion and wisdom, which I recommend to you.

The goal of any spiritual journey is self-discovery, culminating in the realisation that one is whole and complete. The next chapter discusses this goal; that you are full and enough.

ᑭᑭᑭ

FORTY-EIGHT
YOU ARE WHOLE

Our whole endeavour in this lifetime is about trying to complete ourselves. This feeling that I am incomplete and I need something other than myself to complete me is at the foundation of our lives, economy and aspirations. Everything we wish to possess, own, and experience originates from this yearning. I fully acknowledge the power of this feeling and how it propels us to progress towards setting and achieving higher and higher goals, bettering our standard of living and giving our loved ones a life of options and security. I also understand that life would almost be impossible without this 'seeking' attitude.

At the same time, I also remind myself often that this seeking is essentially spiritual. Our ultimate goal is to become complete, whole, and at peace with ourselves. That destination is the grandest aspiration and goal one can have, and one should eventually grow to have one. Finding a mind of contentment, free of anxiety and emotional dependence and so on are only some of the milestones on this grand journey. This destination is very much within our reach. Let it be the north star of our spiritual voyage.

The great contemporary teacher of meditation, Eckhart Tolle, said

"You are not separate from the whole. You are one with the sun, the earth, and the air. You don't have a life. You are life."

Be a great student, son/daughter, husband/wife, professional, leader, a great human being, traveller, adventurer and great grandparent. Don as many roles as you are inspired to but remember why we embarked on this journey in the first place- to feel complete, to become whole. Even in old age, it will be a pity if we do not realise this purpose. To die without knowing what would complete you has been within you all along would be a pity.

To realise that we are much more than this limited self with needs and desires. My favourite philosopher and mystic, Alan Wilson Watts, said

> "It's not true that you came into this world. You came out of it in the same way a flower comes out of a plant, or a fruit comes out of a tree. An apple tree apples, the solar system peoples...You are a function of this total galaxy. ...
>
> ......it does not occur to the ordinary person to regard himself or herself as an expression of the whole universe. It should be obvious that we cannot exist except in an environment of air, earth, water and solar temperature, that all these things go with us and are as important to us as our internal organs such as our heart, brain, stomach and so forth."

We are the universe experiencing itself as a human. Most people don't realise they are an expression of this grand universe. I urge everyone not to neglect and brush aside their spiritual side. Instead, nourish it, pray that you become this whole again, and indeed a path, your path, will light up and show you the way.

The great Christian Mystic Meister Eckhart said,

> "The eye through which I see God is the same eye through which God sees me. My eye and God's eye are one eye, one seeing, one knowing, one love."

You are the universe. You are whole. The universe is writing this chapter, and the universe is reading it.

Spiritual growth is the maturity of understanding. It is not collecting spiritual axioms and truths. It is not the accumulation of specific knowledge but rather a profound understanding of them. The next chapter presents a mental model of different levels of understanding.

ᑭᑭᑭ

FORTY-NINE
TRUE UNDERSTANDING

———•ᘉ•———

What do we mean when we say 'I understand' – in a relationship, in business, in academics, in seeking to know ourselves?

In their book, Understanding by Design (1998), Grant Wiggins and Jay McTighe discuss "Six Facets of Understanding." They came up with these six facets of understanding to help instructional designers check if students deeply understand the idea or concept being taught. In addition, the authors provide a framework that systematically addresses the six levels of understanding. This is the best explanation of what it means to understand something.

Wiggins and McTighe suggest that when a person truly understands something, they can do six things: explain it, interpret it, apply it, have perspective, empathise, and finally, have self-knowledge.

Each of the six facets demonstrates a certain level or degree of understanding. However, one can also see the six facets as different ways of demonstrating understanding.

Most of us who aim to understand something browse online and read about it and may even take notes. Some even discuss it or reflect on it. Memorise it. Most of the 'understanding' endeavours end there. Is this truly enough to develop a deeper and more mature understanding?

A complete and mature understanding ideally involves fully developing all six kinds of understanding. Let us look at each in some more detail:

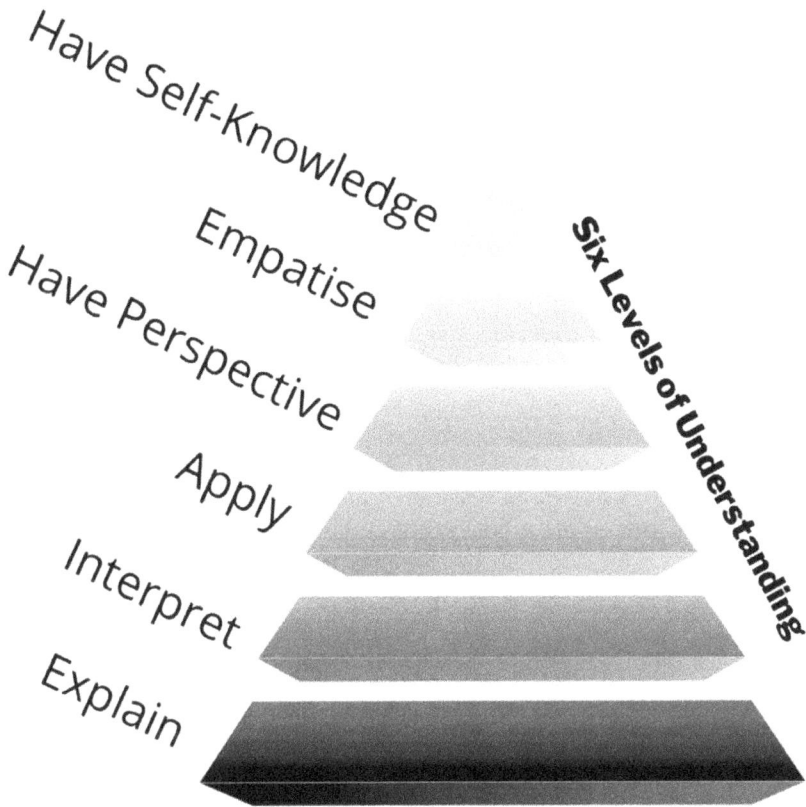

Wiggins & Tighe's Six Facets of Understanding

1. *Explain:*

You can provide well-articulated explanations or theories to expand upon events, actions, and ideas at this first level. In addition, you can provide thorough and justifiable accounts of phenomena, facts, and data.

2. *Interpret*

You can identify meaning in what you have learned through interpretations, narratives, and translations at this level. You can relate it to your life and things happening around you. You can tell meaningful stories, offer apt translations, and provide a revealing historical or personal dimension to ideas and events. Furthermore, you can make it unique or accessible through images, anecdotes, analogies, and models.

3. Apply

At this level, you can demonstrate the ability to adapt effectively whatever you have learned by using the knowledge in new situations and contexts. You can take what you know and use it in everyday life.

4. Have perspective

At this level, you can identify various critical and insightful points of view. You can answer questions like 'Of what value is this idea?', 'How important is this idea?', 'What does this idea enable or empower us to do/achieve/ overcome?'. You can now see and hear viewpoints through critical eyes and ears and understand something from more than your own perspective. You are also able to see the big picture.

5. Empathize

At this level, you can get inside another person's feelings. You can see the world from different viewpoints. This allows you to also appreciate the diversity in thoughts and feelings worldwide. You can find value in what others might find odd, alien, or implausible. You can perceive sensitively based on prior indirect experience.

6. Have self-knowledge

At this final level, you can demonstrate wisdom in knowing how your own personal style, prejudices, projections, and habits of mind, both shape and impede your understanding. You know what you do not understand and why understanding is so hard. You can see the boundaries between your own understanding and that of others. You can see the difference between your own perspective and that of others. All understanding ultimately culminates into self-knowledge. One exhibits true integrity and is willing to act based on what one understands.

This is what it means to truly understand- to rise through all the six facets of understanding. You can clearly see that it is not an easy task, a process, and it may take years of focus, study and practice to intimately get it.

Be it any topic contained within the vast libraries of neuroscience, physics, Vedanta, psychology, mathematics, language, etc. We cannot learn everything about everything. We can only understand some things in depth. Life is short. Think about what matters most to you, what you must deeply understand in this lifetime and then raise your understanding through this. This is helpful even to parents who want to build a good understanding of concepts and values in their young ones. And this mental model also applies to spiritual understanding. Use this model to measure your spiritual understanding.

Understanding goes deeper than data, information, or even gathered wisdom. It is where humanity's most significant potential and glory come from. And it is also life's greatest gift. That is why Leonardo Da Vinci said, 'The noblest pleasure is the joy of Understanding.'

Armed with clarity on the levels of understanding, you can now try to understand where you lose most of your mental and emotional energy. The following chapter discusses the meaning of vicious circles, how to identify them and, through proper understanding, free ourselves from them.

FIFTY

YOUR VICIOUS CIRCLES

---•〇•---

A vicious cycle is a sequence of repeating cause and effect in which two or more elements intensify and aggravate each other, inevitably worsening the situation for you. A vicious circle is punishing, painful, frustrating and hopeless. Here is a simple example of how it is used in daily usage: "debtors were caught in a vicious circle: they could not be freed until they had paid their debt and were not able to pay their debt as long as they were in prison". A vicious cycle can also mean falling victim to the same thought and behaviour patterns. For example, desiring can become a vicious cycle when that which you have, seems insufficient and that which you don't, you long for again and again. Even relationships can become a vicious cycle - you have conflicts with those near you, and you start missing the same people when they leave or when they are away.

The vicious cycle theory finds use in economics too. For example, according to the principle of vicious circle, in under-developed countries, the income level remains low, leading to a low level of saving and investment. Low investment leads to low productivity, which again leads to low income. The same can be applied to a poor man: He does not get enough food, which makes him weak. As a result of weakness, his efficiency reduces; therefore, he gets a lower income and thus becomes poorer or remains poor. It is like trying to be debt-free by paying one credit card bill using another credit card.

Another example is the air conditioning paradox: How do we cool people without heating up the planet? The world is now 1.1 degrees Celsius or 2 degrees Fahrenheit — warmer on average than it was at the dawn of the Industrial Revolution. The earth will only heat more, rendering parts of the world unlivable.

A vicious cycle is a situation in which an attempt to resolve one problem creates new problems that lead back to the original position. It is also defined and applied in the medical field. A condition in which a disorder or disease gives rise to another disease or disorder, which in turn affects the first and makes it worse. For example, the fatter I get, the unhappier I am, so I eat to cheer myself up, which makes me put on more fat—it's a vicious circle. Pleasure requires us to go through pain, and then comes insecurity and fear from holding on to pleasure, requiring us to exert further to invest more.

This expression 'vicious circle' comes from the French *Cercle Vicieux*, which in philosophy means "a circular proof"—that is, the proof of one statement depends on a second statement, whose proof, in turn, depends on the first. It also finds definitions and applications in the field of psychology. For example, in psychology, a vicious circle is a situation or behavioural pattern in which an individual's or group's problems become increasingly difficult because of a tendency to address or ignore them repetitively through unhealthy defensive reactions that compound them. If we are to believe that the root cause of most problems we face in this world is psychological, then this is a helpful definition.

We all think that changing things like a partner, a friend, a boss, a car, a job, or a home can bring us lasting happiness. But, whatever we call a change, upgrade, promotion, growth, or even prosperity is notional. It doesn't work that way. You only change the name and form of your dissatisfaction, suffering and insecurity. It only makes life more complicated and continues, one generation after another. Irrespective of whether it's a king or a pauper, the essential equipment each has, his body and his emotional setup are similar. Whether our longing, suffering or insecurity is physical, intellectual, or mental, it is still emotionally experienced. And it seems no one can escape this situation; it seems impossible.

Identifying your vicious cycles. Be mindful of not falling into their trap. Instead, seek to be free of them. That is the ultimate freedom.

Spirituality is about asking profound questions. One such profound question that has baffled spiritual seekers for millennia is, 'what is the meaning of life?' Unless we find the meaning of our living, living is incomplete. So, next, let us discuss what it means to find the meaning of life.

ᗁᗁᗁ

FIFTY-ONE

THE MEANING OF FINDING MEANING IN LIFE.

Many people drift aimlessly through life or keep changing their goals, running around chasing whatever they choose to call happiness. While some others live the life that their parents or their religion/caste/creed/cult or spouses have in mind for them. One finds ultimate fulfilment in life when one has a deep sense of living meaningfully. Before we begin, let us understand the difference between the meaning *of* life and meaning *in* life.

When we look at the stars and wonder where they all came from, we ask about life's meaning. When a tragedy strikes us, like when someone we love leaves us or bad things happen to a good person, and we wonder why such a thing could happen, we ask about life's meaning. Meaning *of* life is about the big questions, the answers to which we must take on faith or inference.

Whereas meaning *in* life is about what makes our own personal lives worth living. It is answerable, liveable, can help us find solutions to problems we face now, and expresses what we wish we could do in our lifetimes. Whether or not there is any meaning in life, we can always strive to create meaning *in* our lives.

Leading experts on meaning in life, psychologists Frank Martela and Michael F. Steger, in The Journal of Positive Psychology in 2016, defined meaning as having three interrelated elements that contribute to having a sense of meaning in our lives. This definition is helpful because it highlights three central components of meaning:

1. Coherence – This is how one **'thinks'** of meaning in life, putting it together and making sense of it all. Finding coherence means feeling that we can make sense of our lives and how the parts fit together. It is the sense that one's life is characterised by predictability. It is an understanding of the world around us, how it works and how we fit into it.

This is an understanding that things happen in your life for a reason. That does not necessarily mean you can fit new developments into your narrative the moment they happen. Still, you usually can do so afterwards or you have faith that you eventually will. If one feels conflicted when one sees how meaning operates in one's life, then there is dissonance.

2. Significance – This is how one **'feels'** about the meaning in life in one's context. It is the feeling that we have inherent value. It is the degree to which a person believes their life has value, worth, and importance. It is the confidence that we can make a difference in some small or more significant ways and that life is worth living or fulfilling. To the world, you might just be one person, but to one person, you might just be the world. *This is how I feel when I see my daughter; I see my significance. This is the sense that your life matters. If you have high levels of significance, you are confident that the world would be a tiny bit—or perhaps a lot—poorer if you did not exist.*

3. Purpose – This is how meaning in life reflects one's **behaviour** and actions. It is to have a sense of direction in life and have personally important long-term aims or a higher purpose that drives us. The purpose might show up as our goals, but not necessarily. It could be more general, deeply felt intentions or values, such as being a good parent, friend, or romantic partner. Purpose can mean dedicating your time, attention and focus to helping others in your community or joining a cause that can improve the world. *The purpose is the belief that you are alive to do something. Think of purpose as your personal mission statement, such as "the purpose of my life is to share the secrets to happiness" or "I am here to spread love abundantly."*

One may ask how seeking happiness can be different from seeking meaning in life. Research by social psychologist Roy Baumeister and colleagues suggests that satisfying basic needs promotes happiness but not meaning. In contrast, linking a sense of self across your past, present, and future promotes meaning but not happiness.

Meaning and purpose in life have deep ties to our sense of identity, belonging, agency, worth, hope, and many other ways we feel OK in the world. On top of this, meaning helps us integrate all these individual domains into one coherent life experience. When this integrated sense of meaning is lost, we feel alienated from ourselves and the world around us and struggle to find why anything is worth investing in and striving for.

Understanding and Introspection for meaning in life in these three interrelated layers of coherence, significance, and purpose helps us better understand where we stand in our lives, where we have made progress and where we need to focus and work. I feel fortunate to have found meaning through my spiritual pursuit, which is nourished by a diet of these three necessary macro ingredients. At least I have taken the first steps on this fulfilling journey. To have meaning in life is to live fully, where your thoughts, feelings, and actions integrate fully. Integration is the key; they cannot simply be disconnected from each other. And yes, this meaning could be different for each of us, and it is an initiative and effort that each of us needs to take. We cannot live with borrowed or marketed meanings that we are surrounded with all day long. We must craft it ourselves, reflect on it, feel it, and live it. Only then can it be fully savoured.

With this framework of finding meaning in life, i.e. using coherence, significance and purpose, we can now ask the question, 'What is the function of a human being?'. The next chapter takes up this topic.

ᗕᗕᗕ

FIFTY-TWO

THE FUNCTION OF A HUMAN BEING

———❦———

human being =
f(universe)

"Yoga is the journey of the self, through the self, to the self."

The Bhagavad Gita

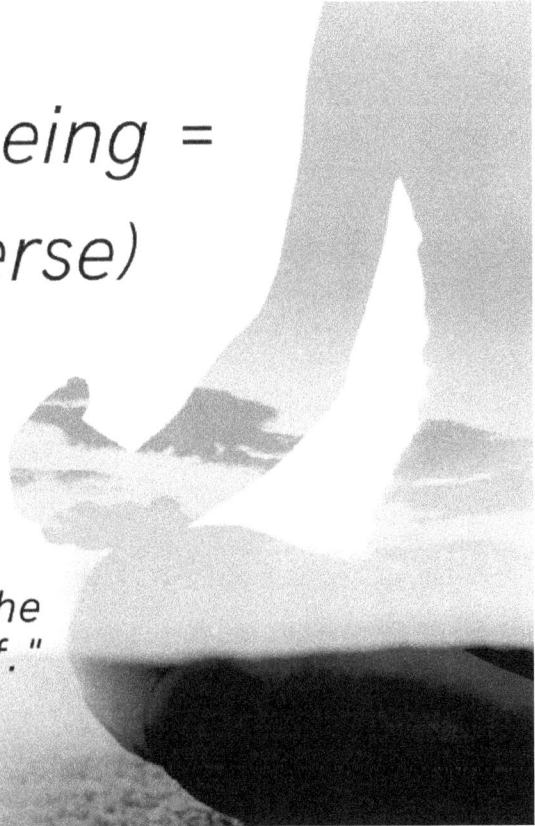

Quote from the Bhagavad Gita

We live in a functional world. For example, the heart's function is to pump blood, the function of the kidneys is to purify the blood, and the function of the lungs is to infuse the blood with oxygen. Even many inanimate objects have functions. For example, the function of a bridge is to enable people to cross from one point to another.

Can a human being also have an intrinsic function? What could be the larger purpose of a human being?

The dictionary reveals that the word 'function' means the kind of action or activity proper to a person, thing, or institution; the purpose for which something is designed or exists; role.

It is life's perennial question to find the purpose and meaning of our existence- to see the function of human life. On the surface, we are meant to only feed, multiply and thrive at the cost of this planet's resources. Is that all that life is all about? To get rich or die trying? To eat, drink and be merry? To serve our maker as the eternal servant. Or to Carpe Diem- seize the day: live for today and make the best of it.

Beingness is the quality, state, or condition of having existence. Beingness, in this sense, belongs to this entire existence, to the universe. Humanness qualifies being-ness, meaning it is like an adjective. Like there can be a specific animal being, tree being, or fish being. Each interacts with the world in a certain way and perceives the world in a certain way.

Similarly, being human also seems like a unique way in which the universe cognises itself, experiences and understands itself, all in the form of a human. Every 'being' is an expression, an act, a persona of this whole universe. And so being human means being whole, undivided, and complete. But at the same time, we humans are uniquely gifted to be self-conscious; we ask questions and seek answers. So then, to be human is to think, feel, and behave as a whole being.

1. To feel human is to relate and connect with other beings. To associate with others - to love, bond, collaborate, team, help, serve, care, parent and protect.

2. To behave humanly is to recognise and respect being-ness in ourselves, the world around us, nature, and our fellow beings. To act in a way as to not hurt ourselves or another.

3. To think humanly is to understand that you are whole; you are this universe cognising a limited aspect of itself.

Being human means embracing ourselves as a unique function of the universe- our flaws and perfections, all of them together. It requires us to acknowledge that the way we perceive the world is limited in many ways. Yet it is possible to understand and assimilate its wholeness.

The universal principles like truth, non-injury, fairness, and so on that many spiritual traditions prescribe for deliberate practice help us be in harmony with ourselves, fellow humans, and nature. Thus, it helps us feel, act, and think well, allowing us to create the inner space to take the next leap of understanding. An ethical life prepares us for the deep intuitive wisdom that frees us from our limited-ness, narrow-mindedness, biases, and frailties and nudges us in the direction of being whole again. It is a journey from the illusion that 'I am in this universe to the understanding that 'The Universe is in me'.

I have been mulling over 'the function of human beings for several weeks after it occurred to me, but I couldn't explain it until this chapter was written. This reinforces my faith in how truth is intuitive and self-revealing. We can only negate what is not true through inductive or deductive reasoning and arrive at the gate of truth. Beyond that, we need to let our intuition guide us and help us take the leap of understanding – the intuitive sense that we are all a function of this universe. So our function is to feel the connection with it, relate to our fellow beings, act in ways that recognise and respect this wholeness in others and finally to understand and realise that fullness in us, know that we are this universe.

The beating heart, the purifying kidneys and the infusing lungs are all aspects of what a human being does. Similarly, what a human being does is but a part, albeit the most critical part, of what the universe does- realising itself.

Spiritual exploration takes us beyond the limited self. It inches us towards an understanding of a higher self, a larger self, the universal self, or a transcendental self, as different spiritual traditions may call it. The next chapter discusses how we have become this global organism.

ᚦᚦᚦ

FIFTY-THREE

WE ARE A GLOBAL ORGANISM

In the science fiction of the 1920s, it was imagined that future humans would grow bigger brains to process more and more information and take more complex decisions and problem-solving. What happened was quite unforeseen. Instead of inflating our brains, we started building a gigantic digital nervous system outside ourselves. This makes the idea of individuality relative and notional: We are individuals to the extent that a finger is 'independent' in the body. It is more appropriate to use the word distinct than independent. It is more accurate to say that an individual is a distinct attribute of the global organism, not a separate entity.

Here are some examples that demonstrate how humans have become a global organism:

Utilities: A typical Indian middle-class home is connected to a larger grid of electricity, cooking gas, water, drainage, internet, telephone, cable tv and community maintenance. All are subscription-based, to be paid for each month and for normal day-to-day living, and are not optional. It is hard to imagine a life without any or all of these.

Communication: A typical middle-class family, for day-to-day communication and social networking, uses cell phones, emails, chats, video conferencing and discussion forums for communication. Life seems impossible, especially without cell phones today.

Work & Compensation: Most of our professional lives are conducted over laptops or cell phones or simply at workplaces which are gigantic organisms of steel, concrete, and network communications. Our money is digital and resides on the server of some bank; our own identity is digital and lives in the national citizen directory and on an office server.

Economy: Trade and commerce are global. In its annual report on global trade status, the World Trade Organization finds that the increasing interconnectedness of the world's economies is a double-edged sword. While this globalisation makes individual countries more vulnerable to short-term shocks, the WTO says, it also allows them to recover far more quickly than they would have in the past.

Relationships: Over the last decade, we have grown farther from our neighbours and our neighbourhood and started mingling with people we have no clue where they live and connect from. Long-distance relationships are commonplace, and we feel and communicate more with virtual strangers than real acquaintances. Even our self-identity and self-esteem depend on how social networks like Facebook, Instagram or LinkedIn evaluate us in their statistical reports.

It is clear from all these examples that we are no longer the individuals or communities we used to be fifty or a hundred years ago. Instead, we live in a highly interconnected world; we are just distinct parts of a global organism – subservient to it, where our individuality is notional. The dictionary defines an organism as an individual form of life, such as a plant, animal, bacterium, protist, or fungus; a body composed of organs, organelles, or other parts that work together to carry on the various processes of life. We are parts of a global organism.

As was imagined in the 20s, we did not grow larger brains. Instead, we develop a brain, a nervous system, outside us. This nervous system runs across our planet's towns, states, countries and continents. And we have become sensitive to the pains and pleasures that are felt thousands of miles away from where we live. Like the bacteria living in our gut have a distinct identity but not a separate existence, we humans have become distinct, not separate, aspects of this global organism. Peter Hesseldahl, in his book, Global Organism, describes this:

> "*It seems like humanity is shifting to a new phase in its evolution. We are no longer individuals, each struggling alone to survive the whims of nature. Increasingly, we're like one global organism, all connected and collectively developing ever more advanced technologies that enable us to transcend our original nature, becoming instead like we want us to be. We have become a new kind of creature; at one level, we are independent individuals – yet simultaneously, humanity behaves*

like a single system. Increasingly, we share the same fate, are mutually interdependent and aware of each other, and are weaving ourselves closer and tighter into this global community of humanity."

Now, where does this understanding leave us? There are two key takeaways. First, if we think we have become more independent and free because of all the technological progress, it's not true. We have become more dependent and at the mercy of our global ecosystem. I am not complaining but rather acknowledging this fact. The second takeaway concerns spirituality. If all of spirituality is considered a journey of self-discovery, then this discovery of our true self has become harder than it has been over the last centuries. Too many layers of conditionings and connections need to be understood, severed, resolved and reintegrated to realise the full glory of our true selves. The conflict between us and our world has grown deeper, and yet it is only apparent. We have grown seemingly insignificant, yet we can realise our fullness of being. Spiritual maturity is to recognise that what we call the "external world" is as much of us as our own body; our skin doesn't separate us from the world, it's a bridge through which the external world flows into us, and we pour into it. We were not born into this world but grew out of it like apples on a tree.

My favourite spiritual writer and philosopher, Alan Wilson Watts, said,

""Through our eyes, the universe is perceiving itself. Through our ears, the universe is listening to its harmonies. We are the witnesses through which the universe becomes conscious of its glory and magnificence."

That is our journey, voyage rather- to discover how the universe is experiencing itself through us.

The acid test of spiritual understanding and growth is how it transforms your attitude, thinking and behaviour in daily living. You cannot restrict spirituality to mental confines. It has to pour into your everyday living and shine in everything you believe, thinks and act, and this is the topic of our next chapter.

ᛈᛈᛈ

FIFTY-FOUR

DO THE RIGHT THING

―――――◆♭◆―――――

Choosing to do the right thing under any given circumstance is our best course of action against making errors and mistakes that may haunt us later. No one wants to live with guilt and regret over doing something that could have been entirely avoidable at a certain point in time. You can call it ethical living or Dharma. It is an attitude. This requires us to choose our actions based on possible consequences. At the same time, these actions need to be aligned and harmonious with the laws of nature. The choice of actions shouldn't create a conflict at any level of our being, physiological, psychological or social.

Of course, one can debate endlessly about what is right under a given circumstance, but the answer is straightforward most of the time. Under the circumstance, we may not understand what's right or even if we know it, it may be a challenging thing to do.

Here is an easy way of making choices in line with Dharma:

1. The action feels right to you at the present moment and is not influenced by your likes/dislikes.

2. The action feels like the one you may not regret in the future, even if things do not go as planned.

3. The action is in harmony with your life principles and values.

4. The action aligns with your responsibilities and assigned duties as a family member.

Acting ethically serves everyone the best – in the family, work or society. Your role as a son, daughter, parent, spouse, sibling, manager, boss, friend, and citizen comes along easily if you act in line with a set of universal ethics.

♭♭♭

FIFTY-FIVE

OUR JOURNEY TO FREEDOM AND INDEPENDENCE

Each of us is on a journey, and we are ultimately seeking freedom. Many call this our spiritual journey, which is unique for each of us.

Each of us seeks freedom in some form- physical, financial, artistic, and emotional. It is a journey to satisfy the core wanting person inside us. It is a journey to find completeness of being, to free ourselves of the constant wanting. To find a place of rest and fulfilment. Yet, while each of us is on this journey, very few realise that it is as much an inner journey as an external one.

So what is spirituality all about in day-to-day life? It all comes down to learning how we choose: in matters of love, work, health, parenting and play. Our spiritual development and maturity direct how we choose in life. To be spiritual is to 'know' before 'acting'- It is to know what is in one's best long-term interest and what serves only the short term. It is to see the difference between the lasting and the fleeting. In the language of Vedanta, it is to know the difference between *Shreyas*, which is ultimately good and *Preyas*, which is momentarily pleasurable. We can either seek freedom on the path of pleasure or on the way of good.

The path of pleasure may give you some sense of freedom, but it is illusory and binds you more than it liberates you. Sloth, vanity, hangovers, addiction, anger, restlessness, confusion, and frustration are only some of its effects. It is the flight of the moth towards the fire. It consumes you and burns you out. This path invariably ends in destruction.

The path of good lightens you at each step and brings freedom from despair. We know how that feels- like the feeling after a good workout, a job done well, being of help to someone in need, contributing to someone's welfare, eating right, having a good night's sleep, a silent retreat, solitude, and prayerfulness. A good act adds to your health, alertness, presence of mind, productivity, generosity, and resourcefulness. It does not just free you; it makes you independent.

The destination of ultimate freedom and independence, or *moksha* as Vedanta calls it, is real and within reach of each of us. And it comes by choosing to favour good at every step of life.

Bondage arises out of freedom.

All of us are striving for some form of freedom or another. It comes naturally to us. We make sacrifices and work hard, sometimes for years, to achieve a certain kind of freedom we seek. It could be emotional, financial, or space to live per one's values. What does not come naturally is to preserve what is hard-won. It just takes one decision to undo years of effort.

Our biggest folly is that we believe that our new decision does not guarantee that we will retain the freedom that allowed us to decide in the first place. Be it parenthood, a new career choice, starting a new business or taking a new responsibility, a new loan, or a new relationship. We take freedom for granted. When things are going well, we think of taking up newer projects. Then when they put the balance out of our life, we feel we have again lost our freedom and have become bound by our new circumstances. This begins a new journey of seeking freedom again. And thus, the cycle of freedom and bondage continues without an end. Never in our lifetime, having once found our freedom, do we rest and say this is it, that I have finally arrived. So let me hang on to this and enjoy this freedom.

Freedom has become a shifting goalpost, a mirage we have fallen in love with chasing without really learning how to live with it and keep it. So, we treat freedom just like money, simply as an end, without ever thinking it could be a means to something higher. People earn and lose freedom just like they make and lose money.

Striving for freedom takes focus and hard work, and each of us has this potential. But only some have the skill or knowledge to preserve and protect our hard-earned freedom. *Yoga* (freedom) + *Kshema* (preservation) is true well-being. Freedom alone, without the skill to keep it, is simply transitory. And so, one moves from one bondage to another with intermediate pauses of freedom.

So, the message here is that freedom alone can guarantee neither well-being nor happiness, and we need the skill to preserve hard-won freedom. How to protect freedom is a topic that needs space for discussion. It includes developing skills like self-awareness, value-based decision-making, resilience, emotional intelligence and, most importantly, clarity of one's life's purpose and ultimate goals. For now, it is sufficient to understand that bondage is chosen out of our freedom, and freedom alone is no guarantee of its protection and preservation.

The next chapter discusses a handy mental model to help us build spiritual intelligence.

ᗡᗡᗡ

FIFTY-SIX

BUILDING SPIRITUAL INTELLIGENCE

There is enough talk about the Intelligence Quotient (IQ) and Emotional Quotient (EQ) in academic and corporate circles today, with several ways of measuring, analysing and building one's intelligence in problem-solving and emotional management. The two are essential in a person's pursuit of security, happiness and values. But are these enough to describe our ability to sail through life successfully? Can we reach the apex of Maslow's pyramid, self-actualisation and self-transcendence, armed with these two?

I have wondered what kind of a person takes to a spiritual path. And if one takes a spiritual path, what kind of a person flourishes, spiritually progresses and grows?

At some point in our lives, we all have spiritual rendezvous where we ask questions we never asked before – about life's meaning, purpose or a higher self. For most of us, these events last a while and then pass like any other experience. But for some of us, this becomes a lifelong quest. People call this pursuit many names – Nirvana, Tawhid, Moksha, Perfection, Beatification and so on. I like to refer to it as the fourth pursuit.

Here I am exploring the intelligence that such a person has or needs to embark on the journey successfully. Many questions came to mind. That's when Lady Luck arranged my encounter with the work of Dabah Zohar, a physicist, philosopher, and management thought leader who has co-authored Spiritual Capital: Wealth we can live by.

She calls this third intelligence spiritual intelligence, built on the foundation of IQ and EQ. She defines spiritual intelligence as the power an individual or organisation can manifest based on their most profound meanings, values and purposes. She then goes on to enumerate the twelve principles that make it up:

Self-Awareness	Knowing what I believe in and value, and what deeply motivates me
Spontaneity	Living in and being responsive to the moment
Being Vision- and Value-Led	Acting from principles and deep beliefs, and living accordingly
Holism	Seeing larger patterns, relationships, and connections; having a sense of belonging
Compassion	Having the quality of "feeling-with" and deep empathy
Celebration of Diversity	Valuing other people for their differences, not despite them
Field Independence	Standing against the crowd and having one's own convictions
Humility	Having the sense of being a player in a larger drama, of one's true place in the world
Tendency to Ask Fundamental "Why?" Questions	Needing to understand things and get to the bottom of them
Ability to Reframe	Standing back from a situation/problem and seeing the bigger picture; seeing problems in a wider context
Positive Use of Adversity	Learning and growing from mistakes, setbacks, and suffering
Sense of Vocation	Feeling called upon to serve, to give something back

12 Principles of Spiritual Intelligence (Source: The Systems Thinker – Spiritual Intelligence: A New Paradigm for Collaborative Action - The Systems Thinker)

Turning to spirituality means seeing beyond our motivations to seek pleasure, security and values in the external world and instead choosing to dive within ourselves, withdrawing from external noise and finding that life's ultimate goal within.

These 12 principles can also serve us as a measure of our spiritual development or progress. So give each of these principles a thought and see how you can relate to them. Another SQ expert and coach, Cindy Wigglesworth, expanded on Danah's work and derived from these 12 principles the 21 skills of spiritual intelligence. She describes them in her book SQ21: twenty-one skills of spiritual intelligence. Based on whether the skill one employs between Self – Another, she divides them into four quadrants:

SQ21: 21 Skills of Spiritual Intelligence

	Self / self focused	Other focused
What You See - Inner World	**1. Self / self Awareness** 1. Awareness of own worldview 2. Awareness of Life Purpose (Mission) 3. Awareness of Values Hierarchy 4. Complexity of inner thought ★ 5. Awareness of Ego self/Higher Self	**2. Universal Awareness** 6. Awareness of interconnectedness of life ★ 7. Awareness of worldviews of others 8. Breadth of Time perception 9. Awareness of limitations / power of human perception 10. Awareness of Spiritual Laws 11. Experience of transcendent oneness
What Other People See – Outer World	**3. Self/self Mastery** 12. Commitment to spiritual growth ★ 13. Keeping Spirit Self in charge 14. Living your purpose and values 15. Sustaining faith 16. Seeking guidance from Spirit *Calm, peaceful at all times*	**4. Social Mastery/Spiritual Presence** 17. Wise and effective teacher / mentor 18. Wise and effective leader / change agent ★ 19. Makes Compassionate AND Wise decisions 20. A calming, healing presence 21. Being aligned with the ebb and flow of life *Compassionate and Wise Action*

21 Skills of Spiritual Intelligence

The best word for spirituality in the Indian wisdom tradition of Vedanta is yogaḥ, meaning joining of inner and outer world or simply absolute knowledge (wisdom). These 21 skills can be seen as the equivalent of Karma Yoga: practised deliberately to develop them as skills. When one understands the 12 principles that stand behind them, it is similar to Jnana yoga- the pursuit of wisdom, a way of developing the skill of higher understanding. When we look at the 12 principles, we can see that each can be acquired – by learning about them, asking clarifying questions, immersing ourselves in their meaning and finally spontaneously living by that understanding.

I can't help but see these parallels and how these ideas are universal- whether arrived at by empirical research or from time-tested traditions.

Living by these principles doesn't mean we stop pursuing pleasure, security and values. On the contrary, it means we see these pursuits in a new light as something that sets the stage for spirituality, an environment of the harmonious and healthy functioning of our minds, bodies, society and ecology. Living by principles allows those few among us who are ready to start their spiritual hike and climb to heights of higher taste, meaning, and purpose.

The most important question to ask ourselves is: Am I ready to start this journey of self-discovery or not?

ᗍᗍᗍ

FIFTY-SEVEN

BALANCING INNER AND OUTER PURSUIT OF WEALTH

———————◦♭◦———————

Who doesn't want to be wealthy? But what does being wealthy mean? Does it only mean acquiring money? What about peace of mind or a good night's sleep – is this wealth not worthy of pursuit? That's why it makes sense to differentiate between inner and outer wealth.

Inner wealth refers to contentment, well-being, health, inner freedom, peace of mind and tranquillity.

In the sacred Vedanta text, Bhagavad Gita (Song Divine), Krishna, the charioteer friend of Arjuna and spiritual master, differentiates between the wealth pursued by Devas (godly) and the wealth pursued by Asuras (demoniac). Spiritual wealth leads to freedom, while the wealth of an Asura leads to bondage. Before Krishna starts describing the wealth of Asura, he first assures Arjuna that he needs not to worry as he is blessed or born with spiritual wealth. I wish he could say the same about most of us.

Krishna continues that in this world, largely there are two types of beings, the divine and the worldly. The divine has also been discussed in Gita, but here I want to explore the part where Krishna describes the characteristics belonging to those of us with a worldly/ practical outlook. The worldly/ practical among us do not know what is to be done and what is to be withdrawn from. So worldly people go with what feels pleasing now without subjecting choices and decisions to any higher level of reasoning. So the worldly need not care for inner cleanliness, proper conduct, or

THINK BETTER AND THRIVE

truthfulness.

The worldly believe that this world is untruthful, without an ethical basis, basically Godless, and is born of blind evolution, where the fittest survive by recourse to any means, where ends justify means. Every achievement is driven by passion and will to survive and nothing else. As a natural consequence, the entire nature, including the other men, women and children, are seen as the 'other' who needs to be ruled over and exploited for profit. Nature needs to be exploited. Thinking becomes narrow and meagre, attitude dominating, and actions cruel. Soon they see no difference between their thriving and the destruction of nature.

Each has bucket lists, wish lists and dream lists with the least concern for the cost at which the items on the list get ticked off. There is no end to what they desire because they believe that if they *will* strongly, the entire universe will conspire to fulfil every wish of theirs. They seek purpose in living which has no foundation nor end goal. Moving from one wish to another, one project to next, one dream to next, they continue endlessly like deer searching for an oasis by chasing after a mirage.

With desires come possessions, and with possessions, fear of losing them. Life becomes a journey of immeasurable concern, anxiety and worry until death, intent upon only the enjoyment of objects of desire. Having concluded, 'This is all there is to Life,' committed to desire and anger and bound by hundreds of fetters of hope, they engage themselves in the accumulation of wealth which can fulfil all desires.

Today, I have achieved this. Tomorrow, I need to achieve that. Vacation plan, retirement plan, second income plan, career plan, fitness plan- one plan after another and some are running parallelly. All that is needed to put you on a chase is some teasing of your senses with a targeted advertisement, a mannequin in a shopping mall, or a billboard that defines what makes a real man or woman. One who has X wants 2X, and one who has 2X is planning for 4X.

Relationships are seen as consisting of friends and foes. Friends must be pleased, and foes conquered or destroyed. It is all about 'I' – I am the ruler; I am the enjoyer; I am successful, powerful, and happy. 'I have wealth. I was born into a very good family. There is no one quite like me. I will perform rituals. I will give. I will enjoy.'

Commitment to pleasure comes with marriage to pain. Even religion or charity becomes a means to an end, either for seeking social approval or an expression of social stature. They revel in their glory, filled with vanity, vain, pride and arrogance. This commitment to pleasure is a doorway to a painful and unfulfilled life, destroying a person. It fills a person with pangs of desire, anger, and greed. Once one is in their grip, there is hardly any escape.

Krishna says,

"*A man who is free from these three gates to darkness, Arjuna, follows what the ultimate good is. Because of that, he reaches the higher end. The one who, being impelled by binding desire, engages oneself casting away the injunctions of the sāstra, gains neither maturity nor happiness (here), much less a higher end.*"

After all the chasing, targeting, planning, and achieving – one remains the same wanting, incomplete, greedy person. Pursuing the worldly and the practical binds us tighter with every new desire. An asura is thus not an evil or immoral person but simply one caught in worldly pursuits.

The ancient Indian philosopher Nagarjuna described pleasure beautifully,

"*There is a pleasure when a sore is scratched, but to be without sores is more pleasurable still. There are pleasures in worldly desires, but to be without desires is still more pleasurable.*"

I want everyone to evaluate our lives and pursuits on this auspicious day. Ask yourself, 'Where am I going?' and where do I want to go? Life is short, even if one lives beyond the life expectancy of his country.

Those wary of worldly life can choose instead to pursue spiritual wealth, the one that frees, not binds. One can choose the divine life. Krishna discusses this in the early part of the 16th chapter of the Bhagavad Gita. Those who are interested to find out more can explore. I would leave you with the hope that our precious lives need not end in this worldly way. Seek divine grace, and your path will light up.

HAPPINESS: Where everything comes together

FIFTY-EIGHT

BETWEEN THE GOOD LIFE AND LIFE GOOD ENOUGH

How much is enough? Can we measure life simply by accumulated wealth? Can there be *good enough* good in our life? Edward Skidelsky and Robert Skidelsky attempted to answer these questions in their 2012 book *How Much is Enough: Money and the Good Life*. They proposed that the "Good Life consists in realising the "basic goods" (or ultimate goods or end-values). And they attempted to list these essential goods (with a note of caution that this may need to be more comprehensive). They are as follows:

Health

Health refers to the whole body functioning, the perfection of our animal nature. Health includes all things needed to sustain life or a reasonable life span but is by no means limited to them. As officially defined by the WHO, good health is complete physical, mental, and social well-being, not merely the absence of disease or infirmity.

Security

Having security means an individual's justified expectation that his life will continue in its accustomed course, undisturbed by war, crime, revolution, or significant social and economic upheavals. It's about conservations of what one already has in one's life. A secondary meaning includes fulfilling basic security needs like having a comfortable home, income for sustenance, decent savings, insurance coverage, etc.

Health. Security. Respect.
Autonomy. Harmony.
Friendship. Leisure.

The Good Life: Simplified

Respect

To respect someone indicates, by some formality or otherwise, that one regards his views and interests as worthy of consideration, as things not to be ignored or trampled on. Respect is a two-way street in all practical situations: giving respect gets you respect. Living a healthy social life with its mannerisms and ground rules wins us respect and accords the same to others.

Authentic Personality

By personality, it is meant the ability to frame and execute a plan of life reflective of one's tastes, temperament, and conception of the good. It means that you live freely as your genuine self. Being authentic requires a certain level of autonomy in life. Autonomy is hard to have if one is bound by things like mortgages which force one to work or live in a restricted manner. Personality, in this sense, can be closely associated with wealth —an individual's total assets minus their liabilities. Authenticity in living confers the freedom to pursue an autonomous life plan.

Harmony with Nature

This involves living with the resolution that humans are an inseparable part of nature and cannot damage it without severely hurting themselves. Harmony with nature is needed to balance the economic, social, and environmental needs of present and future generations.

Friendship

Friendship is a necessarily inadequate translation of the ancient Greek philia, a term encompassing all robust, affectionate relationships. A father, spouse, teacher, and workmate might all be "friends" in our sense. The stoic philosopher Seneca said that friendship caters to the basic need of being understood and understanding another. That makes it a basic 'good.'

Leisure

Leisure is something we do for its own sake, not for something else. This definition contrasts with contemporary use, where leisure is synonymous with relaxation or rest. But leisure is not just time off work but a special activity.

"What is this life if, full of care,
We have no time to stand and stare.
No time to stand beneath the boughs
And stare as long as sheep or cows."
— **W.H. Davies**, Common Joys and Other Poems

The book is important for a couple of reasons—first, its argument for the importance of identifying clear end "goods" beyond mere material wealth. Second, the good life is identifiable and universal.

Do you now understand how much is good enough for you?

ᐅᐅᐅ

FIFTY-NINE
THE SKILL OF HAPPINESS

———•♭•———

Happiness needs to be pursued, not simply desired.

In the ancient Indian Vedic tradition, happiness is described as 'purushartha', meaning 'pursuit', something we need to plan, budget and work for rather than something obtained by wishing for it.

The Vedic tradition talks of four Purusharthas or Pursuits (the word pursuit probably came from Purushartha): Kama (Pleasure or simply Fun), Artha (Security), Dharma (Values) and Moksha (Inner Peace and Freedom). The Kama includes all forms of sensual or intellectual pleasures like novelty, food, status, romance, music, adventure, and entertainment. Anything we do for fun or entertainment is Kama. Artha, includes health, wealth, home, belongingness, security, respect, and relationships. Dharma can be translated as universal values like equality, justice, charity, etc. Finally, Moksha is freedom from emotional suffering, dissatisfaction, craving, and vices. It means true inner peace and poise.

Indeed, all human strivings can be combined into these four pursuits. Happiness can then be seen as an evaluation of one's state of mind and life as an integration of the achievements resulting from these pursuits. It is not static and fixed in time but a rolling evaluation of all that one has achieved in one lifetime in terms of pleasures, securities, values, and freedom.

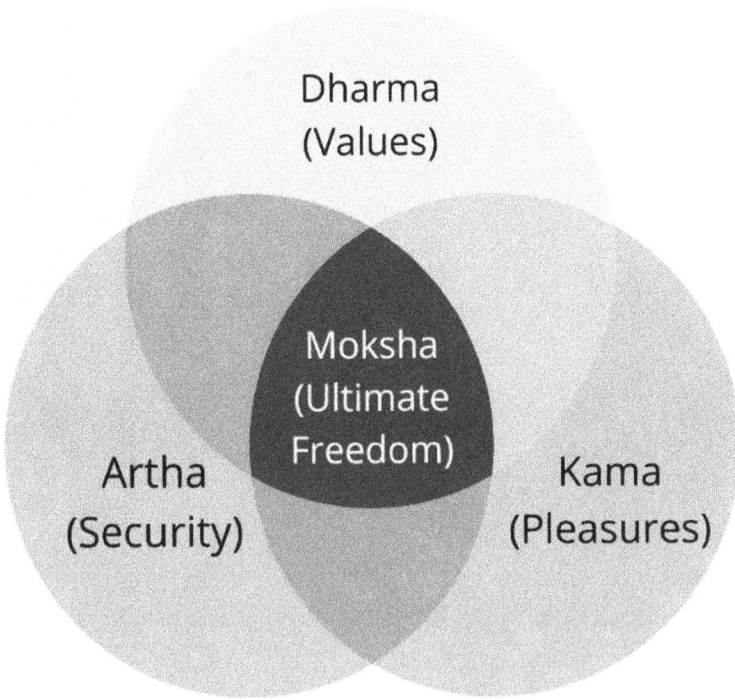

Dharma
(Values)

Moksha
(Ultimate
Freedom)

Artha
(Security)

Kama
(Pleasures)

Happiness is a pursuit

The skill and pursuit of Happiness

You can pursue each of these four pursuits independently and solely. For example, one can pursue wealth alone, with life's only goal to maximise one's net worth, paying no heed to values, pleasures, or inner peace. Similarly, one can be a hedonist. A hedonist is always seeking newer, variegated pleasures and trying to maximise them without thinking about whether they are providing him health, safety, or security. Yet happiness arises only when the Purusharthas align with each other and do not conflict. Pursuing only one may lead you into a wild goose chase for happiness.

Happiness is not wishful thinking or simply a rumination of what could be or could have been. It is an active striving to achieve. Happiness cannot

THINK BETTER AND THRIVE

be achieved by merely positive thinking. Pursuing happiness requires intellectual energy and genuine effort. It requires clarity of one's goals. It requires the acknowledgement that, in the end, one has only a limited time, energy and will to spend on accomplishing these goals. And finally, one needs a plan that allocates and balances resources across the four pursuits.

Happiness is the skill of choosing, prioritising, and executing actions in the value-driven pursuit of security and pleasures. It is the pursuit of that knowledge of the truth that culminates in inner peace and happiness.

Do not just desire happiness. Work for it.

Learning the skill of happiness

Fortunately, today there is a lot of good research available on happiness. By relying on philosophers' careful thinking and using scientific methods, we can have better answers to questions that have vexed humanity for millennia. And these answers only get more accurate and precise over time. One such enlightening research is from Selin Kesebir, Associate Professor of Organisational Behaviour at LBS, who posits that happiness is not about what we have and do not have. Instead, it's a skill, and you can learn it like we can learn to speak a new language or play a musical instrument.

> *"It is a skill of the mind, a capacity to shape the way that we see, process and interpret our reality and the things around us. It can be developed like any other competence."*

The quality of our happiness, says Kesebir, is contingent on the health of our relationship with reality, ourselves and other people. And we understand that happiness comes from within.

Kesebir recommends that we adopt five attitudes as part of the Happiness skillset:

1. **Know that life is complex, and suffering is to be expected:** Accept this. Letting go of expectations about an easy and perfect life and accepting the inevitability of change and loss can mitigate frustration when things go wrong.

2. **Expect to have negative experiences and emotions and accept them:** If suffering is to be expected, we need to sometimes expect to feel negative emotions. Being happy doesn't mean feeling good all the time. Happy

people have their share of negative emotions. Getting comfortable with sometimes being uncomfortable is key to happiness.

3. **Stop arguing with reality:** If something is a fact, fighting or resisting is simply a waste of our time and energy. Understand that some problems are like gravity; they are simply facts of life and cannot be changed. As the pandemic has shown us, railing against things over which we have no control won't change anything — it's futile. Far better to accept facts and move on.

4. **Adopt a positive outlook:** Our attention is like a spotlight; it never gives us the complete picture. We need to realise that reality is larger than what our attention is presenting us. Under uncertainty, we can interpret the same event through different lenses, some more positive than others.

5. **Please don't buy into everything your mind says:** Happier people can look at their thoughts from a distance and hear and observe their emotions and inner voice without being carried away by what is going on in their heads. They instead question the validity of those voices and aim at a more truthful and constructive inner voice.

In another research paper, Pelin Kesebir from the University of Wisconsin-Madison suggests that happiness becomes more achievable if we cultivate the following:

1. Healthy habits of the body

Studies consistently show that cultivating healthy habits of the body, such as eating well (e.g., increased consumption of fruits and vegetables), exercising, and getting enough sleep improves well-being

2. Healthy relationship with ourselves

We have healthy self-esteem. Self-esteem refers to a feeling born from the I's evaluation of me—a general sense of comfort and happiness with all the things one is. A love for oneself and a love for life typically go together, explaining the link between happiness and self-esteem. Healthy or optimal self-esteem entails a firmly grounded sense of self-worth and calm self-confidence.

3. Healthy habits of the heart and mind (i.e. virtues)

Happiness and Virtuous Living have a circular relationship - one reinforces the other. Virtue leads to happiness, and there is support for the notion that happiness leads to virtuous behaviour.

4. Healthy relationships with others

THINK BETTER AND THRIVE

The desire to belong is a fundamental human motivation. And its satisfaction through love, friendship and close emotional ties is robustly linked to well-being. Man is essential to man's happiness. Cultivating happiness requires developing close relationships characterised by mutual trust, caring, and understanding.

5. Healthy connection to a larger beyond

Transcending the self and connecting to something larger than the self (e.g., God, universe, nature) has been regarded as a recipe for happiness across ages. Self-transcendent connections are a powerful source of meaning and purpose. They are critical ingredients of well-being. Self-transcendent emotions such as compassion, gratitude, and awe have also been linked to greater physical and emotional well-being. They echo the insight that self-transcendence might be a more promising strategy for cultivating happiness than focusing heavily on the self.

The key message here is happiness is a Skill made up of part attitude and part practice, and it is something we do with our minds, intentions and actions rather than something we get.

Epicurus's Happiness Hack

Epicurus is the most misunderstood of all philosophers. The pleasure principle propounded by him is largely misinterpreted. The wrong ideas have fuelled an entire generation of 'Carpe Diem' and 'Wine, Dine & Be Merry- for there is not tomorrow' generation.

I want to make this chapter super simple, so I will list the key takeaways from his philosophy of living a happy and fulfilling life.

1. Seek necessary pleasures, shun unnecessary pleasures

Epicurus distinguishes between necessary and unnecessary desires. Necessary desires are essential for survival, health, and fitness of the body-mind-sense complex. These include the desire to be free of pain, the desire to have a family, friends, nourishing food, a place to rest comfortably, an engaging occupation that pays decently, and the desire for inner tranquillity and harmony in life.

Unnecessary desire is that whose fulfilment comes with a lot of exertion and which we can very well do without. 'Beyond a certain point, we can't extend pleasure; we can only vary it,' writes one of my favourite writers Eric

Weiner. A swankier car, the latest fitness watch, a larger TV, a new job, a new pair of shoes, and those extra muscles don't come without exertion. Yet, they only give you slightly different variants of the same pleasure you otherwise enjoyed. So it's worth asking the question, 'is it necessary?'.

2. Seek Ataraxia, not pleasure

Only when we are in pain, do we need to seek pleasure, a condition that inevitably produces greater pain. To eliminate this pain-pleasure-pain cycle, we need to cultivate a mindset in which there is no pain. Thus, the aim is not the positive pursuit of pleasure. The purpose is rather the attaining of a neutral state, best described as "peace of mind" or " Shanti " of the Vedanta or "emptiness," as the Buddhists refer to it. The Greek word Epicurus uses for this state is Ataraxia, which means "freedom from worry." It is when you feel rested, fresh, active and sensitive. And when pleasure comes, welcome it wholeheartedly while it lasts. Consciously stay away from the hedonic treadmill where all of life is spent for the next dopamine kick.

3. Cultivate the wisdom to understand when pain is necessary

We need the wisdom to see which pleasures induce pain and which pains are required to produce joy. For example, some pleasures lead to greater pain, like getting drunk on alcohol, getting high on drugs, or smoking your lungs out, so the wise will shun behaviours that threaten their health and long-term pleasure capacity. On the other hand, specific pains, like sadness, can lead to an appreciation for life. A painful activity, like exercise, can lead to a healthy body-mind which is a highly pleasurable state. We should not, therefore, get rid of all negative emotions but only those that lead to unnecessary pain. This, by the way, is also one of the main conclusions that positive psychologist Ed Diener outlines in his latest research on the empirical basis of happiness.

4. Lasting happiness is found within

The philosopher is the happiest of all people, for he chooses the stable pleasures of knowledge over the temporary and volatile pleasures of the body. Epicurus says that if one practices these precepts, he will become a "god among men," for he will have achieved an immortal state even in a mortal body. The secret to happiness lies in reducing our dependence on external things. This keeps us from the anxiety of obtaining them, the insecurity of keeping them and the disappointment of losing them.

5. Happiness flourishes when exercised with like-minded people

Friendship is a necessary ingredient that sweetness the deal of happiness that life has to offer us. For one who has tasted it once, it is the essential ingredient. Friends are needed, not a company in getting wasted on weekends but rather as sparring partners for your accumulated wisdom.

Epicurus said,

> "*Of all the means procured by wisdom to ensure happiness throughout life, by far the most important is the acquisition of friends.*"

The quality of friends you gather reflects your knowledge and wisdom. He further said,

> "*"Exercise yourself in these precepts, day and night, both by yourself and with one who is like-minded; then never, either in waking or in one's dreams, will you be disturbed but will live as a god among men. For man loses all semblance of mortality by living in the midst of immortal blessings."*"

So, those are five Happiness Hacks of Epicurus that I wished to share with you, and I am happy I could do it finally in this chapter.

ϸϸϸ

SIXTY

LIFE: THE JOURNEY OF LETTING GO

—◆♡◆—

Life will put everything you believe to test.

There comes a day when everything you believe and take pride in being, will be put on trial, questioned, challenged and put to the test.

You will be asked to narrate your life story, and people will judge your choices, decisions and responses to situations. They will challenge your claim over your achievements. They will challenge your education, your upbringing, and your beliefs. Do you believe you gave your best? Then prove it. Do you think you loved, supported and helped someone through their ups and downs? You are probably lying. Can you prove it? Do you have beautiful memories or special moments? What if it was all faked? They will put everything you believe yourself on trial, and the judgement will be at the mercy of strangers.

What are you proud of? Are you proud of being a good mother, a good father or a good friend? Then they will challenge that. Have you been a good son, a good daughter or a good employee? Finally, you'll be asked to prove it to a complete set of strangers. They will tell you that you are otherwise. They will validate your entire being.

Can you be trusted? Are you loyal? Are you faithful? Are you a good person? Are you a normal person? Prove it. Are you even for real? Or are you a story made up to entertain yourself, oblivious and unrelated to the real world, a work of fiction? Or are you a story in the heads of other people who made it up to serve their interests?

Who are you?

Be a Lamp unto Yourself

You come to this life alone and leave alone. There is nothing to hold on to in this world except your being.

At least once a day, drop everything on your mind - your worries, projects, tasks, aspirations for some time and just be - be with yourself. Relish that pure joy of being and perfect peace. Commune with the light within you. To be alive, to experience I-ness, to breathe, to experience being is in itself a miracle. Revel in the light of your being.

Whenever you're all by yourself, try to watch your thoughts instead of getting lost in your thoughts. As long as you identify with the mind, you cannot be contented. We keep moving from one job to another, one relationship to another, one ideology to another- all out of discontentment, thinking change will bring happiness, bring contentment. We are all victims of a machine that produces thoughts continuously, said Paul Brunton and 'meditation is the process of regaining control over this machine'.

Learn from yourself, understand yourself, and watch yourself- the light is in you. No one else can do this on your behalf. It's your journey, and you walk alone. There is no need to seek it outside in a deity, in a Guru, in Books, or in places of Pilgrimages: Ishwara or the light of God is already in you. The more you seek it outside, the more elusive it becomes. The kingdom of God is within you. Search within.

Buddha's final message to his pupils was to Be a light unto yourself.

Krishna said in the Bhagavad Gita, *Atman Atmani uddharet* which means ' Lift yourself by yourself'.

Make that effort. Jesus said in Luke, 'Be careful, then, that the light within you is not darkness.' We need to discover the light of god, the essence of being in ourselves.

Learning to let go

Everyone knows we do not live forever and that life, this life, is short. There comes a day when we need to leave behind the things we hold most dear to our hearts. The people we love, our achievements, our wealth, our possessions, even our own lives, everything is left behind when we die.

In this life journey, we lose more than we gain as we grow older. It is a journey of letting go. But few of us can come to terms with this reality, and even fewer can realign their journey to accommodate this reality. Losing anything of value always leads to suffering. It is a roller coaster ride of negative emotions. So then, is it possible to live without suffering? Is there a life design that can minimise/ insure/ protect us from this?

Here are some ways I think we can best come to terms with this reality and lead happy lives:

1. Understand the transitoriness of life and its gifts

That life's gifts, our potentialities are transitory- that they do not last forever- our strength, intelligence, beauty, wealth, youth- nothing lasts forever.

> "An ancient Sanskrit proverb says:
> यथा काष्ठं च काष्ठं च समयेाता महोदधौ ।
> समेत्य च व्यपयेाता तद्वद् भूतसमागमः ॥
> Just as logs of wood floating in a river/ocean meet and then separate, all our associations here are momentary – will have to end."

It needs a stoic attitude towards life to face this reality. To see through life requires we pause, take a step back and look at things objectively. Begin every new venture with the full knowledge of this reality and then live life accordingly.

2. Focus on what matters most

As a person in this world, what matters is that part of us lives after we are gone. Your LinkedIn profile, your Instagram likes, or that date with a stranger- none of these matters so much after you are gone. Instead, what will matter most is what our life experiences taught us, how (or if) we found lasting peace and freedom and how we are remembered by those whose lives we touched while we lived.

It is called the *Obituary Exercise*. Take a blank sheet of paper and draft your obituary – what you would want to be written about you when you have passed away many years from now. Write whatever comes to mind. Use words, phrases, and sentences. Do not overthink this exercise. Do not edit, censor, analyze or critique your thoughts. Take 10-15 minutes to complete this exercise.

You can revisit this exercise in the future, so do not try to perfect your answer now. Questions you should ask yourself as you do this exercise:

· What or who did you impact or change? Why?
· What character traits and values did you consistently demonstrate over your life? At your core, who were you?
· Who did you care for? How did you impact or change this person/these people?
· What were significant accomplishments in your life? At the ages of 40, 50, 60, and 70?
· What did you show interest in? What were you passionate or enthusiastic about?
· What was your legacy?

Think big. Imagine possibilities. Recall inspiring dreams and thoughts you have had in the past. After this exercise, think about what choices, which paths and what priorities you need to set to realize that obituary.

3. Learn something from all good and bad experiences

One of my favourite philosophers, Arthur Schopenhauer, said

"*Mostly it is the loss that teaches us about the worth of things.*"

Anyone can learn from their own mistakes. We know even animals can do that. That makes them trainable. They learn by the carrot and stick method or the operant conditioning method. The real differentiator in great learners is their ability to learn from mistakes and the losses of others. One of my earliest mentors and fatherly figures, Shrikant Gokhale (I called him Gokhale uncle), told me, 'If you realise and learn what I have learnt by age 50 by the time you are 25, you get to live 25 bonus years'. Learn from everything.

4. Letting go may be in your best long-term interest

Andrea Mathews, in her book 'Letting go of Good' describes how holding on is a form of 'bargain' and how this bargain brings pain. She says, 'Letting go means being willing to allow life to carry you to a new place, even a deeper truer rendition of self. Holding on means trying to push life into the place of your making or be damned.'

Do not fall for the sunk cost fallacy. The sunk cost fallacy is our tendency to include the value of past costs in a future decision or trade-off. For example, we continue to invest further in them just because we are already invested in a particular relationship, project, skillset, or job. We need to realise that this new investment can pay better dividends elsewhere. Like that expensive pair of jeans, you once bought and never wore and do not even get rid of just because you've paid for it. So, think long-term. See if you can say with high probability that it is in your best interest to hold on to someone or something.

5. Prepare for life's final journey

Letting go is always a tough call. It is always hard to take that decision. In life, while we must sometimes let go of people and things, we also ultimately need to prepare to let go of life. Live conscious that one day we will bid goodbye to our bodies, and it is ok to do so.

Accepting one's mortality can be one of the most liberating feelings. First, however, we must find a way to best process this reality for ourselves. Processing mortality does not mean we need to control how we die; that is impossible. Instead, we need to learn to live with this acceptance.

Here is an extract from Sherwin B. Nuland's beautiful book, How We Die: Reflections of Life's Final Chapter:

> "The art of dying is the art of living. The honesty and grace of the years of life that are ending are the real measures of how we die. It is not in the last weeks or days that we compose the message that will be remembered, but in all the decades that preceded them. Who has lived in dignity dies in dignity?"

I hope this does not paint a very gloomy picture of life and helps us think and act better when it comes to letting go.

THE END

References

Health:

- It is a state of health and well-being and, more specifically, the https://brainly.ph/question/5755085
- Feel-good hormones: How they affect your mind, mood and body. https://www.health.harvard.edu/mind-and-mood/feel-good-hormones-how-they-affect-your-mind-mood-and-body
- Physical fitness - Wikipedia. https://en.wikipedia.org/wiki/Physical_fitness
- How much physical activity do adults need? | Physical Activity | CDC. https://www.cdc.gov/physicalactivity/basics/adults/index.htm
- Physical Activity for Different Groups - Centers for Disease Control .... https://www.cdc.gov/physicalactivity/basics/age-chart.html
- Getting Started with Physical Activity | Healthy Weight, Nutrition, and .... https://www.cdc.gov/healthyweight/physical_activity/getting_started.html
- Sit and Reach Test: How to Measure Lower Back Flexibility - Verywell Fit. https://www.verywellfit.com/sit-and-reach-flexibility-test-3120279
- Cadence Push-Up Test - Topend Sports. https://www.topendsports.com/testing/tests/pushup.htm
- Body Mass Index (BMI) - Topend Sports. https://www.topendsports.com/testing/tests/BMI.htm
- What Should I Eat? - The Nutrition Source. https://www.hsph.harvard.edu/nutritionsource/what-should-you-eat/
- You'll Never Change Your Life Until You Change Something ... - Lifehack. https://www.lifehack.org/articles/productivity/youll-never-change-your-life-until-you-change-something-you-daily.html
- It all comes down to what you do daily - John Maxwell. https://www.johnmaxwell.com/blog/it-all-comes-down-to-what-you-do-daily/
- Clear, James. *Atomic habits: An easy & proven way to build good habits & break bad ones.* Penguin, 2018.
- Sinclair, David A., and Matthew D. LaPlante. *Lifespan: Why we age—And*

why we Don't have to. Atria books, 2019.
- Emotional intelligence - Wikipedia. https://en.wikipedia.org/wiki/Emotional_intelligence
- How to Improve Your Emotional Intelligence - Harvard DCE. https://professional.dce.harvard.edu/blog/how-to-improve-your-emotional-intelligence/
- Active listening - Wikipedia. https://en.wikipedia.org/wiki/Active_listening
- If— by Rudyard Kipling | Poetry Foundation. https://www.poetryfoundation.org/poems/46473/if---
- Reiss, S. (2001). Who am I?: The 16 Basic Desires That Motivate Our Actions and Define Our Personality, Jeremy P. Tarcher/Putnam, New York

Spirituality:

- Hanh, Thich Nhat. *The art of living.* Random House, 2017.
- Vicious Circle of Poverty - Economics Discussion. https://www.economicsdiscussion.net/poverty/vicious-circle-of-poverty/4584
- Climate change has made air conditioning a vital necessity. It also https://www.vox.com/science-and-health/23067049/heat-wave-air-conditioning-cooling-india-climate-change
- Vicious circle - Idioms by The Free Dictionary. https://idioms.thefreedictionary.com/vicious+circle
- Three Simple Ways to Find the Meaning of Life - The Atlantic. https://www.theatlantic.com/family/archive/2021/10/meaning-life-macronutrients-purpose-search/620440/
- Having a sense of meaning in life is good for you - The Conversation. https://theconversation.com/having-a-sense-of-meaning-in-life-is-good-for-you-so-how-do-you-get-one-110361
- Meaning | Action for Happiness. https://actionforhappiness.org/10-keys/meaning
- The Global Organism | PETER HESSELDAHL. http://peterhesseldahl.dk/in-english/the-global-organism.html

Parenting:

- 5 Ways Social Media Affects Teen Mental Health - Verywell Family. https://www.verywellfamily.com/ways-social-media-affects-teen-mental-health-4144769
- Violent discipline - UNICEF DATA. https://data.unicef.org/topic/child-protection/violence/violent-discipline/
- A Violent Education: Corporal Punishment of Children in US Public https://www.hrw.org/reports/2008/us0808/11.htm
- Shouting, slapping to denying food: Indian parents use 30 different https://timesofindia.indiatimes.com/life-style/parenting/toddler-year-and-beyond/shouting-slapping-to-denying-food-indian-parents-use-30-different-ways-of-abuse-according-to-a-unicef-report/photostory/76243993.cms
- Violence against children and children's rights - Our World in Data. https://ourworldindata.org/violence-against-rights-for-children
- Convention on the Rights of the Child | UNICEF. https://www.unicef.org/child-rights-convention
- Physical discipline is harmful and ineffective. https://www.apa.org/monitor/2019/05/physical-discipline
- Corporal punishment against children and the law - Times of India Blog. https://timesofindia.indiatimes.com/blogs/legally-speaking/corporal-punishment-against-children-and-the-law/
- Becoming a vegetarian - Harvard Health. https://www.health.harvard.edu/staying-healthy/becoming-a-vegetarian
- Corrupting the Youth: Should Parents Feed their Children Meat? https://link.springer.com/article/10.1007/s10677-021-10223-2
- 25 Nonviolent Discipline Options - Suzuki Association of the Americas. https://suzukiassociation.org/news/25-nonviolent-discipline-options/
- Convention on the Rights of the Child | UNICEF Lebanon. https://www.unicef.org/lebanon/convention-rights-child
- What are the emotional needs of a child? - CPD Online College. https://cpdonline.co.uk/knowledge-base/safeguarding/emotional-needs-of-a-child/
- Understanding the Emotional Needs of a Child by Age. https://masandpas.com/emotional-needs-of-a-child/
- Are parents spending less time with their kids? - Our World in Data.

https://ourworldindata.org/parents-time-with-kids
- Karpman drama triangle - Wikipedia. https://en.wikipedia.org/wiki/Karpman_drama_triangle
- On Children by Kahlil Gibran - Poems | Academy of American Poets. https://poets.org/poem/children-1

Love:

- Kelly, Matthew. The rhythm of life: Living every day with passion and purpose. Simon and Schuster, 2004.
- Ayn Rand Lexicon. http://aynrandlexicon.com/lexicon/love.html
- The Power of Two - Gallup.com. https://news.gallup.com/businessjournal/111826/power-two.aspx
- Kelly, Matthew. The Seven Levels of Intimacy: The Art of Loving and the Joy of Being Loved. Simon and Schuster, 2005.
- Pragmatic Reasons for Getting Married - The School Of Life. https://www.theschooloflife.com/article/pragmatic-reasons-for-getting-married/
- Infidelity | Psychology Today. https://www.psychologytoday.com/us/basics/infidelity
- Why do people cheat in relationships – Scientific American https://www.scientificamerican.com/article/why-do-people-in-relationships-cheat/?amp=true
- Triangular theory of love - Wikipedia. https://en.wikipedia.org/wiki/Triangular_theory_of_love
- Triangular theory of love - Hofstra University. https://www.hofstra.edu/pdf/community/slzctr/stdcsl/stdcsl_triangular.pdf
- Triangular theory of love | Psychology Wiki | Fandom. https://psychology.fandom.com/wiki/Triangular_theory_of_love

Work:

- Knapp's Relationship Model - Communication Theory. https://www.communicationtheory.org/knapps-relationship-model/

REFERENCES

- Barker, Joel Arthur. "Discovering the Future: The Business of Paradigms." The Journal for Healthcare Quality (JHQ) 13.5 (1991): 65.
- A Simple Way to Map Out Your Career Ambitions - Harvard Business Review. https://hbr.org/2018/11/a-simple-way-to-map-out-your-career-ambitions
- Seven vital trade-offs you will face at work and how to deal with them. https://economictimes.indiatimes.com/wealth/earn/seven-vital-trade-offs-you-will-face-at-work-and-how-to-deal-with-them/articleshow/64231405.cms
- Can I Trade In Two Cars For One - Trade Choices. https://tradechoices.blogspot.com/2018/02/can-i-trade-in-two-cars-for-one.html
- Trade-off - Wikipedia. https://en.wikipedia.org/wiki/Trade-off
- Consumer Vs Producer. https://www.peprimer.com/consumer-vs-producer.html
- Assign3 - 1. People Face Tradeoffs To get one thing, we…. https://www.coursehero.com/file/16166847/Assign3/
- Opportunity Cost | English meaning - Cambridge Dictionary. https://dictionary.cambridge.org/dictionary/english/opportunity-cost
- 10 Principles of Economics - LinkedIn. https://www.linkedin.com/pulse/10-principles-economics-amberlynn-lani
- How to get lucky — Almanack of Naval Ravikant. https://www.navalmanack.com/almanack-of-naval-ravikant/how-to-get-lucky
- Honor Yourself: Live with Integrity — Frank Sonnenberg Online. https://www.franksonnenbergonline.com/posters/honor-yourself-live-with-integrity/
- Honour & Integrity. https://www.bobritchie.ca/post/honour-integrity
- Sabatier, G. (2020). *Financial Freedom: A Proven Path to All the Money You Will Ever Need*. Penguin.

The Author In His Own Words

Like many of you, I play different roles. I am:

- *a Business-to-Business Marketing professional with over eighteen years of experience in Strategic Marketing and Digital Enablement.*
- *a Father of an 11-year-old daughter who is the centre of our family universe*
- *a Son to wonderful parents who gave me an excellent middle-class upbringing and who now live a happy retired life*
- *a Seeker and a student of Vedanta, studying under the guidance of traditional teacher*s

I am a humanist who believes that one must do everything in one's capacity to reach one's full potential of happiness in one's lifetime. Happiness is a journey of holistic development of an individual leading to greater physical, emotional, spiritual and intellectual health while, at the same time, making positive contributions towards one's family, work and social life. My travels for work and leisure have taken me to over twenty countries exploring diverse arts, cultures, worldviews and traditional wisdom.

Ten ways that make me

Our ways of thinking, feeling, behaving, and decision-making defines us and make us the person we are. We often attempt to define ourselves professionally but seldom at a personal level. However, I always wanted to make a disclosure to my daughter, Aanya, at some place in this book about this personal side and describe it briefly. So I take the opportunity now. So, here are ten ways, in no order, that I believe make me the person I am and influence my thinking, my work and my relationships:

1. Pursuing Self-enquiry

Since my school days, I have been in awe of the universe and life on earth and wondered what our place and purpose are here. I have asked myself these fundamental questions and sought answers to them. Who am I? Am I my thoughts, my actions, my sensations, or am I someone more or different than these? Am I what I am because I think so? And so many such questions have nudged me on this journey of self-inquiry. With exposure to evolutionary and humanistic psychology and the ancient Indian wisdom tradition of Vedanta, I finally seem to be making progress. I am beginning to create a coherent, integrated, contradiction-free worldview and life philosophy.

2. Committing to Mentors and Spiritual teachers

Through my childhood days to this date, I have felt the need to approach those accomplished few amongst us to guide me with the best course of action when faced with ambiguity or help me think more systematically and rationally. A school teacher, a friend of my father's, a priest, a reclusive old man, a preacher, a professor, a boss, a philosopher, a scientist, a Saint, a spiritual teacher- they had come in many forms to me and helped me think better. They presented themselves to me when I needed guidance, motivation and a little hand-holding from time to time. I have never shied away from seeking such people, either. When I think back, many good life decisions I made were in association with mentors, teachers and coaches. Unfortunately, I can also see some bad decisions that I took which did not involve any guide or mentor. I have learnt so much from these teachers and mentors and will be ever grateful to them.

3. Health over gratification

If and when I am faced with a choice between a lifestyle disease and a lifestyle change, I have and will always choose a lifestyle change. I would change my behaviour than depend on medication. I understand sometimes we need to take recourse to drugs to make a quick recovery, which is fine. But I also believe with changes in food choices and activity levels, the medication should taper off to a zero or maintenance level at some point. I have diabetes and hypertension in my family, and it seems one or both of these might affect me someday. But I know these can be reversed and managed with lifestyle changes. So if I had to choose, I would choose health over medication.

4. Challenging own beliefs

Every generation inherits a basket of beliefs from their parents and another from social and news media. Beliefs that challenge current beliefs are seldom inherited beliefs. Many of the beliefs we hold are largely a result of conditioning during our upbringing. But how many of us question the beliefs we hold on dearly to our bosoms? I always have. From belief in an omnipotent God to rituals, the afterlife, morals, ethics and even values. For me, it is not just enough to scrutinise them but also important to put them to the test. Besides, I even challenge holding beliefs that may contradict each other. Also, cognitive dissonance – the uneasiness caused by the gap between beliefs and behaviour bothers me. For many of us, it is easy to compartmentalise beliefs and behaviours without bothering much about how they integrate. I find it extremely hard to do.

5. Prioritizing learning and self-development

In recent years, I have dedicated a substantial amount of time to learning and acquiring new knowledge and skills. I spend about 10% of my daily time studying, reading, researching or taking an online course. I could easily attribute a lot of good things and progress I have done at work to this habit.

6. Reason over Sentiments

Sentiments and emotions play a big role in the daily life of Indians and influence everything from politics, parenting, relationships, and business. In an extreme form, sentimentality is defined as exaggerated and self-indulgent tenderness, sadness, or nostalgia. Proper reasoning is a tendency I have developed in the last ten years. As a college youth, I once subscribed to a popular spiritual tradition of India that thrives on the followers' emotional weaknesses, with its founding principles grounded in sentimentality. They conditioned me to become one. This and other experiences where I burned my fingers taught me always to put reason above gross sentiments. Sentimentality may have advantages as such people may come across as more loving or lovable. Still, the reason is a superior guide most of the time. The reason is the power of our minds to think, understand, and form judgements logically. Today, I put reason above sentimentality. It hurts people sometimes, but in the end, it serves them well too.

7. Choosing mindful engagement over mindless

entertainment

I have grown up watching the people around me, dedicating the best times of their lives to watching cricket and tennis. It is a passion millions share in our country to this date. To top up this, we have daily reality TV and Live News which put the last nail in the coffin of imagination and creativity. It is extremely hard to subscribe to this routine. There is too much at stake. We can neither participate nor contribute to what happens in sports, television, or events. I could never subscribe to being a passive spectator sitting on the sidelines and cheering cricketers and politicians. Either you play, coach in sports, or vote in an election- watching it is not really doing anything. But that's just my take. Yes, I have been a victim of Netflix binge-watching a couple of times, but that's really about that. I probably binge-read, but I don't consider it mindless. Time is precious and the most limited resource we have. I wish to make every day count in a mindful way.

8. Love of Reading

My love for reading came partly from being an introvert who loved solitude and partly from my never-ending curiosity to know and to find things out. When I started reading outside my curriculum in my school days, I was deeply fascinated by the universe and all the mysterious bodies that float in the endless ether. I would voraciously drink from these books, the deep oceans, extinct civilisations, lost treasures, voyages of discovery, the inventions and discoveries that made our century, the great historical personalities and their biographies. Reading is a love that I carry to this day, even more so since I can now afford to buy books that I may never read! My grandmother was a voracious reader of fiction and trivia magazines. I would like to think that I got this from her.

9. Applying mental models across contexts

We think in terms of mental models. We all construct these mental models of reality through which we make sense of the real world. We also learn new models in our academic journeys. These could be psychological models, business models, economic models, strategy models, parenting models, leadership models and so on. A familiar model could be the Varnaashrama model from the Bhagavad Gita or Maslow's hierarchy of needs model. I love to think in terms of models, apply them and put them to work in my professional and personal life. Besides, I am fascinated by taking a great mental model from one context and applying it in completely another context of life. For example, we know the model of compounding that we apply in finance. It is fascinating to see how we can apply this to our habits, learning and relationships. Trust me, many great models are already proven in certain contexts and are simply waiting for surprising outcomes when applied in a different context. Proceed with some caution and common sense, though!

10. *Pursuit of freedom over bondage*

I, for one, have always favoured individual freedom- the right to think, speak and act as one wants as long as you are not hurting others. Freedom means I am not enslaved to another person's beliefs and control. One step further, freedom for me also means I am not enslaved to my own emotions, biases and cravings. Any binding desire or expectation is enslaving. And I have always sought to be a free man, free from being a wanting person in the first place, free from emotional dependence. I seek Moksha, the ultimate freedom from all kinds of bondage. I always believed this kingdom lies within us, ready and waiting only to be claimed one day. This yearning has defined me and made me the person I am today. That may be why this is my most unique, defining trait.

I know my daughter, Aanya, will grow up to be her person one day, perhaps different from me. This note will tell her that it is okay to be so. I wish that she inherits whatever little good I have and not my defects and I hope she becomes a much better person than me in every way. I thank my parents for letting me become my person and make my own choices.

I hope the readers can use this note as an example of how they can articulate what makes them who they are. For those who know me already or do not quite know me yet, this note can be of interest and help. Thank you for having made it this far. I hope you enjoyed reading this book and find it useful in whichever little way it can make your life better.

ᗞᗞᗞ

Printed in the USA
CPSIA information can be obtained
at www.ICGtesting.com
CBHW071058070224
4085CB00054B/1415

9 798889 098379